THE INTERNATIONAL
COOKIE
COOKBOOK

NANCY BAGGETT
PHOTOGRAPHS BY DENNIS M. GOTTLIEB

STEWART, TABORI & CHANG
NEW YORK

Originally published in hardcover in 1988

Paperback edition published in 1993 by
Stewart, Tabori, & Chang
575 Broadway
New York, NY 10012

Library of Congress Cataloging-in-Publication Data

Baggett, Nancy, 1943-
  The international cookie cookbook / Nancy Baggett;
photographs by Dennis Gottlieb.
    p. cm.
    Includes index.
    ISBN 1-55670-041-5 (cloth)
       1-55670-328-7 (paper)
    1. Cookies.   I. Title.
TX772.B28   1988
641.8'654—dc19   88-15310
                           CIP

Distributed in the U.S. by Workman Publishing
708 Broadway, New York, New York 10003

Distributed in Canada by Canadian Manda Group
P.O. Box 920 Station U, Toronto, Ontario M8Z 5P9

Distributed in all other territories (except Central and South
America) by Melia Publishing Services
P.O. Box 1639, Maidenhead Berkshire SL6 6YZ, England

Central and South American accounts should contact Export
Sales Manager at Stewart, Tabori & Chang

Printed in Italy
10 9 8 7 6 5 4 3 2 1

Design: *Joseph Rutt*
Food stylist: *Susie Harrington*
Prop stylists: *Adrienne Abseck*
           Laurie Jean Beck
           Nancy Mernit
Cover design: *Amanda Wilson*
Cover food stylist: *Dolores Custer*
Frontispiece: *Black Walnut Icebox Cookies*
(recipe on page 65).

ACKNOWLEDGMENTS

Many people had a part in creating *The International Cookie Cookbook*. My heartfelt thanks go to the following:

To photographer Dennis Gottlieb, whose extraordinary contribution to this book speaks for itself.

To my editor, Leslie Stoker, for her enthusiasm, guidance, and dedication to publishing fine quality books.

To the suppliers who generously furnished special equipment used in testing the recipes: the Maid of Scandinavia Company for a wide variety of European kitchen utensils and supplies; Williams-Sonoma for several cookie stamps and irons; master craftsman Don Dillon for handcarved speculaas and springerle molds; and Brown Bag Cookie Art for assorted ceramic cookie molds.

To fellow IACP members who helped me gather cookie recipes from around the globe. Jacki Passmore of Australia, Annabel Langbein of New Zealand, and Sinclair Philip and Margaret Fraser of Canada all provided assistance.

To my kitchen assistants and testers who helped with the baking. Jene Springrose tested many recipes, helped develop several others, and generously shared her expertise throughout the project. Selvin Martinez, Nilene Mosher, Denise Donahue, Jennifer Levine, and Nicole Jensen cheerfully measured, mixed, shaped, and baked batch upon batch of cookies. Lindy Griffith, Gary Hunt, and JoAnn Tater also aided with testing, and the TIS group helped with tasting and rating.

To Jean Favors and Ruth Glick, for advising with the design and helping to decorate the German cookie house, and Pat Massey for decorating the Honey Lebkuchen cookies.

To Susan Bellsinger, Polly Clingerman, Christine Tischer, Sally Churgai, Lucy Gerspacher, Jean Favors, Elizabeth Dietrich, Jo Simons, Marie Kahn, Diane Garrett, and Marie Chmilewsky Ulanowicz for kindly sharing recipes from their personal collections.

To my agent and friend, Linda Hayes, who provided personal as well as professional support, and my family, Roc and David, who offered encouragement and served as enthusiastic tasters throughout the project.

CONTENTS

INTRODUCTION   *6*

CHAPTER 1
Baking Cookies: The Basics   *8*

CHAPTER 2
American & Canadian Cookies   *14*

CHAPTER 3
Latin American Cookies   *70*

CHAPTER 4
British Isles Cookies   *86*

CHAPTER 5
Scandinavian Cookies   *108*

CHAPTER 6
Western European Cookies   *138*

CHAPTER 7
Southern European Cookies   *192*

CHAPTER 8
Eastern European Cookies   *216*

APPENDIX   *236*

CREDITS   *237*

INDEX   *237*

INTRODUCTION

WELCOME TO THE WORLD OF COOKIES! FOR me it's a magical realm, filled with some of life's simplest, but most wonderful sensory experiences: the heady aroma of Ginger Thins baking, the rich, soul-satisfying taste of Chocolate Drop cookies still warm from the oven, and the pleasing crunch of Lemon Snaps.

No one could ask for a more rewarding or interesting task than writing an international cookie cookbook. It has given me the excuse to spend hours with old recipe files and heirloom cookbooks, and the opportunity to "know" several fine home bakers of past generations from the recipes and baking notes they left behind. It has led me into the kitchens and lives of cooks on several different continents. I will not forget the German grandmother who, to be sure I was translating all the spices in her recipe correctly, took me to her cupboard and let me sniff the contents of each little jar. Researching has also let me explore and appreciate the traditions and confront the languages of a variety of nations. Thank goodness for Scandinavian friends with impeccable English or I would still be puzzling over the Danish word for cream of tartar.

There are many other sweet memories associated with writing *The International Cookie Cookbook*. I recall one of our magical Christmases in Europe when the entire family pitched in to build a traditional cookie house, or *Knusperhaus,* for my then seven-year-old son. It was the recollection of his look of wonder and the sheer fun of the activity that inspired me to include a cookie house in this book. There are images of times spent in the homes of friends and acquaintances in a number of countries. Often, I was struck by their great love and appreciation for their own traditional foods and culture, and I have tried to convey this respect for the past in this book.

As the large chapter of U.S. and Canadian recipes presented here suggests, there are also personal memories as American as chocolate chip cookies (which are certainly as American as apple pie!). I recall quite vividly the childhood pleasure of helping my grandmother decorate our holiday sugar cookies, and of routinely checking my lunchbox on the way to school to see what cookies my mother had packed. And there are a host of enduring "grownup memories" associated with recipes I've gathered over several decades from American relatives, colleagues, and friends.

Of course, the point of *The International Cookie Cookbook* is not recollections, but actually recreating these wonderful sweets. Recipes are what this book is really about. With that in mind, I've spent many long, but gratifying hours working with the recipes, selecting, writing, and rewriting, testing and retesting to *make certain* that you will be able to produce delectable cookies in your own kitchen. My hope is that these cookies will match or even surpass those of your memories.

Hungarian Jam-Filled Butter Cookies (recipe on page 231).

CHAPTER 1

BAKING COOKIES: THE BASICS

COOKIES ARE TRULY ONE OF LIFE'S SIMPLE PLEAsures. Not only are they enjoyable to eat, but they're also fun and easy to make. The equipment needed is minimal, and most cookie recipes involve only a few basic cooking techniques. A little measuring, mixing, shaping, and baking, and voilà—irresistibly fragrant, fresh-from-the-oven cookies.

Besides relying on a good recipe, there is only one secret to making delicious cookies—using top-quality ingredients. Fresh ingredients will ensure a wonderful homemade flavor that cannot be obtained any other way.

Following are some brief comments on the basic techniques, ingredients, and equipment called for in *The International Cookie Cookbook*. The information is designed to answer questions, clarify details, and generally help you get the most from these recipes in your own kitchen.

INGREDIENTS

Baking powder and baking soda. These are both leaveners, but they cannot be used interchangeably. Baking powder must be stored airtight and used promptly or it loses its leavening power. In addition, stale baking powder may leave an unpleasant aftertaste.

Baking soda only works as a leavening agent in conjunction with some acid in the dough. It also promotes browning. Baking soda has a tendency to form lumps, and lumpy baking soda should never be stirred into dry ingredients or added to a batter. Carefully crush any lumps between the fingers or with the back of a spoon until completely powdery, then combine with other ingredients.

Butter. Unsalted butter is called for throughout this book. It has a fresher, more delicate flavor than salted butter, partly due to the addition of special cultures that bring out the rich, sweet taste. Although unsalted butter has a shorter refrigerator shelf life than salted butter (in which the salt acts as a preservative), it keeps extremely well in the freezer. Simply allow it to thaw to the desired temperature before using.

Don't confuse unsalted butter with "sweet cream butter." This designation indicates only that the butter was churned from sweet cream, not whether salt has been added. Check the label to be sure.

If you can't obtain unsalted butter or prefer to use salted, omit any salt called for in the recipe. Never substitute whipped butter, as it contains more air (and consequently less butter) than the same quantity of unsalted butter.

Chocolate Products. A number of different chocolate products are called for in the recipes in this book, including unsweetened, bittersweet, semisweet, milk chocolate, white chocolate, semisweet chocolate chips, and unsweetened cocoa powder (not the presweetened mix for making hot cocoa). These ingredients cannot be used interchangeably because they contain varying amounts of sugar, cocoa butter, and chocolate liquor (the chocolatey essence), all of which affect both the texture and flavor of the cookies. Note carefully what is specified in each recipe and do not substitute unless alternatives are suggested.

Some cooks are confused about the terms "unsweetened" and "bittersweet" chocolate. Unsweetened is chocolate liquor and cocoa butter and tastes quite bitter. Bittersweet, like semisweet chocolate, is sweetened, but is not as sweet as milk chocolate.

Although bittersweet and semisweet chocolates are not exactly the same and yield slightly different results, some of the recipes have been tested using both, and either chocolate may be used whenever specifically indicated. Bittersweet chocolate must contain at least 35 percent chocolate liquor, while semisweet has at least 15 and usually no more than 35 percent, so bittersweet generally imparts a smoother, mellower, and sometimes more subtle chocolate flavor. Bittersweet is usually slightly less sweet than semisweet chocolate. Keep these differences in mind if you are given a choice between the two in a particular recipe.

Chocolate is a temperamental ingredient and should be handled exactly as indicated in the recipes. For example, when melting chocolate and butter over direct heat, make sure to place in a heavy saucepan and warm very slowly to avoid scorching. When melting chocolate in a double boiler, be sure the water just barely simmers or the steam produced can cause the chocolate to suddenly harden (called seizing) and become unmanageable.

Dried fruits. Dried fruits such as raisins, dates, currants, figs, apricots, and prunes used in cookies and cookie fillings should be plump, moist, and fresh. Don't use fruits that have dried out and hardened. Not only will they lack flavor and remain too hard, but they may even draw the moisture from the dough and cause your cookies to be dry and crumbly.

Eggs. All the recipes have been tested using eggs graded "large." Since the texture of most cookies depends on a precise ratio of sugar, fat, egg, and flour, it is best not to make substitutions.

In recipes that call for egg whites to be beaten, the whites must be absolutely free of any yolk. The mixing bowl and beaters must also be free of any traces of grease, or the whites will not increase in volume properly.

Flour. Either all-purpose or unbleached flour can be used in these recipes. Unless a recipe specifies otherwise, measure and use flour unsifted. To measure correctly, dip the appropriate graduated measuring cup into the flour until overfull. Level off the flour with a straight-edged spatula or knife.

Nuts. Use only fresh, top-quality nuts. All nuts become stale rapidly and can develop an off-taste that will adversely affect your cookies. Freeze nuts that are not going to be used promptly. Thaw them thoroughly prior to adding them to cookie recipes.

A number of recipes call for toasting nuts. This helps bring out their flavor and in some instances makes them crisper. In the case of hazelnuts, toasting also helps loosen the hulls, which taste slightly bitter and should thus be removed. For your convenience, instructions for hulling hazelnuts are included in recipes whenever the procedure is required.

Spices and flavorings. Use fresh spices and store them airtight. When kept for long periods, spices not only lose their characteristic flavor, but can also develop an unappealing musty taste.

When recipes call for vanilla, almond, and other such flavorings, use "pure" extracts rather than artificial or imitation. Imitation flavorings usually lend an artificial taste.

Sugar. Recipes always specify whether granulated, powdered, light brown or dark brown sugar should be used. Avoid brown sugar that has hardened and become lumpy; the lumps will remain after beating. Also, don't use the method suggested by some manufacturers of softening hardened brown sugar by heating it in the oven. The warm sugar will cause the fat in the recipe to overheat and soften too much. And if you allow the sugar to cool, it will harden again.

When powdered sugar is called for, it should be measured unsifted unless the recipe specifically calls for sifted powdered sugar.

TECHNIQUES

Preheating the oven. All baking times given in this book are based on results obtained using a thoroughly preheated oven. Allow at least ten and preferably fifteen minutes for preheating. If you have an oven thermometer, use it to be sure the desired oven temperature has been reached before beginning baking and to check for temperature drifts between batches.

Assembling and measuring ingredients. Even though most cookies are fairly simple to make, it's important to work carefully. Always start by reading through the recipe. Also, take care to measure ingredients accurately. Too much or too little fat, flour, sugar, and other basics, for example, can dramatically affect the shape and amount of spreading, the crispness, and, of course, the taste of the cookies.

To measure dry ingredients, use the appropriate cup from a graduated set of measuring cups and overfill slightly. Then level off the top with a straight-edged knife or spatula.

A 1- or 2-cup marked measuring cup with a spout works best for liquid ingredients. When measuring liquids, be sure the cup rests on a flat surface and check from eye level.

Measure tablespoonfuls and teaspoonfuls of items in the ingredient list with a standard set of measuring spoons. Overfill the appropriate spoon, then level off the top with a straight-edged knife or spatula. When instructed to drop cookie dough by teaspoonfuls or tablespoonfuls, however, use a plain flatware teaspoon or tablespoon, *not* a measuring spoon.

Mixing and beating. Most cookies require relatively little beating and mixing. However, unless a recipe calls for sifting the dry ingredients, it's important to stir them together very thoroughly so the salt, leaveners, spices, etc., are evenly distributed throughout the flour. Unless a recipe specifies otherwise, once the dry ingredients are added to the creamed mixture don't beat vigorously, as this develops the gluten in the flour and can cause toughness.

Forming cookies. You may notice that a number of the recipes call for rolling out the dough between sheets of waxed paper instead of on a floured surface. Besides eliminating the kitchen mess associated with working on a floured surface, this technique has several advantages. The dough can be rolled quite thin without any chance of overflouring. Also, the rolled-out dough sheets can be easily transferred to a tray or cookie sheet and chilled in the refrigerator. Once the dough is cold, the waxed paper can be quickly peeled off and the cookies cut out and arranged on baking sheets. The only trick is to make sure to turn the dough over and check the underside frequently, smoothing any creases that form in the bottom sheet of paper.

Recipes in this book not only describe how to shape dough into cookies, but specify cookie size in inches. This information is necessary in order to accurately estimate baking time and recipe yield. It doesn't mean that you must meticulously measure cookies and make them exactly the right size. It does mean, however, that if your cookies are larger or smaller than specified, the yield and baking time will be different and you should take this into account.

Baking cookies. When baking cookies, allow at least two inches of space around each baking sheet so that the hot air can circulate freely. In some ovens two sheets of cookies can be baked at once without crowding, although you'll probably need to reverse the pans from front to back about halfway through baking to ensure even browning. If two sheets seem cramped, you may want to use large sheets and bake only one pan of cookies at a time.

Checking for doneness. A minimum and maximum baking time is specified for all recipes, but a number of unpredictable factors, such as temperature of the dough, type of baking sheet, and reliability of the oven can cause variations. As a result, the recipes always include an alternate measure of doneness, such as the degree of brownness or firmness of the cookies sought, to help you determine when a batch is ready. Unless you are completely familiar with a recipe, it's a good idea to begin checking a minute or two before the cookies are supposed to be done. They can always be baked longer, if necessary, but there is no way to correct for overdoneness.

Cooling cookies. Many cookies are easiest to remove from baking sheets at a particular point in their cooling process (when they are just firm enough not to tear or crumble but still flexible enough not to break), so specific recipe directions have been included to guide you. As soon as the cookies are firm enough, transfer them to wire racks using a spatula. To promote cooling, allow ample space between cookies on the racks. Then let them stand until cooled completely.

Storing. Store cookies airtight. They should be completely cooled first, or they will release steam in the container and may become soggy. The recipe will indicate if they need to be packed in a particular fashion. Some cookies, especially those topped with chocolate, should be refrigerated until serving time.

It is best to store only one kind of cookie in a container at a time. Moist, chewy cookies packed with crispy ones will cause the crisp cookies to go limp. Spicy cookies stored with mild ones will cause the mild cookies to taste of spice.

Despite the conventional notion that cookies can be successfully stored airtight at room temperature for two or three weeks or longer, I've found that most varieties taste best within the first day or so of baking. Cookies won't spoil if held longer, but the wonderful, fresh flavor gradually fades, and some kinds also dry out.

Freezing helps preserve the just-baked taste, so I recommend freezing any cookies that will not be eaten within a few days. They should be packed airtight with as little headroom or air space in the container as possible. If you plan to freeze the cookies for more than a week or so, it's best to double wrap them. Otherwise they will begin to pick up flavors from the freezer. Even when carefully wrapped, most cookies begin to taste stale if frozen for more than a month or two.

EQUIPMENT

Baking sheets. I find that the best baking sheets for cookies are plain (metallic finish) aluminum with one or more very narrow rims. Non-reflective finishes, especially dark-colored ones, tend to disrupt the normal browning process. Deep rims, such as those around "jelly-roll" pans, can interfere with the circulation of hot air over the tops of the cookies.

Aluminum cookie sheets are readily available in two weights, medium and very light weight. Besides durability, the advantage of the sturdier medium-weight sheets is that they hold and distribute heat more evenly and, thus, help prevent cookies from burning on the bottom or browning unevenly. The thin, flexible, light-weight sheets heat up and bake cookies quite rapidly, which promotes maximum browning and crispness, but also means cookies have to be very carefully watched and pans often have to be reversed during baking. It is possible to minimize the chance of burning by stacking one lightweight sheet on top of another and using them as a single, heavier unit.

Although you can certainly use several different kinds of baking sheets at once, keep in mind that each may produce a slightly different amount of browning and require a slightly different baking time. If you want all the cookies in a batch to look uniform, bake them on the same kind of sheet.

Cookie cutters. A number of recipes in this book call for cookie cutters of a particular size and shape. This is simply to indicate how the cookies are traditionally prepared, not to suggest that certain cutters must be used. It's fine to substitute what you have.

Electric mixer. Although many cookie doughs can be mixed by hand, an electric mixer is a great aid in cookie making and is called for throughout this book. Stand mixers normally beat ingredients more quickly and efficiently than do hand-held models. They are also more convenient to use, since they free up both hands for working at other tasks. However, small hand-held mixers will do a perfectly satisfactory job.

Food processor and electric blender. A food processor is required for a few recipes in this book and may be used in preparing several others. It is also extremely handy for grating chocolate and chopping nuts.

A few recipes call for using an electric blender. Do not try to substitute a food processor for a blender unless this is suggested in the recipe. The two don't always yield the same results.

Measuring cups and spoons. You should have a graduated set of plastic or metal measuring cups for measuring dry ingredients. The handiest sets of cups include ¼- ⅓-, ½-, ⅔-, ¾-, and 1-cup measures, but most have fewer, usually ¼-, ⅓-, ½-, and 1-cup. The smaller sets will work, of course, but you'll have to do a little math and more measuring. A glass or plastic 1- or 2-cup marked measuring cup is preferred for measuring liquids, but is not recommended for dry ingredients. A set of measuring spoons is also required.

Spatulas. A thin-bladed spatula (sometimes called a pancake turner) is nearly indispensable for removing most types of cookies from baking sheets. A spatula with a metal blade usually works best, since the blades of plastic or wooden spatulas are often too thick to wedge under thin cookies and lift them up neatly. Use a spatula with a blade wider than the cookies or they may break apart when lifted.

You also need a rubber or plastic spatula (sometimes called a scraper) for scraping down the sides of the mixing bowl and for folding fragile mixtures such as beaten egg whites.

Timer. While not absolutely essential, a timer is especially handy for cookie baking. It is easy to become preoccupied with readying one pan of cookies and to forget another pan in the oven until it's too late.

The electric or battery powered digital timers are the most accurate and are a good investment if you bake frequently. Of course, the mechanical wind-up type can also be used.

RESOURCE LIST

Maid of Scandinavia
3244 Raleigh Avenue
Minneapolis, Minnesota 55416
Telephone: 1-800-328-6722

Wide range of baking supplies and ingredients,
including cookie cutters and molds, pizzelle
and krumkake irons, coarse crystal (pearl)
sugar and sanding sugar, kransekake ring pans,
and madeleine pans. Good source of hard-to-
find European items.

Williams-Sonoma
P.O. Box 7456
San Francisco, California 94120
Telephone: 1-800-541-2233

Assorted baking equipment and ingredients
available through nationwide retail stores or
mail order.

Brown Bag Cookie Art
Hill Design, Inc.
77 Regional Drive
Concord, NH 03301
Telephone: 1-800-228-4488

Assorted decorative and functional ceramic
cookie molds.

D. D. Dillon's Carvings
850 Meadow Lane
Camp Hill, PA 17011
Telephone: 1-717-761-6895

Decorative and functional hand-carved
basswood cookie molds in traditional American
and European designs, including speculaas,
springerle, and shortbread molds.

INFORMATION FOR COOKIE CUTTER AND RECIPE COLLECTORS AND HOBBYISTS

"Cookies" Newsletter
Phyllis Wetherill
5426 27th Street, N.W.
Washington, D.C. 20015

Cookie Cutter Collectors' Club
1167 Teal Road, S.W.
Dellroy, Ohio 44620

CHAPTER 2

AMERICAN & CANADIAN
COOKIES

ALMOST EVERYBODY IN THE UNITED STATES AND Canada loves cookies, and not just because they taste so good. For many of us, cookies call to mind warm kitchens and pleasant family times. We recall sampling cookies straight from mother's or grandmother's oven, or we remember measuring, mixing, and decorating cookies as part of old-fashioned holiday fun.

The variety of cookies baked in American and Canadian kitchens is incredible—zippy ginger snaps, fragile lace wafers, caramel slices, iced sugar cookies, crunchy oatmeal crisps, lemon bars, and simple butter cookies are just a few of the standards. Part of the reason for the diversity is that our nations were settled mostly by immigrants who brought their cookie-making traditions along to the New World. Scandinavian-style spritz are prepared in many homes across the United States, for example, and shortbread is as popular in Canada as it is in Great Britain.

Nevertheless, our best-loved cookies are uniquely our own. Probably *the favorite* in the United States is the chocolate chip cookie, created around 1935 by Mrs. Ruth Wakefield of the Toll House Restaurant in Massachusetts. Her inspired pairing of buttery dough and bits of chopped chocolate (chocolate chips were invented later to go in Toll House Cookies) made American cookie history and has led to such current variations on the chocolate chip theme as Brown Sugar-Chocolate Chunk Supreme, Double Chocolate Chews, and sinfully sumptuous White Chocolate Chunk-Macadamia Nut cookies, all of which appear in this chapter. As of yet, chocolate chip cookies aren't often prepared outside North America, so only our youngsters know the pleasure of sneaking chocolate bits from the mixing bowl!

The second most popular cookie here is, doubtless, the brownie, another chocolate indulgence in fudgy bar form. A particular favorite in Canada today is a super-rich chocolate bar cookie, the Nanaimo Bar, named after the city of Nanaimo in British Columbia.

Chocolate or not, our cookies tend to be rich, chewy-moist, and full of flavor. Ingredients like molasses, brown sugar, and lemon enliven a number of popular recipes. Two other typical ingredients are peanut butter and pecans, both products of plants indigenous to the southern half of the continent. While both peanut butter and pecan cookies seem commonplace to us, they are hallmark recipes of North American cookery. Clearly, they show us at our best.

Lemon Bars (recipe on page 16).

LEMON BARS

United States

An extra-buttery shortbread crust combines with a tangy lemon layer in this modern American favorite. It's easy *and* good.

Directions are provided for preparing the shortbread layer by hand or with a food processor.

SHORTBREAD

1¼   *cups all-purpose or unbleached white flour*
⅓   *cup powdered sugar*
10   *tablespoons (1¼ sticks) cold unsalted butter, cut into small pieces*

FILLING

1½   *cups granulated sugar*
¼   *cup all-purpose or unbleached white flour*
4   *large eggs*
     Finely grated zest of 2 large lemons
⅓   *cup fresh lemon juice*

DECORATION

2 to 3 tablespoons powdered sugar

Preheat the oven to 350 degrees F. Lightly grease a 7½- by 11¾-inch shallow flat baking pan.

To prepare the shortbread by hand, sift flour and powdered sugar into a medium bowl. Sprinkle butter pieces over flour mixture. Using a pastry blender, forks or the fingers, work butter into flour until mixture resembles fine meal. Add 2 teaspoons cold water and toss with a fork until mixture begins to hold together. If necessary, add a bit more water, but be very careful not to over moisten. (To prepare dough with a food processor, combine flour and powdered sugar in a processor fitted with a steel blade. Process in on/off pulses for about 5 seconds to mix. Sprinkle butter pieces over flour mixture. Process in on/off pulses for about 1 minute, or until butter is cut into dry ingredients and mixture resembles coarse meal. Add 2 teaspoons cold water and process in on/off pulses until dough just begins to hold together and form a ball. Add a bit more water if necessary, but do not over moisten or over process.)

Turn dough into prepared baking pan and using fingers or the back of a wooden spoon, press it out toward edges to form a smooth, uniformly-thick layer.

Place in center of the oven and bake for 15 to 17 minutes, or until just beginning to color at the edges.

Meanwhile, prepare the filling. Combine granulated sugar and flour in a small deep bowl. Add eggs and beat with a fork until frothy. Add lemon zest and lemon juice and beat until smooth.

Remove shortbread from the oven and let stand for 3 or 4 minutes. Pour filling evenly over shortbread and return pan to oven. Bake for 21 to 23 minutes longer, or until the filling appears set when lightly touched in the center and edges are beginning to color.

Remove from the oven. Place pan on a wire rack. Let stand until completely cooled. When cool, sift 2 to 3 tablespoons powdered sugar lightly over the top. Using a sharp knife, cut into small bars or squares. Carefully remove bars from pan with a spatula.

Lemon bars are best served within 48 hours of baking. They do not freeze well.

Makes 20 to 24 small bars.

DOUBLE CHOCOLATE CHEWS

United States

A rich, chewy, brownie-like cookie plumped with chocolate chips and dusted with powdered sugar, this is a favorite in many American households.

1¾ cups all-purpose or unbleached white flour
1½ teaspoons baking powder
¼ teaspoon salt
⅓ cup flavorless vegetable oil
4 ounces unsweetened chocolate, coarsely chopped
1⅔ cups granulated sugar
4 large eggs
1¾ teaspoons vanilla extract
⅛ teaspoon almond extract
¾ cup semisweet chocolate chips

DECORATION
¼ cup powdered sugar

In a medium mixing bowl, stir together flour, baking powder, and salt and set aside. Combine oil and chocolate in a medium-sized heavy saucepan and warm over lowest heat, stirring occasionally, until chocolate melts. Remove saucepan from heat and stir in sugar using a large wooden spoon. Add eggs, one at a time, and stir until well blended. Stir in vanilla and almond extracts.

Pour chocolate mixture into dry ingredients and stir until very thoroughly mixed. Add chocolate chips and stir until evenly distributed. Cover dough and refrigerate for at least 1½ hours or up to 48 hours, if desired. If refrigerated for more than 2 hours, let dough warm and soften slightly before shaping and baking.

Preheat the oven to 350 degrees F. Grease several baking sheets and set aside.

Roll chilled dough between palms to form 1¼-inch diameter balls. Space them about 2 inches apart on greased baking sheets.

Place in upper third of the oven and bake for 11 to 13 minutes or until just beginning to firm in the center. Reverse baking sheets from front to back halfway through baking to ensure even cooking. Remove from oven and let stand for 1 minute, then transfer cookies to wire racks to cool. Lightly dust cookies with powdered sugar shortly before serving.

Store cookies in an airtight container for up to a week. They may also be frozen and decorated with powdered sugar after they thaw.

Makes 35 to 40 2½-inch cookies.

Overleaf: *Grandmother Ellison's Oatmeal Cookies and Sugar Cookies (recipes on pages 20–21).*

Sugar Cookies

United States

Crisp, buttery, and slightly sweet, these appealing sugar cookies are nice for the holidays served decorated with nonpareils, colored sugar, or piped icing. They are also good served plain for no particular occasion. An old favorite in my family, these cookies were made by my mother, and her mother before her. Guests always ask for the recipe.

3¾ cups all-purpose or unbleached white flour
2¾ teaspoons baking powder
¼ teaspoon salt
1 cup (2 sticks) unsalted butter, slightly softened
1⅔ cups granulated sugar
2 large eggs
2½ teaspoons vanilla extract

DECORATION (OPTIONAL)
Colored sugar or nonpareils

ICING (OPTIONAL)
1⅔ cups powdered sugar
½ teaspoon light corn syrup
¼ teaspoon vanilla extract
Food coloring, if desired

Thoroughly stir together flour, baking powder, and salt and set aside.

Place butter in a large mixing bowl and beat with an electric mixer on medium speed until light. Add sugar and beat until fluffy. Add eggs and vanilla, and continue beating until thoroughly blended and smooth. Gradually beat in about half the dry ingredients. Stir in remaining dry ingredients using a large wooden spoon. Divide dough in thirds. At this point the cookies may be baked, or dough thirds may be wrapped tightly in plastic wrap and stored for up to 48 hours in the refrigerator or 10 days in the freezer. (Allow dough to warm up before rolling and cutting.)

To bake the cookies immediately, preheat the oven to 375 degrees F. Grease several baking sheets. Place one-third of dough between large sheets of waxed paper and roll out to ⅛-inch thick. Check underside of dough frequently and smooth out any wrinkles in the paper. Slide dough onto a tray or baking sheet and refrigerate for about 15 minutes, until chilled and slightly stiffened. Roll and chill remaining two dough pieces in the same manner.

Working with one dough sheet at a time (keep the others refrigerated), turn dough over so the underside is facing up. Peel off waxed paper; then replace it loosely. Turn dough right side up again and peel off and discard top sheet of waxed paper. Using assorted 2- to 3½-inch cutters, cut out dough. Then, using a spatula, transfer cookies to baking sheets, spacing them about 1½ inches apart. (If cookies of differing sizes are prepared, group them by size on separate baking sheets for even baking.) Gather dough scraps and re-roll between sheets of waxed paper. Repeat the chilling and cutting out process. Repeat with the second and third dough sheets. If not adding icing, decorate cookies with colored sugar or nonpareils, if desired.

Place in the center of the oven and bake for 7 to 10 minutes or until cookies are just beginning to tinge with brown at the edges. Remove baking sheets from oven and allow cookies to firm up for 2 minutes. Using a spatula, immediately transfer cookies to wire racks to cool. Decorate with icing, if desired.

To prepare icing, sift powdered sugar into a mixing bowl. Add corn syrup, vanilla, and 2½ teaspoons water and stir until thoroughly blended and smooth. If mixture is too thick to pipe through a pastry bag fitted with a fine writing tip, add enough water to reach desired consis-

Maple Wafers

United States

Homey and easy-to-make, these very thin wafers are golden brown and crisp. Since the taste of real maple syrup is much more subtle than that of artificial maple extracts, the wafers also have a very mild flavor.

Like lace cookies, maple wafers spread a great deal on the baking sheet and must be removed quickly before they become brittle. Therefore, it's best to bake only one sheet at a time.

¾	cup pure maple syrup
10	tablespoons (1 stick plus 2 tablespoons) unsalted butter
1	cup all-purpose or unbleached white flour
2½	tablespoons granulated sugar
¼	teaspoon baking soda
	Pinch of salt
1	large egg
1¼	teaspoons vanilla extract

In a 2-quart saucepan, bring maple syrup to a boil over medium-high heat. Boil, uncovered, for 4 minutes or until syrup is reduced to a generous ½ cup. Add butter and allow mixture to return to a boil. Boil for 2 minutes longer. Remove saucepan from heat and let stand until mixture cools to warm.

Preheat the oven to 375 degrees F. Grease several baking sheets very generously. Sift together flour, sugar, baking soda, and salt; set aside.

Using a large wooden spoon, vigorously stir egg and then vanilla into the butter-maple mixture. Add dry ingredients and stir until thoroughly incorporated; mixture will be fluid. Drop batter neatly onto baking sheets by small rounded teaspoonfuls, spacing mounds about 3½ inches apart. (Do not crowd, as the wafers may run together.)

Place in the oven and bake for 5 to 6 minutes, or until wafers are rimmed with light brown and golden in the middle. Reverse baking sheet from front to back about halfway through baking to ensure even browning. Near the end of the baking wafers will brown rapidly, so watch them carefully to avoid burning. Remove baking sheets from oven and let stand on a wire rack for 1 minute. Then, using a metal spatula, quickly transfer wafers to wire racks before they become brittle. (If they firm up before all can be removed, return baking sheet to oven for 1 or 2 minutes to soften them slightly.) Let wafers stand until cooled completely. Allow baking sheets to cool completely before reusing, and thoroughly grease between batches.

Wafers may be stored in an airtight container for up to 1 week. Freeze for longer storage.

Makes about 40 3¼- to 3¾-inch cookies.

LEMON WAFERS

United States

Simple, crisp-tender cookies with wonderful flavor and a golden tan color, these are made from an old recipe passed along to me by a Maryland farm family.

1	cup all-purpose or unbleached white flour
1½	tablespoons cornstarch
⅛	teaspoon baking soda
⅛	teaspoon salt
⅔	cup (1 stick plus 3 tablespoons) unsalted butter, slightly softened (see Note)
¾	cup granulated sugar
1	large egg
1	teaspoon vanilla extract
¼	teaspoon lemon extract
	Finely grated zest of 2 medium lemons (about 2 teaspoons)

Preheat the oven to 375 degrees F. Lightly grease several baking sheets and set aside.

In a small, deep mixing bowl, stir together flour, cornstarch, baking soda, and salt and set aside.

Combine butter and sugar in a small mixing bowl and beat with an electric mixer on medium speed until light and fluffy. Add egg and continue beating until thoroughly blended and smooth. Add vanilla and lemon extracts, and beat for 30 seconds longer. Gradually add dry ingredients beating until thoroughly incorporated. Stir in lemon zest until well mixed.

Drop dough onto baking sheets by scant teaspoonfuls about 3½ inches apart, keeping mounds as smooth and even as possible. (Do not crowd the cookies or make them too large, as they spread a great deal.)

Place on the upper oven rack and bake for 7 to 8 minutes, or until cookies are golden brown around the edges. Remove baking sheet from the oven and let cookies firm up for 30 seconds. Then, using a spatula, carefully but quickly transfer cookies to wire racks before they become brittle. (If they firm up before all can be removed, return baking sheet to the oven for 1 or 2 minutes to soften them slightly.) Let stand until cool. Allow baking sheets to cool between batches; otherwise dough will spread too much.

Store wafers in an airtight container for 3 or 4 days. Freeze for longer storage.

Makes 35 to 40 3- to 3½-inch wafers.

Note: The butter should be slightly soft, but not at all melted. If dough is too warm when dropped onto baking sheets, it will spread too much during the first minutes of baking. (Over-warm dough can be cooled in the refrigerator a minute or two between batches, if necessary.)

WHITE CHOCOLATE CHUNK-MACADAMIA NUT COOKIES

United States

A sumptuous combination of white chocolate, macadamia nuts, brown sugar, and butter, this recipe was inspired by a very popular white chocolate-nut cookie in the Mrs. Fields repertoire.

The cookies are chewy-crisp, fragrant, and incredibly rich. They are also large and an eye-catching pale gold with white chocolate chunks. People always rave about these cookies.

¾   cup (1½ sticks) unsalted butter, slightly softened
½   cup packed light brown sugar
8   ounces imported white chocolate
1½   cups all-purpose or unbleached white flour
¾   teaspoon baking powder
½   teaspoon baking soda
¼   teaspoon salt (see Note)
3   tablespoons granulated sugar
1   large egg
1   teaspoon vanilla extract
½   cup coarsely chopped macadamia nuts, preferably unsalted

Place butter in a heavy medium-sized saucepan over medium-low heat and heat until butter boils and bubbles very gently but steadily. Adjust heat as necessary to prevent butter from burning, and continue simmering uncovered for 4 to 5 minutes or until it is golden but not browned, stirring frequently. Be very careful not to burn butter. Immediately remove pan from heat and stir in brown sugar. Pour into a large mixing bowl and refrigerate 50 to 60 minutes, or until mixture resolidifies but is not hard. (To speed chilling, place butter in freezer for about 30 minutes, but don't let it get too hard.)

Preheat the oven to 350 degrees F. Grease several baking sheets and set aside. Grate 3 ounces of the chocolate. Coarsely chop remaining chocolate. Set the two aside separately.

Thoroughly stir together flour, baking powder, baking soda, and salt and set aside. Remove bowl from the refrigerator and beat cooled butter-brown sugar mixture until lightened. Add granulated sugar and beat until fluffy and smooth. Beat in egg and vanilla. Beat in dry ingredients. Add grated chocolate, *half* of the chopped chocolate, and nuts and stir until well combined.

Roll dough into generous 1½-inch balls. Dip top of each ball into remaining chopped white chocolate, pressing lightly to imbed some pieces in the dough. Space balls, chocolate-studded tops up, about 2¼ inches apart on baking sheets. Press down balls just slightly with heel of hand.

Place on *center oven rack* and bake for 9 to 11 minutes or until just tinged with brown. Reverse baking sheets from front to back halfway through baking to ensure even browning. Be very careful not to overbake. Remove baking sheets from the oven and let stand for 4 or 5 minutes. Using a spatula, transfer cookies to wire racks to cool.

Store in an airtight container for 3 to 4 days. Freeze for longer storage.

Makes 25 to 27 3- to 3¼-inch cookies.

Note: Reduce salt to ⅛ teaspoon if salted macadamia nuts are used. Unsalted macadamias are preferred for this recipe, but they are hard to find.

Chocolate Chip Cookies (recipe on page 33) and
White Chocolate Chunk-Macadamia Nut Cookies.

Chunky Macadamia Nut-White Chocolate Cookies

United States

The search for the best American white chocolate-macadamia nut cookie goes on! This recipe—which yields crunchy, slightly crumbly textured cookies studded with whole macadamia nuts and white chocolate bits—was inspired by the Blue Chip Cookie Company in San Francisco. This adaptation was created by a home economist friend, Jene Springrose, so she could enjoy these rich, nutty cookies after she moved away from the West.

2   cups all-purpose or unbleached white flour
¾   teaspoon baking soda
½   teaspoon baking powder
⅛   teaspoon salt
½   cup (1 stick) unsalted butter, slightly softened
½   cup solid vegetable shortening, at room temperature
¾   cup packed light brown sugar
2   tablespoons granulated sugar
1   large egg
1½   teaspoons vanilla extract
8   ounces top-quality white chocolate chips, or 8 ounces imported white chocolate, chopped
7   ounces salted, whole macadamia nuts

Preheat the oven to 375 degrees F. Lightly grease several baking sheets.

Sift together flour, baking soda, baking powder, and salt and set aside. In a large mixing bowl, beat butter and solid shortening until lightened. Add brown and granulated sugars, and beat until fluffy and smooth. Beat in egg and vanilla. Beat in the dry ingredients. Add white chocolate and macadamia nuts, and stir until evenly distributed throughout.

Drop dough by large, rounded teaspoonfuls onto baking sheets, spacing cookies about 2½ inches apart. Flatten tops of cookies slightly with the blade of a table knife or long-bladed spatula.

Place in center of the oven and bake for 8 to 9 minutes, or until tops are golden and edges are lightly browned. Reverse baking sheets from front to back halfway through baking to ensure even browning. Be very careful *not* to overbake. Remove baking sheets from the oven and let stand for 2 or 3 minutes. Using a spatula, transfer cookies to wire racks to cool.

Store in an airtight container for up to a week. Freeze for longer storage.

Makes 35 to 40 2¾-inch cookies.

CHOCOLATE ICEBOX SLICES

United States

A good, crisp chocolate cookie that's also convenient. The dough logs can be stored in the refrigerator or freezer to be sliced and baked as needed.

2¼   cups all-purpose or unbleached white
      flour
⅓   cup unsweetened cocoa powder
½   teaspoon baking powder
1   cup (2 sticks) cold unsalted butter,
      cut into pieces
1   cup granulated sugar
1   large egg
2   teaspoons vanilla extract
4   ounces bittersweet or semisweet
      chocolate, finely grated

Thoroughly stir together the flour, cocoa powder, and baking powder in a large bowl. Using a pastry blender, fork or fingertips cut the butter into dry ingredients until mixture resembles fine crumbs.

In a medium bowl, combine sugar, egg, and vanilla and beat with a fork until well blended. Stir in grated chocolate. Pour egg mixture into flour mixture and stir until thoroughly incorporated. Knead until mixture becomes cohesive.

(Or combine flour, cocoa powder, and baking powder in the bowl of a food processor fitted with a steel blade and process with on/off pulses for 5 seconds to blend ingredients. Sprinkle butter over dry ingredients and process with on/off pulses for about 1½ minutes, or until mixture resembles fine crumbs. In a medium bowl, combine sugar, egg, and vanilla and beat with a fork until well blended. Stir in the grated chocolate. Add egg mixture to processor. Process with on/off pulses until ingredients are just blended, being careful not to overprocess.)

Divide dough in half. Spoon each half onto a sheet of waxed paper, and shape and roll each into a smooth, uniformly thick log about 2 inches in diameter and 8½ inches long. Slide logs onto a large tray or baking sheet and chill until firm enough to slice—about 1 hour in the refrigerator or about 35 minutes in the freezer. (Dough can be sliced and baked immediately, or wrapped tightly and stored in the refrigerator for up to 4 days or in the freezer for up to 2 weeks to be sliced and baked as needed. Allow frozen logs to thaw slightly before slicing.)

Preheat the oven to 350 degrees F. Lightly grease several baking sheets. Using a sharp knife, cut the dough crosswise into scant ¼-inch-thick slices. Space slices about 1½ inches apart on baking sheets.

Place in the center of the oven and bake for 9 to 11 minutes, or until almost firm on top. The baking time will vary somewhat depending on the temperature of the dough. Remove from the oven and let cookies cool on baking sheets for about 3 minutes. Using a spatula, transfer to wire racks and let cool completely.

Store in an airtight container for up to a week. Freeze for longer storage.

Makes 50 to 60 2¾-inch slices.

CHOCOLATE-TIPPED PECAN BARS

United States

There are many versions of this super-rich bar cookie around the United States today. Some recipes specify cutting the bars into diamonds, others into squares or rectangles. In this version, the cookies are thinnish rectangles with a narrow end dipped in a glossy chocolate glaze.

SHORTBREAD

³⁄₄	cup all-purpose or unbleached white flour
1	tablespoon granulated sugar
¹⁄₈	teaspoon salt
¹⁄₄	cup (½ stick) cold unsalted butter, cut into small pieces
1	to 1½ tablespoons light cream

PECAN TOPPING

1½	cups chopped pecans
¹⁄₃	cup (5¹⁄₃ tablespoons) unsalted butter
½	cup packed light brown sugar
2	tablespoons honey
2	tablespoons granulated sugar
1	tablespoon light cream
1½	teaspoons vanilla extract

CHOCOLATE GLAZE

1½	ounces semisweet chocolate
½	ounce unsweetened chocolate
2	teaspoons solid vegetable shortening
1	teaspoon honey

Preheat the oven to 350 degrees F.

To prepare shortbread, thoroughly stir together flour, sugar, and salt in a large mixing bowl. Add butter and cut into dry ingredients with a pastry blender or forks until the mixture resembles coarse meal. Add 1 tablespoon cream and toss until well distributed and dough begins to bind together when pressed into a ball. If necessary, add more cream by teaspoons until a dough forms, but do not over-moisten. (Alternatively, combine dry ingredients and butter in food processor bowl fitted with a steel blade and process in on/off pulses until the mixture resembles coarse meal, being careful not to over-process. Add 1 tablespoon cream and process in on/off pulses until dough begins to hold together. Add a bit more cream if needed to bind dough, but do not over-moisten.)

Turn dough into an ungreased 8-inch square baking pan and press out toward edges to form a smooth, evenly thick layer.

Place in the center of the oven and bake for 12 minutes. Remove shortbread from oven and set aside to cool slightly.

To prepare the pecan topping, spread pecans in a large baking pan and toast, stirring several times, for 5 to 6 minutes. Place butter in a medium, heavy saucepan over medium heat and heat until melted and bubbling. Simmer over medium heat for 2 minutes, adjusting heat if necessary and being careful not to burn butter. Stir in brown sugar, honey, and granulated sugar. Stirring frequently, bring mixture to a boil. Boil for 3 minutes, then remove from heat. Add toasted pecans, cream, and vanilla and stir until well combined. (The proportion of nuts to sugar-butter mixture will seem high but it is correct.) Spread pecan mixture evenly over shortbread.

Return to the oven and bake at 350 degrees for 20 to 22 minutes, or until topping is bubbly and golden brown. Remove baking pan from the oven and place on a wire rack to cool to warm before cutting. (If dough is too warm when cut

bars will be crumbly; if it's too cool, it will be too firm to cut easily, so check frequently.)

Carefully cut into 16 equal squares with a sharp knife. Then, cut squares in half to form rectangular bars. Using a spatula, transfer bars to a wire rack set over a sheet of waxed paper.

To prepare glaze, combine semisweet and unsweetened chocolate, solid shortening, and honey in a small, heavy saucepan and warm over low heat, stirring occasion-ally, until completely melted and runny; be careful not to burn. Working quickly before glaze cools and stiffens, dip one narrow end of each bar into glaze. Return bars to rack and let stand for at least 45 minutes, or until the glaze sets.

Store refrigerated in an airtight container for up to a week. Bars may be frozen if desired. Keep refrigerated after thawing.

Makes 32 2-by-1-inch bars.

CHOCOLATE CHOCOLATE CHIP COOKIES

United States

A nice, extra-large, chocolatey cookie studded with chocolate chips.

1 cup quick–cooking oats
2½ cups all-purpose or unbleached white flour
1½ teaspoons baking powder
1 teaspoon baking soda
¼ teaspoon salt
12 ounces (2 cups) semisweet chocolate chips
1 cup plus 5 tablespoons (2 sticks plus 5 tablespoons) unsalted butter, slightly softened
1 cup packed light brown sugar
⅓ cup granulated sugar
2 large eggs
2½ teaspoons vanilla extract

Process the oats to a powder in a food processor or blender. (If using a blender, stop motor and stir oats several times to pulverize evenly.) Combine oats, flour, baking powder, baking soda, and salt in processor or a bowl and blend well. Place 1 cup of the chocolate chips in the top of a double boiler and warm over gently simmering water, stirring occasionally, until melted and smooth; set aside.

In a large mixing bowl, beat butter until light and fluffy. Add brown and granulated sugars and beat until fluffy and smooth. Beat in eggs and vanilla. Beat in the melted chocolate and about half the dry ingredients. Add remaining 1 cup chocolate chips and remaining dry ingredients and stir until thoroughly incorporated. Cover bowl and refrigerate for 20 to 30 minutes or until the dough is firm enough to be shaped into balls.

Preheat the oven to 350 degrees F. Grease several baking sheets. Shape dough into 1½-inch balls and space them about 2¼ inches apart on baking sheets. Gently pat down the tops of the balls *just slightly*. (Don't actually flatten the balls or the cookies will spread too much and lose their moist, chewy texture.)

Place in the upper third of the oven and bake for 9 to 11 minutes or until just beginning to become firm in the center. For very moist cookies be careful not to overbake. Remove from the oven and let stand on baking sheets for 3 or 4 minutes. Transfer cookies to wire racks and let stand until cool.

Store in an airtight container for up to a week. Freeze for longer storage.

Makes 40 to 45 2½-inch cookies.

Chocolate Chip Cookies

United States

Great flavor, a fine chocolate aroma, and a chewy-crisp texture make this chocolate chip cookie a favorite. It is similar to the chocolate chip cookie sold in Mrs. Fields' shops.

Chopped walnuts are included as an optional ingredient, but I like this particular cookie better without them.

1²/₃ cups rolled oats
1½ cups all-purpose or unbleached white flour
1 teaspoon baking soda
¾ teaspoon baking powder
¼ teaspoon salt
¾ cup (1½ sticks) unsalted butter
²/₃ cup granulated sugar
²/₃ cup packed light brown sugar
1 large egg
2 teaspoons vanilla extract
1 6-ounce package semisweet chocolate chips
1 3-ounce bar top quality milk chocolate, finely chopped
¾ cup chopped walnuts (optional)

Preheat the oven to 375 degrees F. Grease several baking sheets and set aside. Place oats in a food processor or blender and grind to a fine powder. Set aside.

Stir together flour, baking soda, baking powder, and salt. Place butter in a large mixing bowl and beat until lightened. Add granulated and brown sugars, and beat until fluffy and smooth. Beat in egg and vanilla. Add dry ingredients and beat until well blended. Add oats, chocolate chips, chopped chocolate, and nuts (if used) and stir until distributed throughout.

Roll dough pieces between palms to form 1½-inch balls. Space balls about 2½ inches apart on baking sheets. Flatten slightly with the heel of the hand.

Place in upper third of the oven and bake for 8 to 10 minutes, or until just tinged with brown. Reverse baking sheets from front to back halfway through baking to ensure even browning. Be very careful not to overbake. Remove baking sheets from the oven and let stand for 3 to 4 minutes. Using a spatula, transfer cookies to wire racks to cool.

Store in an airtight container for up to a week. Freeze for longer storage.

Makes about 30 3½-inch cookies.

Caramel Walnut Slices

Canada

Homey, golden-colored icebox cookies rich with the taste of nuts and caramel. This very old recipe—which has been updated somewhat—comes from Winnipeg. The cook's original notes suggest that the dough can be stashed in the icebox and baked up in time for tea.

Since this recipe calls for preparing caramel, be sure to work carefully: Hot caramel reaches a high temperature and will burn if it contacts the skin.

1	cup (2 sticks) plus 2 tablespoons unsalted butter, slightly softened
2¼	cups packed light brown sugar
2	cups chopped walnuts
2	large eggs
2¾	teaspoons vanilla extract
3⅔	cups all-purpose or unbleached white flour
¾	teaspoon baking soda
¼	teaspoon baking powder
½	teaspoon salt

Place butter in a large glass or metal mixing bowl (do not use plastic as the hot caramel may melt it); set aside. Grease a large baking sheet.

To prepare the caramel, combine brown sugar with ⅓ cup water in a 2-quart saucepan. Place over medium-high heat and bring to a foaming boil, stirring constantly. Start timing when the mixture begins to boil and boil for 3 minutes, stirring and scraping the bottom of the pan with a wooden spoon to prevent scorching; the caramel will boil harder and darken gradually as it cooks. Quickly pour all *except* ½ cup of the caramel over the reserved butter. Set saucepan and remaining ½ cup caramel aside. Stir caramel and butter together for about 30 seconds, or until butter is partially melted and the two are well combined.

Return saucepan to the heat and bring remaining ½ cup caramel to a boil once again. Boil, stirring, for 2 minutes. Immediately remove from the heat and add 1 cup of the walnuts, stirring until they are coated with the syrup. Quickly turn mixture out onto baking sheet. Set aside for 8 to 10 minutes, or until mixture hardens. Remove from baking sheet and place in a heavy plastic bag. Using a mallet or the back of a heavy spoon, pound mixture into very small pieces.

Beat the caramel-butter mixture with an electric mixer on low speed until the butter is completely melted and the mixture has cooled to warm. Beat in the eggs and vanilla until well blended. In a separate bowl, combine flour, baking soda, baking powder, and salt and stir to blend. Gradually beat about half the dry ingredients into the butter mixture. Stir in caramel-coated walnut pieces and remaining dry ingredients using a large wooden spoon. (Set aside remaining 1 cup walnuts for garnish.) Cover and refrigerate the dough for 10 to 20 minutes, or until firm enough to shape into logs.

Divide dough in half and place each half on a long sheet of waxed paper. Shape into two 11½- by 2¼-inch logs, rolling each back and forth on waxed paper until smooth and evenly shaped. Sprinkle each log with ½ cup of the remaining walnuts, turning logs to coat all sides evenly and gently pressing nuts into the dough. Carefully slide the logs onto a baking sheet and refrigerate until firm, about 1½ hours.

Logs may be cut and baked immediately or wrapped tightly and refrigerated for up to 2 days. They may also be frozen for up to a week and then partially thawed in the refrigerator prior to cutting and baking.

Preheat the oven to 375 degrees F. Grease several baking sheets. Using a sharp knife, cut logs into generous ⅛-inch-thick slices. Place on baking sheets about 1 inch apart.

Place in the center of the oven and bake for 10 to 12 minutes, or until just tinged with golden brown all over; exact baking time will vary considerably, depending on the temperature of the dough when used. Reverse baking sheets from front to back halfway through baking to ensure even browning. Remove from the oven and let stand for several minutes. Using a spatula, transfer the cookies to wire racks and let stand until completely cooled.

Store cookies in an airtight container for up to a week. Freeze for longer storage.

Makes 60 to 65 3-inch cookies.

CHOCOLATE CHIP ICE CREAM SANDWICHES

United States

A small dessert shop in Myrtle Beach, South Carolina, serves ice cream sandwiches like these. The crisp and flavorful cookies, chock full of small chocolate chips, are sandwiched around a good vanilla ice cream.

The sandwiches can be put together well in advance and stored in the freezer if desired. However, the cookies will gradually lose their crispness as they absorb moisture from the ice cream. I prefer to freeze the cookies separately and then assemble the sandwiches within a day or so of when they will be eaten.

3¾ cups all-purpose or unbleached white flour
1 tablespoon unsweetened cocoa powder
2 teaspoons baking powder
½ teaspoon baking soda
½ teaspoon salt
1 cup plus 3 tablespoons (2 sticks plus 3 tablespoons) unsalted butter, slightly softened
1¾ cups packed dark brown sugar
3 tablespoons light corn syrup
2 large eggs
1 tablespoon vanilla extract
1 12-ounce package semisweet chocolate mini-chips (see Note)
1 to 1¼ quarts (approximately) vanilla ice cream, slightly softened

Thoroughly stir together flour, cocoa powder, baking powder, baking soda, and salt. Set aside.

Place butter in a large mixing bowl and beat with an electric mixer on medium speed until light and fluffy. Add brown sugar and corn syrup and beat until well-blended and light. Add eggs and vanilla and continue beating until thoroughly blended and smooth. Gradually add dry ingredients, beating until thoroughly incorporated. Add chocolate chips, and stir until evenly distributed.

Divide dough in half. Roll each half out between two large sheets of waxed paper to a ¼-inch thickness. Check underside frequently and smooth out any creases that form. Transfer to a large tray or baking sheet and refrigerate for about 25 to 30 minutes, or until cold and firm but not stiff. (To speed chilling, place dough in freezer for about 15 minutes, being careful not to allow it to become too cold and hard.)

Preheat the oven to 375 degrees F. Lightly grease several baking sheets and set aside. Carefully turn over chilled dough and peel waxed paper from the underside. Replace paper and turn dough right side up again. Peel off and discard waxed paper. Using a 2½-inch round cookie cutter or the rim of a 2½-inch glass, cut out cookies. Transfer cookies to baking sheets with a spatula, spacing them about 2½ inches apart. Gather dough scraps and re-roll between sheets of waxed paper. Return dough to a tray and refrigerate it several minutes. Meanwhile, cut out second dough sheet. Re-roll scraps, chill, and continue cutting out until all dough is used.

Place in the center of the oven and bake for 9 to 11 minutes, or until just barely tinged with brown at edges. Remove from oven and let cookies cool on baking sheets for 2 minutes. Using a spatula, immediately transfer cookies to wire racks and let stand until cooled completely. Place cookies in freezer and chill thoroughly before assembling ice cream sandwiches.

To assemble sandwiches, spread 2½ to 3 tablespoons just slightly softened ice cream over the flat side of one cookie using a table knife or long-bladed spatula. Working quickly so ice cream doesn't melt, place another cookie on top of ice cream and press down lightly. Place sandwiches, slightly separated, on a waxed paper-lined tray and freeze until firm. Pack sandwiches in heavy plastic bags.

Store in freezer for up to 2 weeks. If you prefer the cookie portions to be crisp, assemble the sandwiches only a day or two ahead.

Makes about 55 cookies or 27 3¼-inch cookie sandwiches.

Note: Mini-size chocolate chips are required because regular-size chocolate chips become too hard and difficult to bite when frozen. They also make the cookies too "lumpy" to roll out to the desired thickness.

Brown Sugar-Chocolate Chunk Supreme Cookies

United States

Rich, chewy-crisp cookies enriched with the taste of brown sugar, butter, and chunks of bittersweet and white chocolate. This chunky chocolate variation on the traditional chocolate chip cookie theme is nearly irresistible! *And* the recipe is very easy to make.

2   cups all-purpose or unbleached white flour
1   teaspoon baking powder
½   teaspoon baking soda
¼   teaspoon salt
1¼ cups (2½ sticks) unsalted butter, slightly softened
½   cup packed light brown sugar
¼   cup packed dark brown sugar
1   large egg
1½ teaspoons vanilla extract
5   ounces imported bittersweet or dark chocolate, chopped moderately fine
3   ounces imported white chocolate, chopped moderately fine

Preheat the oven to 375 degrees F. Grease several baking sheets and set aside.

Thoroughly stir together flour, baking powder, baking soda, and salt and set aside. Place butter in the bowl of an electric mixer and beat until lightened. Add the light and dark brown sugars, and beat until fluffy and smooth. Beat in the egg and vanilla. Beat in the dry ingredients. Add bittersweet chocolate and white chocolate and stir until distributed throughout. Drop dough onto baking sheets by heaping teaspoonfuls about 2½ inches apart.

Place in center of the oven and bake for 9 to 11 minutes, or until edges are lightly browned. Reverse baking sheets from front to back about halfway through baking to ensure even browning. Be very careful not to overbake. Remove from oven and let stand for 2 or 3 minutes. Using a spatula, transfer cookies to wire racks to cool.

Store in an airtight container for up to 3 or 4 days. Freeze for longer storage.

Makes 35 to 40 3-inch cookies.

FUDGE BROWNIES

United States

It is hard to find a man, woman, or child in the United States who doesn't love brownies. And there are almost as many recipes for these simple bar cookies as there are cooks.

For most Americans, the richer, darker, and more chocolatey brownies are, the better—in which case, these will win high marks. They are dense, moist, and fudgelike without being gummy. They have a shiny top and an intense chocolate flavor and aroma.

¾ cup all-purpose or unbleached white flour
1½ cups powdered sugar
2 tablespoons unsweetened cocoa powder
¾ teaspoon baking powder
⅛ teaspoon salt
4 ounces bittersweet or semisweet chocolate
6 tablespoons unsalted butter
1½ tablespoons dark corn syrup
2 large eggs
1½ teaspoons vanilla extract
⅛ teaspoon almond extract

Preheat the oven to 350 degrees F. Line an 8-inch square baking pan with aluminum foil, allowing foil to overlap two ends of the pan by about 2 inches. Grease foil.

Sift together flour, powdered sugar, cocoa powder, baking powder, and salt and set aside.

Place chocolate and butter in a large heavy saucepan and place over lowest heat, stirring frequently, until just melted and smooth. Remove from heat and stir in the corn syrup. Let stand until mixture cools to lukewarm. When cooled, add eggs, one at a time, beating them into chocolate with a large wooden spoon. Stir in vanilla and almond extracts. Add dry ingredients and stir until well blended and smooth. Turn batter out into baking pan, spreading it evenly to edges.

Place in the middle of the oven and bake for 22 to 25 minutes, or until the center top just begins to feel firm when pressed. (For moister brownies bake for minimum time; for slightly firmer ones, bake the maximum time.) Remove from the oven, place pan on a wire rack, and let stand for at least 15 to 20 minutes. Then, using overhanging foil as handles, carefully lift brownie from pan and place on rack to cool completely. Carefully peel foil from bottom and set brownie right side up on a cutting board. Using a large sharp knife, mark and then cut brownies into 2-inch squares or 2- by 2⅝-inch bars.

Store in an airtight container for 2 or 3 days. Freeze for longer storage.

Makes 12 2-by-2⅝-inch bars or 16 2-inch squares.

Butterscotch Brownies (recipe on page 41), Fudge Brownies, and Extra Chocolatey Brownies with Shiny Chocolate Glaze (recipe on page 40).

Extra Chocolatey Brownies with Shiny Chocolate Glaze

United States

Designed for chocolate lovers, these dark, dense brownies have an intense chocolatey flavor and a shiny, bittersweet chocolate glaze. If you prefer your brownies plain, or don't have time to prepare the glaze, these are also very good unglazed.

1/4 teaspoon instant coffee powder or granules
1 1/2 tablespoons boiling water
5 tablespoons unsalted butter
6 ounces bittersweet or semisweet chocolate, broken or chopped into large pieces
2 large eggs
3/4 cup granulated sugar
2 teaspoons vanilla extract
2/3 cup all-purpose or unbleached white flour
2 tablespoons unsweetened cocoa powder
1/2 teaspoon baking powder
1/4 teaspoon salt

GLAZE (OPTIONAL)
1/2 tablespoon unsalted butter
1 teaspoon light corn syrup
1/3 cup powdered sugar, sifted after measuring
3 ounces bittersweet or semisweet chocolate, broken or chopped into small pieces
1 ounce unsweetened chocolate, broken or chopped into small pieces
1 teaspoon vanilla extract

Preheat the oven to 350 degrees F. Line an 8-inch square baking pan with aluminum foil, allowing foil to overlap two ends of the pan by about 2 inches. (To fit the foil, invert pan and mold foil around the bottom. Turn pan right side up and fit the foil neatly inside, turning overlapping edges outside.) Grease the foil.

Combine the coffee and boiling water in a small cup and set aside until the coffee dissolves. Place butter in a small heavy saucepan and melt over low heat. Stir in chocolate and continue warming over low heat for 1 minute longer. Remove from the heat and let stand, stirring occasionally, until chocolate melts and mixture is smooth.

Place eggs in a medium bowl and beat lightly with a fork. Stir in the sugar, vanilla, and coffee mixture and set aside.

Sift together flour, cocoa, baking powder, and salt. Stir dry ingredients into the egg mixture. Add melted chocolate and stir until well-blended and smooth. Turn batter out into foil-lined pan, spreading it evenly to the edges.

Place on the center oven rack and bake for 27 to 30 minutes or until center top is firm to the touch. (For very moist brownies bake the minimum time; for firmer ones bake longer.) Transfer pan to a wire rack and let stand for at least 15 to 20 minutes. Then, using the overhanging foil edges as handles, carefully lift brownie from the pan and place on the wire rack to cool completely. Carefully peel foil from the bottom of brownie and return it to a rack set over a sheet of waxed paper.

To prepare glaze, place butter, corn syrup, powdered sugar, and 3 tablespoons water in a small heavy saucepan over medium heat. Bring to a boil, stirring, and remove from the heat. Stir in chocolate and set aside, stirring occasionally, until chocolate is melted and mixture is smooth. Stir in vanilla. Let stand until cool and slightly thickened.

Spoon glaze onto brownie, spreading it quickly and evenly over the top and sides with a long-bladed spatula or large knife. If desired, draw the tip of a knife across the glaze vertically and horizontally at ¼-inch intervals to decorate (see photo on page 39). Let brownie stand for at least 45 minutes, or until glaze sets. (Or place in the refrigerator for about 25 minutes to set glaze more quickly.)

Transfer brownie to a cutting board and cut into 2-inch squares with a large sharp knife. For neatest appearance, use a ruler to measure before cutting, and clean knife blade after each cut with a damp paper towel.

Store brownies in an airtight container and refrigerate for up to 2 or 3 days.

Makes 16 2-inch squares.

Butterscotch Brownies

United States

The following recipe for this popular American bar cookie is adapted from one given to me by a superb Washington, D.C. cook and hostess, Polly Clingerman.

These brownies are shiny on top and rather chewy. They smell heavenly as they bake.

1   cup (2 sticks) unsalted butter
1⅔   cups packed light brown sugar
2   cups all-purpose or unbleached white flour
1½   teaspoons baking powder
½   teaspoon salt
3   large eggs
2½   teaspoons vanilla extract
1   cup chopped pecans or walnuts (optional)

Preheat the oven to 350 degrees F. Line an 11¾- by 7½- by 2-inch flat baking pan with aluminum foil, allowing foil to overlap two ends of the pan by about 2 inches. (To measure and fit foil, turn the pan upside down and mold foil around bottom. Remove foil, turn pan right side up and fit molded foil neatly into pan.) Grease foil.

Place butter in a large heavy saucepan over medium heat; melt and bring to a boil. Simmer for 5 minutes, stirring occasionally and adjusting heat so that the butter gently bubbles and turns slightly golden but does not burn. Add brown sugar, stirring. Immediately remove saucepan from heat and let stand until mixture cools to lukewarm.

Sift together flour, baking powder, and salt and set aside. Add eggs and vanilla to cooled butter-brown sugar mixture, and stir vigorously with a large wooden spoon. Add dry ingredients and stir until thoroughly incorporated. Gently fold in nuts.

Spoon batter into foil-lined baking pan, spreading it out evenly to the edges.

Place in upper third of oven and bake for 35 to 40 minutes, or until center top is golden brown and feels almost firm when tapped. Remove from the oven, transfer pan to a wire rack, and let stand for at least 20 minutes. Then, using the overhanging foil as handles, carefully lift brownie from pan and place it on rack until completely cooled. Peel foil from the bottom and transfer the brownie right side up to a cutting board. Mark and cut crosswise into 6 strips and lengthwise into 4 strips to yield 24 bars.

The brownies may be stored in an airtight container for up to 2 days. Freeze for longer storage.

Makes 24 2-inch square brownies.

Toasted Coconut Dream Bars

United States

In this version of the popular dream bar cookie, the coconut and nuts are lightly toasted to bring out their rich flavor and aroma. The filling is not as sweet as in some recipes.

Dream bars are easy to make and are always well received.

PASTRY
⅔ cup all-purpose or unbleached white flour
¼ cup (½ stick) cold unsalted butter, cut into small pieces

FILLING
1¼ cups shredded or flaked, sweetened coconut
1 cup chopped pecans or walnuts
2 large eggs
½ cup packed light brown sugar
1½ tablespoons all-purpose or unbleached white flour
Pinch of salt
1¼ teaspoons vanilla extract

ICING
3 tablespoons unsalted butter, at room temperature
1¼ cups powdered sugar
2 teaspoons fresh lemon juice
1¼ teaspoons vanilla extract

Preheat the oven to 350 degrees F. Lightly grease an 8-inch square baking pan.

To prepare the pastry dough, combine flour and butter in a small bowl. Using a pastry blender or forks cut in the butter until the mixture resembles fine crumbs.

Sprinkle over 2 teaspoons cold water and lightly stir or knead the dough until it begins to hold together. (Alternatively, combine flour and butter in the bowl of a food processor fitted with steel blade and process in on/off pulses for about 1 minute, or until the mixture resembles coarse crumbs. Add the 2 teaspoons cold water through the feed tube. Continue processing in on/off pulses until dough just begins to form a ball.) Place dough in baking pan and press toward edges to form a smooth, even layer. Bake for 10 minutes; set aside.

To prepare filling, spread coconut and nuts in separate baking pans and toast, stirring frequently, for 8 to 10 minutes or until coconut is very lightly tinged with brown. Remove from the oven and set the nuts and all but 2 tablespoons coconut aside to cool slightly. Continue toasting remaining 2 tablespoons coconut until lightly browned; set aside for the garnish.

In a small bowl, beat eggs with a fork until frothy. Add brown sugar, 1½ tablespoons flour, salt, and vanilla and continue beating until smooth. Stir in the lightly toasted coconut and pecans until thoroughly combined. Spread mixture evenly over pastry dough in baking pan.

Place in the oven and bake for 20 to 23 minutes, or until top is firm and golden brown. Remove from the oven and place pan on wire rack to cool slightly.

Meanwhile prepare the icing. In a mixing bowl, combine butter and powdered sugar. Add lemon juice and vanilla and stir until smooth. Add enough water to yield a spreadable consistency, about 2 teaspoons. When baked square has cooled to warm, spread icing thinly over the top. Immediately sprinkle top with reserved 2 tablespoons toasted coconut. Let stand until set. Cut the square crosswise into thirds then lengthwise into fifths to yield 15 bars.

Store in an airtight container for 2 or 3 days. Freeze for longer storage.

Makes 15 1½-by-2½-inch bars.

NANAIMO BARS

Canada

This is one of Canada's favorite cookies. It is named for the British Columbian city of Nanaimo, though no one is absolutely certain why.

Nanaimo bars consist of three rich, almost candy-like layers, including a chocolate-coconut-walnut base, buttercream filling, and dark chocolate top.

The following recipe was inspired by two different Nanaimo bar versions printed in *Canadian Living Magazine*, one containing a plain vanilla buttercream and the other a more sophisticated orange-Grand Marnier filling. My version is designed so you can make the bars either way.

BOTTOM LAYER

5   tablespoons unsalted butter
3½   ounces semisweet chocolate, coarsely chopped
1   cup grated or shredded sweetened coconut
1   cup graham cracker crumbs
1   cup finely chopped walnuts

BUTTERCREAM LAYER

1   large egg yolk
1   tablespoon milk or orange liqueur, such as Grand Marnier
½   cup (1 stick) unsalted butter, slightly softened
¾   teaspoon vanilla extract
     Very finely grated zest of 1 medium orange (optional)
1⅓   cups powdered sugar

TOP LAYER

2   ounces unsweetened chocolate, coarsely chopped
2   ounces semisweet chocolate, coarsely chopped
1   tablespoon solid vegetable shortening

Grease an 8-inch square flat baking pan.

To prepare the bottom layer, melt the butter, stirring occasionally, in a heavy, medium saucepan over medium heat. Reduce heat to very low and stir in the chocolate. Warm, stirring, until the chocolate is melted and smooth. Immediately remove from the heat. Stir in coconut, graham cracker crumbs, and walnuts and continue stirring until evenly distributed. Turn mixture out into the baking pan, and press it with fingertips or spoon out over the pan bottom to form a firm, evenly thick layer. Cover and refrigerate for at least 20 minutes, or until cool to the touch. (To speed up the cooling, place the pan in the freezer instead.)

To prepare buttercream layer, beat egg yolk and milk (or liqueur) in a small mixing bowl until well blended. Add butter, vanilla, and orange zest (if used) and beat until the mixture is light and fluffy. Gradually add powdered sugar and continue beating until the mixture is smooth and creamy. Using a blunt knife, evenly spread the buttercream layer over the bottom layer. Cover baking pan and return it to the refrigerator (or freezer) until the buttercream layer is cool and firm, but *not* hard.

To prepare top layer, place the semisweet and unsweetened chocolates and shortening in a small heavy saucepan and warm over lowest heat, stirring occasionally, until melted. Cool until *just barely warm* to the touch. Pour chocolate over the buttercream layer and, using a blunt knife, spread it out into an evenly thick layer, working quickly, as the chocolate will quickly begin to set. Cover and refrigerate until the chocolate sets but is not yet hard. Then, using a sharp knife, cut through the chocolate to mark into bars. For small bars, mark and cut into 8 sections horizontally and 4 sections vertically. For larger bars mark and cut it into 8 sections horizontally and 3 sections vertically.

Cover and refrigerate bars for several hours, or until very cold, before cutting all the way through. Remove from pan using a spatula.

The bars may be stored, refrigerated, for up to a week. Freeze for longer storage.

Makes 24 or 32 small bars.

Pecan Butter Icebox Cookies with Orange Zest

United States

Pecans and oranges are both grown in the American Southwest and have been successfully paired there in a number of popular and delicious dishes, most notably orange-pecan pie. This fine icebox cookie recipe was given to me by a friend, cookbook author Susan Belsinger, who combed the Southwest for regional specialties while researching *New Southwestern Cooking*.

The cookies are crisp and buttery and prove just how enticing the pecan-orange combination can be.

1   cup coarsely chopped pecans
    Zest of 1 medium orange, trimmed of
    all white membrane
1   cup granulated sugar
1   large egg
1   cup (2 sticks) cold unsalted butter,
    cut into small pieces
1   teaspoon vanilla extract

½   teaspoon salt
2   cups all-purpose or unbleached white
    flour

Preheat the oven to 325 degrees F.

Spread pecans in a single layer in a large baking pan and toast in the oven, stirring occasionally, until very fragrant and just tinged with brown, 8 to 10 minutes. Remove them from the oven immediately and let stand until completely cooled. Place pecans in a food processor fitted with a steel blade and process until finely ground. Empty ground pecans onto a sheet of waxed paper or a small plate.

Place zest and sugar in the food processor and process until zest is very finely minced. Add egg and process about 1 minute. Sprinkle butter, vanilla, and salt over mixture and continue processing 1 minute longer, or until well combined. Sprinkle ground pecans evenly over mixture and process briefly. Add flour and process until just incorporated.

Divide dough into thirds. Place each third on a sheet of plastic wrap and shape and roll each into a smooth, uniformly thick log about 1¾ inches in diameter. Slide logs onto a large tray or baking sheet and refrigerate for at least 1 hour, or overnight, if desired. (Logs may also be frozen, well wrapped, for up to 10 days and thawed slightly before slicing and baking.)

Preheat the oven to 350 degrees F. Lightly grease several baking sheets. Using a sharp, heavy knife, cut dough crosswise into ¼-inch slices, and place them about 1 inch apart on baking sheets.

Place in upper third of the oven and bake for 10 to 12 minutes, or until edges are golden brown. Baking time will vary somewhat depending on temperature of dough. Remove baking sheets from the oven and let cool for about 3 minutes. Using a spatula, transfer cookies to wire racks and let stand until completely cooled.

Store in an airtight container for up to a week. Freeze for longer storage.

Makes 60 to 70 2- to 2¼-inch cookies.

PECAN CRISPS

United States

These crispy, melt-in-the-mouth icebox cookies combine the flavors of toasted pecans, brown sugar, and fresh, sweet butter.

The recipe makes two logs of dough which can be stored in the freezer for up to two weeks, to be sliced and baked as needed.

1¼ cups chopped pecans
2⅓ cups all-purpose or unbleached white flour
½   teaspoon baking soda
½   teaspoon salt
½   cup (1 stick) unsalted butter, slightly softened
½   cup packed light brown sugar
½   cup powdered sugar
1   large egg
½   cup flavorless vegetable oil
1   teaspoon vanilla extract

Preheat the oven to 325 degrees F. Spread pecans in a single layer in a large baking pan and toast in the oven for 7 to 8 minutes, stirring occasionally, until fragrant and browned. Remove from the oven and set aside until cool. Thoroughly stir together flour, baking soda, and salt.

In a large mixing bowl, combine butter, brown and powdered sugars, and beat until fluffy and smooth. Add egg, oil, and vanilla and beat until well mixed. Beat in dry ingredients. Stir in half of toasted, cooled pecans.

Cover and refrigerate dough for 1 hour, or until slightly firm. Divide dough in half. Lay each half on a 15-inch long sheet of waxed paper and shape into smooth 2-inch diameter logs about 9½-inches long. Sprinkle half of remaining pecans over each log, pressing and patting them into the surface. Wrap logs tightly and freeze for at least 4 hours, or until very firm. The dough may be placed in plastic bags and frozen for up to 2 weeks, if desired.

Preheat the oven to 375 degrees F. Grease several baking sheets. Remove one log from freezer, cut quickly into ¼-inch-thick slices, and place 1½ inches apart on baking sheets. (Leave second log in the freezer until just before slicing and baking.)

Immediately place in upper third of the oven and bake for 9 to 11 minutes, or until nicely colored all over and slightly darker around edges. Reverse baking sheets from front to back halfway through baking to ensure even browning. Using a spatula, transfer the cookies to wire racks and let stand until completely cooled.

Store in an airtight container for up to a week. Freeze for longer storage.

Makes 55 to 60 2½-inch cookies.

Pecan Crisps and Pecan Praline Cookies
(recipe on page 48).

PECAN PRALINE COOKIES

United States

These are sweet, slightly chewy cookies plumped with crunchy bits of pecan praline (caramelized pecans). Since pecans are indigenous to the American South, they are used often in Southern cooking. The technique for preparing the praline is classic French. Not surprisingly, the basic recipe was provided by a cook in New Orleans. The praline may be prepared far in advance if desired.

PRALINE
1   cup chopped pecans
1/3 cup granulated sugar

DOUGH
1½   cups all-purpose or unbleached white flour
1¼   teaspoons baking powder
¼   teaspoon baking soda
¼   teaspoon salt
½   cup (1 stick) unsalted butter, slightly softened
1   cup packed light brown sugar
2   tablespoons granulated sugar
1   large egg
2   teaspoons vanilla extract

Preheat the oven to 325 degrees F.

To prepare praline, spread pecans evenly in a large baking pan. Place in the oven and toast, stirring frequently, for 8 to 10 minutes, until fragrant and toasted but not burned. Remove from the oven and set pecans aside to cool. Butter a heatproof platter or plate and set aside.

Combine the sugar with 2 tablespoons water in a small, heavy saucepan and place over medium-high heat. Bring to a boil, swirling mixture in the pan several times to dissolve sugar. Cover and boil for 2 minutes. Uncover and cook 2 to 2½ minutes longer, or until syrup thickens slightly, bubbles and turns deep amber, but *not* dark brown. Immediately add toasted pecans to syrup, stirring to coat with mixture; be careful not to splash as the mixture is extremely hot. Quickly turn praline mixture onto buttered platter. Let the mixture stand about 10 minutes or until completely cooled. Transfer praline to a heavy plastic bag. Using a mallet or the back of a heavy spoon, crack the mixture into tiny pieces. The praline may be used immediately or stored in an airtight container in the refrigerator or freezer for up to a month. Allow praline to come to room temperature before using.

Preheat the oven to 375 degrees F. Lightly grease several baking sheets and set aside. Combine flour, baking powder, baking soda, and salt and stir until well mixed; set aside.

Place butter in a small mixing bowl and beat with an electric mixer on medium speed until light and fluffy. Add brown and granulated sugars, egg, and vanilla and continue beating until very smooth and well blended. Add half of dry ingredients and beat until well blended. As the dough stiffens, stir in remaining dry ingredients with a spoon until thoroughly blended. Place a generous 1/3 cup pecan praline in a shallow bowl and set aside. Using a large spoon, stir remaining praline into dough until evenly distributed.

Pull off portions of dough and roll between palms into 1-inch balls. Dip top of each ball into the reserved praline to coat lightly. Space balls, praline side up, about 2 inches apart on greased baking sheets.

Place in the center of the oven and bake for 10 to 11 minutes or until cookies are

48

just barely brown at the edges. Reverse baking sheets from front to back halfway through baking to ensure even browning, and be careful not to overbake. Remove cookies from oven and let stand on baking sheets for 2 minutes. Using a spatula, transfer cookies to wire racks to cool completely.

Store in an airtight container for up to a week. Freeze for longer storage.

Makes about 30 2¾-inch cookies.

OLD-FASHIONED SOUR CREAM DROP COOKIES

United States

Homey, cake-like cookies with a mild flavor and incredibly light, tender texture. The original recipe—which I've adapted slightly—is from Washington, D.C. resident Jean Favors, who has been making these cookies for more than twenty years.

DECORATION
2   tablespoons granulated sugar
¼   teaspoon finely grated lemon zest, or
     ½ teaspoon ground cinnamon

DOUGH
3   cups all-purpose or unbleached white
     flour

½   teaspoon salt
½   teaspoon baking soda
½   teaspoon baking powder
⅛   teaspoon ground cinnamon
⅔   cup (1 stick plus 3 tablespoons)
     unsalted butter, slightly softened
1⅓   cups granulated sugar
2   large eggs
2¼   teaspoons vanilla extract
3 to 4 drops lemon extract
¼   teaspoon finely grated lemon zest
1   cup dairy sour cream

Preheat the oven to 400 degrees F. Grease several baking sheets. In a small bowl, stir together granulated sugar and lemon zest (or cinnamon) until well mixed; set aside.

Sift together flour, salt, baking soda, baking powder, and cinnamon. Place butter and sugar in a large mixing bowl and beat until lightened and fluffy. Beat in eggs, one at a time. Add vanilla and lemon extracts and lemon zest and beat until well blended. Alternately add dry ingredients and sour cream, beginning and ending with dry ingredients and adding about a third of the total at a time.

Drop dough by generous teaspoonfuls onto baking sheets, spacing cookies 2 inches apart. Lightly sprinkle each cookie with some of the sugar-lemon mixture.

Place in upper third of the oven and bake for 10 to 12 minutes or until edges are barely tinged with brown. Reverse baking sheets from front to back halfway through baking to ensure even browning. Remove baking sheets from the oven and let stand for a minute or two. Transfer cookies to wire racks and let stand until cooled completely.

Store in an airtight container for 2 or 3 days. Freeze for longer storage.

Makes 45 to 50 2½-inch cookies.

49

Overleaf: Peanut Butter Sandies (recipe on page 53).

Pecan Lace Cookies

United States

Pecan lace cookies are about as Southern as you can get. They are rich with the taste of brown sugar, butter, and pecans—ingredients Southern cooks love to use.

I consider these fragile, brittle-crisp wafers America's answer to Italy's famous Florentine cookies. Not quite as elegant perhaps, but just as irresistible. Although it isn't really traditional, for special occasions I like to drizzle a little bittersweet chocolate glaze over the wafers. If this seems like gilding a lily to you, just serve the cookies plain. They're yummy that way too.

Since part of the appeal of pecan lace cookies is their brittle, caramelized consistency, prepare them on a dry day. Otherwise, they may absorb too much moisture from the air and end up slightly chewy. Also, handle the wafers carefully; they are so lacy and thin you can see right through them.

1	cup coarsely ground pecans
2/3	cup (1 stick plus 2½ tablespoons) unsalted butter
3/4	cup packed dark brown sugar
1/3	cup light corn syrup
1/4	teaspoon salt
1	cup quick cooking oats
2	tablespoons all-purpose or unbleached white flour
2	teaspoons vanilla extract

CHOCOLATE GLAZE (OPTIONAL)
1½	teaspoons solid vegetable shortening
2	ounces semisweet chocolate, coarsely chopped

1½ ounces unsweetened chocolate, coarsely chopped

Preheat the oven to 325 degrees F. Spread the pecans in a large baking pan. Place in oven and toast for 6 to 7 minutes, or until very fragrant and tinged with brown. Remove from the oven and set aside to cool. Reset the oven temperature to 375 degrees F. Grease several baking sheets and set aside.

Place the butter in a heavy medium saucepan and bring to a boil over medium heat. Lower the heat slightly and gently simmer, stirring occasionally, for 4 minutes. Stir in sugar, corn syrup, and salt and continue heating for about 1 minute, until the mixture is smooth and well-blended. Remove saucepan from the heat. Stir in oats, flour, and vanilla until well-blended. Fold in toasted pecans.

Spoon dough onto baking sheets by *very small* teaspoonfuls, spacing them about 4 inches apart. Don't crowd cookies or make them too big, as even very small portions will spread into large rounds. (It is normal for dough to stiffen as it cools.)

Place in the upper third of the oven and bake for 6 to 8 minutes, or until the cookies are deep golden brown all over and just slightly darker at the edges. Reverse baking sheets from front to back halfway through baking to ensure even browning. Remove from the oven and let cookies stand on baking sheets for about 1 minute, until firmed slightly. Then using a spatula, quickly transfer them to wire racks. (If cookies cool too quickly and become too brittle to be removed from baking sheets easily, return them to the oven for 1 minute to soften again.) Set racks over waxed paper if planning to glaze cookies. Let the wafers stand until cooled completely, then glaze, if desired. Be sure to regrease baking sheets before reusing.

To prepare glaze, place shortening in a small, heavy saucepan and melt over lowest heat. Stir in semisweet and unsweetened chocolates and warm, stirring frequently, until melted and smooth. Immediately remove saucepan from the heat. Using a spoon, drizzle a thin stream of glaze back and forth across the wafers in a random pattern. (If the glaze starts to cool and stiffen as you work, rewarm it slightly.) Let wafers stand for 1 hour, or until glaze sets.

Store in an airtight container for up to a week. If glazed, the cookies must be stored in the refrigerator. Unglazed cookies may be frozen for longer storage. Glaze them after thawing.

Makes 50 to 60 3¼-inch wafers.

PEANUT BUTTER SANDIES

United States

A wonderful "sandy"-crisp texture combines with peanutty goodness in this all-American kids' favorite. These are great for after-school snacks. Adults like them too.

2   cups all-purpose or unbleached white flour
1   teaspoon baking powder
½   teaspoon baking soda
¼   teaspoon salt
1   cup powdered sugar
½   cup flavorless vegetable oil
½   cup smooth peanut butter
6   tablespoons unsalted butter, slightly softened
½   cup packed light brown sugar
1   large egg
1½   teaspoons vanilla extract

DECORATION
¼   cup chopped unsalted, skinless peanuts (optional)

Preheat the oven to 350 degrees F. Grease several baking sheets and set aside.

Sift together flour, baking powder, baking soda, and salt; set aside. Sift powdered sugar. In a large mixing bowl, combine oil, peanut butter, and butter and beat until blended. Add powdered and brown sugars, and beat until fluffy and smooth. Beat in egg and vanilla. Beat or stir in dry ingredients until thoroughly mixed.

Shape dough into generous 1¼-inch balls with the palms and place on baking sheets about 2 inches apart. Using the bottom of a glass dipped in cold water, flatten each cookie slightly to about 1½-inches in diameter. If desired, sprinkle cookies lightly with peanuts; pat them down to imbed slightly.

Place in upper third of the oven and bake for 10 to 12 minutes, or until just tinged with brown around the edges; reverse baking sheets from front to back halfway through baking to ensure even browning. Remove baking sheets from oven and let cool for 2 to 3 minutes. Transfer cookies to wire racks with a spatula and let stand until cool.

Store in an airtight container for up to a week. Freeze for longer storage.

Makes 30 to 35 2½-inch sandies.

PEANUT BUTTER-KISS COOKIES

United States

I've never come across an American child who didn't like these peanut butter-kiss cookies, and a lot of adults rate them highly, too. Youngsters also find this recipe fun and easy to make, and particularly seem to enjoy tucking a chocolate candy kiss into the center of each cookie. Of course, a few chocolate kisses always disappear as the cookies are being made!

Some peanut butter cookies tend to be heavy, but these are airy light and very smooth. Although the peanut butter-chocolate flavor combination is very appealing, the chocolate kisses can be omitted from this recipe to make good, plain peanut butter rounds. If you wish to do this, simply roll the dough into balls as described in the recipe, press down with the heel of the hand *just slightly*, and proceed with baking.

1²/₃ cups all-purpose or unbleached white flour
¹/₃ cup cornstarch
¹/₂ teaspoon baking powder
¹/₂ teaspoon baking soda
¹/₂ cup (1 stick) unsalted butter, slightly softened
¹/₃ cup smooth-style peanut butter
²/₃ cup powdered sugar
¹/₃ cup packed dark brown sugar
1 large egg
2 teaspoons vanilla extract
35 to 40 chocolate candy kisses (about 6 ounces)

Preheat the oven to 350 degrees F. Grease several baking sheets and set aside. Thoroughly stir together flour, cornstarch, baking powder, and baking soda in a bowl.

In a large mixing bowl, beat butter and peanut butter with an electric mixer on medium speed until very light. Sift in the powdered sugar. Add brown sugar and beat until very light and smooth. Beat in egg and vanilla. Gradually beat in the dry ingredients until thoroughly incorporated but not overmixed.

Pull off small portions of dough and roll, one at a time, between palms to form 1¼-inch balls. Holding each ball, press a chocolate kiss, flat-side-down, deep into the center of the dough. Then mold the dough up around the chocolate kiss with the fingertips so that only the top ¼ inch of the kiss remains visible. Continue forming cookies in this manner, spacing them about 2 inches apart on baking sheets.

Place in the center of the oven and bake for 9 to 11 minutes, or until lightly browned at the edges and beginning to brown on top. Remove baking sheets from the oven and let stand for 3 to 4 minutes. Then transfer cookies to wire racks and let stand until cooled completely.

Store in an airtight container for up to a week. Freeze for longer storage.

Makes about 35 2-inch cookies.

ORANGE-DATE PINWHEELS

United States

This recipe yields attractive and homey icebox cookies with a slightly crisp dough and a chewy filling. It is based on an old "receipt" from North Dakota.

After the pinwheel dough logs are formed they can be refrigerated or frozen, then sliced and baked as needed.

FILLING

10	ounces (approximately 2 generous cups) chopped pitted dates
⅔	cup orange juice
	Grated zest of 1 medium orange
3	tablespoons packed light brown sugar
¼	teaspoon ground cinnamon
¾	cup finely chopped walnuts or pecans

DOUGH

3⅓	cups all-purpose or unbleached white flour
¾	teaspoon baking powder
¼	teaspoon salt
¼	teaspoon ground cinnamon
¾	cup (1½ sticks) unsalted butter, slightly softened
⅔	cup granulated sugar
⅔	cup packed light brown sugar
2	large eggs
1	teaspoon vanilla extract
	Grated zest of 1 medium orange

To prepare filling, combine dates, orange juice, orange zest, brown sugar, and cinnamon in a medium saucepan and place over medium heat. Simmer, stirring, for 5 to 6 minutes, or until mixture is soft and most of the liquid is absorbed. (If dates were dry and absorb all the liquid, add 1 tablespoon water.) Stir in nuts. Remove from heat, cover, and set aside to cool. (Filling can be made up to 48 hours in advance and refrigerated. Allow it to warm up and soften slightly before using.)

To prepare dough, thoroughly stir together flour, baking powder, salt, and cinnamon. Place butter in a large mixing bowl and beat until light. Add granulated and brown sugars, eggs, and vanilla, and beat until fluffy and well blended. Add orange zest and beat a few seconds longer. Gradually beat in half the dry ingredients. If mixer motor labors, stir in remaining dry ingredients by hand until thoroughly incorporated.

Wrap dough in plastic wrap and refrigerate for about 1½ hours, or until firm. (The dough may be held up to 24 hours but should be allowed to warm up slightly before rolling out.)

To form pinwheel logs, roll dough out on a very lightly floured surface into a 12-by 18-inch rectangle. Cut and patch dough as necessary to make sides of the rectangle straight. Lift dough several times to make sure it isn't sticking. Spread filling evenly over entire surface of dough. Working from longer side of rectangle, tightly roll up dough and filling jelly-roll style. Gently stretch and smooth log from center to form an evenly thick 24-inch log. Cut log in half crosswise. Gently stretch out halves until each is evenly thick and about 14 inches long. Wrap logs in plastic wrap, and place on a tray or baking sheet. Refrigerate for at least 2 hours or freeze for at least 1 hour to firm logs enough to be cut neatly. (Or freeze logs, tightly wrapped, for up to 2 weeks; allow dough to thaw partially in refrigerator before cutting.)

Preheat the oven to 350 degrees F. Generously grease several baking sheets. Using a large sharp knife, cut chilled logs

GINGERBREAD PEOPLE

United States

Much loved by American children (and adults who remember when they were), these large spicy cookies are easy to make, fun to decorate, and even more fun to eat. Gingerbread people are attractive simply garnished with raisins for eyes and cinnamon "red hot" candies for buttons, but, if desired, icing may also be piped on to suggest facial details or the outline of clothing. Prepare the homemade icing given here and pipe through a pastry tube fitted with a fine writing tip, or use a commercial tube of decorator icing.

1 cup light molasses
2 large eggs
5½ to 6 cups all-purpose or unbleached white flour
2½ teaspoons ground ginger
2½ teaspoons ground cinnamon
½ teaspoon ground cloves
¾ teaspoon baking soda
¼ teaspoon baking powder
1 cup (2 sticks) unsalted butter, slightly softened
1 cup packed light or dark brown sugar
Finely grated zest of 1 large lemon
Finely grated zest of 1 large orange

DECORATION
Raisins
Cinnamon "red hot" candies

ICING (OPTIONAL)
1¼ cups powdered sugar
⅛ teaspoon vanilla extract
Drop of food coloring, if desired

Place molasses in a small saucepan, bring almost to a simmer, and remove from the heat. Add eggs, one at a time, beating mixture with a large wooden spoon. Set mixture aside until tepid.

Thoroughly stir together 4 cups of the flour, the ginger, cinnamon, cloves, baking soda, and baking powder and set aside.

Place butter in a large mixing bowl and beat with the mixer on medium speed until light and fluffy. Beat in brown sugar, lemon zest, and orange zest until well blended and smooth. Gradually beat in cooled molasses mixture until incorporated. Beat in flour-spice mixture. Using a large wooden spoon, stir in 1½ cups more flour until blended and smooth. If dough seems too soft and moist to handle, gradually stir in another ½ cup flour. However, keep in mind that dough will become more firm as it chills. Divide dough into thirds and wrap each third in plastic wrap. Refrigerate for at least 1½ hours and up to 24 hours. (Or freeze in plastic bags for up to a week. Set out frozen dough to warm up slightly before baking.)

Preheat the oven to 350 degrees F. Grease several baking sheets and set aside.

Working with one third of the dough at a time (leave the other portions refrigerated), roll dough on a lightly floured work surface to ¼-inch thickness. Lift dough several times and dust rolling pin frequently to prevent the dough from sticking. Cut out cookies using a gingerbread person cutter. Using a spatula, transfer cookies to baking sheets, and space them about 2 inches apart. Add the raisins for eyes and cinnamon red hots for buttons.

Place in center of the oven and bake for 11 to 13 minutes or until edges are just tinged with brown. Remove from oven and let stand on sheets for 2 to 3 minutes. Using a spatula, transfer cookies to wire racks and let cool completely. Decorate with a light piping of icing, if desired.

BLACK WALNUT ICEBOX COOKIES

United States

Black walnut fans love these crisp, fragrant cookies, and they have even won over people who thought they didn't care for the distinctive taste of this North American nut.

The following is an adaptation of an old North Carolina recipe. Friends who grew up in the Tar Heel state say the aroma and flavor remind them of home.

1	cup finely chopped black walnuts
2½	cups all-purpose or unbleached white flour
1	teaspoon baking powder
¼	teaspoon baking soda
¼	teaspoon salt
⅔	cup (1 stick plus 3 tablespoons) unsalted butter, slightly softened
⅔	cup packed light brown sugar
½	cup granulated sugar
1	large egg
1	large egg yolk
1½	teaspoons vanilla extract
1	large egg white

Preheat the oven to 325 degrees F. Spread walnuts out evenly on a baking pan, place in the oven and toast for 8 to 10 minutes, stirring occasionally, until fragrant and lightly toasted; make sure nuts don't burn. Remove from the oven and set walnuts aside to cool.

Thoroughly stir together flour, baking powder, baking soda, and salt. Place butter in a large mixing bowl and beat with an electric mixer on medium speed until light and fluffy. Add brown and granulated sugars and beat until well blended and light. Add egg, egg yolk, and vanilla and continue beating until thoroughly blended and smooth. Gradually beat in about half the dry ingredients until thoroughly incorporated. As dough stiffens, stir in remaining dry ingredients by hand. Add half of the walnuts and stir until evenly distributed. Reserve remaining walnuts for garnish.

Divide dough in half. Lay each half on a 15-inch long sheet of waxed paper and shape into a smooth log, 2 inches in diameter by about 9½ inches long. Wrap logs and chill for at least 2½ hours or until very firm. Dough may be refrigerated for 2 to 3 days, if desired. Or, freeze it for up to 2 weeks. Allow to thaw in the refrigerator until dough softens to firm before slicing.

Preheat the oven to 375 degrees F. Grease several baking sheets. Working with one log at a time (leaving the other refrigerated), cut dough into 3/16-inch thick slices with a sharp knife. Space cookies 1¼ inches apart on baking sheets.

In a small bowl, combine egg white with ½ tablespoon of water and beat well. Using a pastry brush or paper towel, lightly brush 3 or 4 cookies with egg white wash, then quickly sprinkle tops lightly with some of the remaining chopped walnuts. Continue in this manner, brushing a few cookies at a time, until all are garnished.

Place on the center rack of the oven and bake for 8 to 10 minutes, or until nicely browned at the edges and golden all over. Reverse baking sheets from front to back halfway through baking to ensure even browning. Remove from the oven and let cookies cool on baking sheets for 1 to 2 minutes. Then transfer them to wire racks, using a spatula, and let stand until completely cooled.

Store the cookies in an airtight container for up to a week. Freeze for longer storage.

Makes 60 to 70 2¼-inch cookies.

Pennsylvania Dutch Pumpkin Whoopie Pies

United States

Whoopie pies are huge, soft, chewy-moist cookies sandwiched together with a creamy filling. I have seen whoopie pies that are made with chocolate and very sweet vanilla cream, but these hearty, homey Pennsylvania Dutch whoopies are flavored with a lively blend of pumpkin and spices and accented with a smooth, not-too-sweet cream cheese filling. They remind me a little of a cream cheese-iced carrot cake, but in cookie form. This recipe comes from my sister, Sally Churgai, who lives in Pennsylvania Dutch country.

For convenience, the filling can be made a day ahead and stored in the refrigerator until needed.

4²/₃ cups all-purpose or unbleached white flour
1 tablespoon cream of tartar
2 teaspoons baking soda
1 teaspoon baking powder
¹/₄ teaspoon salt
1 tablespoon plus 2 teaspoons ground cinnamon
1¹/₂ teaspoons ground ginger
1¹/₂ teaspoons ground allspice
1 cup (2 sticks) unsalted butter, slightly softened
1 cup flavorless vegetable oil
2¹/₃ cups packed dark brown sugar
1¹/₄ cups fresh or canned unsweetened pumpkin puree
1 large egg
2 large egg yolks

1 tablespoon vanilla extract
¹/₄ teaspoon finely grated lemon zest
1¹/₃ cups quick-cooking oats

FILLING
12 ounces cream cheese, slightly softened
2 large egg whites
¹/₄ teaspoon vanilla extract
¹/₄ teaspoon finely grated lemon zest
2³/₄ cups powdered sugar

Preheat the oven to 350 degrees F. Generously grease several baking sheets and set aside.

Thoroughly stir together the flour, cream of tartar, baking soda, baking powder, salt, cinnamon, ginger, and allspice in a large bowl. Place butter and oil in a large mixing bowl and beat with an electric mixer on low speed until well mixed. Increase speed to medium and continue beating until lightened and fluffy. Add brown sugar and beat until smooth. Beat in pumpkin puree, egg, egg yolks (reserve the extra whites for the filling), vanilla, and lemon zest. Gradually beat in the flour mixture. If the mixer motor labors, stir in the last of the flour mixture by hand. Using a large wooden spoon, stir in oats until thoroughly incorporated.

Using an ice cream scoop or rounded serving spoon, drop about 2½ tablespoons of dough at a time onto the baking sheet, spacing mounds at least 4 inches apart and making them as round as possible. Using a blunt knife and swirling in a circular motion, spread each dough mound out into an evenly shaped, 2¾-inch diameter round.

Place in the upper third of the oven and bake for 10 to 12 minutes, or until just slightly darker at the edges. Remove from the oven and let cookies stand on baking sheets for 3 minutes. Using a spatula, carefully transfer cookies to wire racks, and let stand until cooled completely before assembling.

To prepare filling, beat together cream cheese, egg whites, vanilla, lemon zest, and half of powdered sugar in a mixing bowl. Gradually add remaining powdered sugar and beat until well blended and smooth. Refrigerate the mixture, uncovered, for at least 15 minutes, or cover and hold in the refrigerator for up to 24 hours before assembling cookies.

To assemble the whoopie pies, spoon about 2 tablespoons filling in the center of the flat side of half the cookies; the filling will spread out toward the edges. Let stand a few minutes to allow filling to set slightly. Then center remaining cookies, flat side down, over the filling on each cookie, trying to match rounds so that the tops and bottoms are the same size. Gently press down until the filling spreads just to the cookie edges, and is about ¼-inch thick. Let cookies stand on a flat surface for about 30 minutes, until filling sets somewhat; otherwise tops may slide off.

Store refrigerated in an airtight container for up to a week, or pack the whoopies into individual plastic bags and refrigerate. Freeze for longer storage.

Makes 18 to 20 3¾- to 4-inch sandwich cookies.

SOOKE HARBOUR HOUSE SALAL BERRY COOKIES

Canada

This recipe was created by Martha Russell, a chef at the Sooke Harbour House restaurant in British Columbia, and graciously shared with me by its owner, Sinclair Philip. This unusual recipe is made with part whole wheat flour and uses wildflower honey instead of sugar. It also calls for salal berries, small tart berries that grow along the Pacific Northwest coast. Huckleberries can be substituted, although the taste will not be exactly the same.

DOUGH
$1\frac{1}{3}$ cups all-purpose or unbleached white flour
1 cup whole wheat flour, preferably whole wheat pastry flour
$\frac{1}{2}$ teaspoon baking soda
$\frac{1}{2}$ cup (1 stick) unsalted butter, slightly softened
$\frac{1}{2}$ cup wildflower honey
1 large egg
$\frac{1}{2}$ cup finely ground walnuts

FILLING
$\frac{1}{3}$ cup whole hazelnuts
1 cup salal berries
2 to 4 tablespoons wildflower honey

To prepare dough, thoroughly stir together white flour, whole wheat flour, and baking soda in a bowl.

Place the butter and honey in a mixing bowl and beat with a electric mixer on medium speed until fluffy and smooth. Beat in the egg until blended. Beat in the walnuts. Using a large wooden spoon, stir in the dry ingredients until incorporated but not over-mixed. Press the dough into a ball, wrap in plastic wrap, and refrigerate for at least 2 hours, or until very cold but not hard.

Preheat the oven to 325 degrees F. Spread hazelnuts in a baking pan, place in the oven and toast, stirring occasionally, for 16 to 18 minutes, or until skins begin to loosen and the nuts just begin to color. Remove from the oven and set aside to cool briefly.

When hazelnuts are cool enough to handle, remove the dark hulls by vigorously rubbing a handful of nuts at a time between the fingers or in a clean kitchen towel, discarding the bits of hull as you work. It's usually difficult to remove hulls entirely, but the hazelnuts should be relatively clean. Finely chop hazelnuts and set aside. Reset oven temperature to 375 degrees F. Grease several baking sheets.

Combine salal berries and 2 tablespoons of the honey in a small, heavy saucepan. (If the berries are very tart or you prefer a slightly sweeter filling, add 1 or 2 more tablespoons honey.) Place over low heat and simmer until the berries begin to render their juices. Increase heat to medium-high and cook, stirring, for 4 to 5 minutes, or until the excess liquid has evaporated from the saucepan and the mixture has thickened slightly. Stir in chopped hazelnuts and set the filling aside to cool.

To prepare for baking, remove about a quarter of the dough from the refrigerator. Using a rolling pin, roll out dough to $\frac{1}{8}$-inch thick on a lightly floured surface, dusting rolling pin frequently and lifting the dough several times to make sure it isn't sticking. Cut out rounds, using a $2\frac{3}{4}$-inch round cutter or the rim of a drinking glass. Working quickly before the rounds warm up and become too soft to handle, transfer to baking sheets with a spatula, spacing them about 1½ inches apart. Place 1 teaspoon filling in the center of a round and immediately fold half of dough round over the filling to form a turnover. Crimp edges closed with the fingers or the tines of a fork dipped in flour. Continue forming the turnovers. Combine dough scraps and refrigerate until cold. Continue rolling, cutting, and filling portions of dough in this manner until all dough is used.

Place in the upper third of the oven and bake cookies for 8 to 10 minutes, or until edges are tinged with brown, reversing baking sheets from front to back about halfway through baking to ensure even browning. Remove from the oven and let cookies stand on baking sheets for 3 minutes. Transfer cookies to wire racks and let stand until cooled completely.

DATE ROCKS

United States

These are old-fashioned American drop cookies, plump with dates and fragrant with spice. The name comes from their irregular shape. They are *not* hard, but rather, chewy-crisp.

This heirloom recipe was passed down through four generations of an Ohio family.

1¾ cups all-purpose or unbleached white flour
½ teaspoon baking soda
1 teaspoon ground cinnamon
1 teaspoon ground cloves
¼ teaspoon ground allspice
⅛ teaspoon salt
¾ cup (1½ sticks) unsalted butter, slightly softened
1 cup granulated sugar
2 large eggs
1½ teaspoons vanilla extract
10 ounces pitted dates, diced moderately fine (about 2 cups diced)

Preheat the oven to 375 degrees F. Grease several baking sheets and set aside.

Thoroughly stir together flour, baking soda, cinnamon, cloves, allspice, and salt; set aside. Place butter in a large mixing bowl and beat until lightened. Add sugar and beat until fluffy and smooth. Beat in eggs and vanilla. Vigorously stir in dry ingredients. Fold in dates, mixing until distributed throughout.

Drop dough by generous teaspoonfuls about 2 inches apart on baking sheets.

Place in the upper third of the oven and bake for 11 to 13 minutes or until just tinged with brown; reverse the baking sheets from front to back halfway through baking to ensure even browning. Remove from the oven and let stand on baking sheets for 1 minute. Transfer cookies to wire racks to cool completely.

Store in an airtight container for up to a week. Freeze for longer storage.

Makes 35 to 40 2¼- to 2½-inch cookies.

CHAPTER 3

⌂

LATIN AMERICAN
COOKIES

THE SPANIARDS FIRST ARRIVED IN WHAT IS NOW called Latin America nearly five hundred years ago, and the foods of Mexico, and Central and South America have never been the same since. In the course of colonization, an Old World culture and established cuisine were superimposed upon the cookery and traditions of the native Indian societies. The effects are evident today, even in such simple foods as cookies.

It was the early Spanish explorers who brought sugar cane and the technology of sugar mills to the New World. With cane sugar widely available, local cooks began what has become a strong tradition of candies, cookies, and other desserts. Throughout the region, the tastes of brown sugar and caramelized sugar are so well liked that they often serve as principal flavorings in recipes. For example, brown sugar is featured in the Cuban Brown Sugar Cookies and both brown and caramelized sugar appear in the Colombian Brown Sugar-Peanut Bars, a delicious modern version of a very old Indian recipe.

In addition to sugar cane, the Spaniards and other Europeans also introduced oranges, limes, cinnamon, almonds, and dairy products, not to mention their knowledge of how to use these ingredients effectively in baked goods. While the cookies presented in this chapter have a decidedly New World character, many have borrowed

from the traditions of Spain. The festive Mexican Seville Cookies are fragrant with orange, lemon, and lime zest and the amusing Piglet sugar cookies are flavored with cinnamon and orange. Little Sugar Dusties, which are shaped into bite-sized balls and rolled in cinnamon sugar, are reminiscent of several tender, sugar-dusted shortbreads found in Spain today.

Of course, some of the pre-Hispanic indigenous ingredients are used in Latin American cookies, too. Mexican Wedding Cookies generally feature the rich, sweet taste of pecans, a nut native both to Mexico and the southern United States. The unusual but delicious Cornmeal Cookies feature a staple in traditional Indian cookery, cornmeal, and are decorated with pine nuts, which grow wild in Mexico. Peanuts, another native foodstuff used by the ancient Indians, are frequently called for in recipes, including the Costa Rican Peanut-Coconut Cookies in this chapter.

Coconut often appears in desserts in the tropical areas of Latin America, although it is unclear whether the coconut palm is a native or an introduced plant. Like the numerous other culinary elements, it has simply been incorporated into recipes because creative cooks know it yields cookies that are uncommonly good.

Brown Sugar-Peanut Bars (recipe on page 72).

Brown Sugar-Peanut Bars

(Cucas)

Colombia

These cookies are based on an old Colombian recipe and feature an appealing combination of brown sugar and peanuts, both very popular ingredients in South and Central American baked goods. In this updated recipe, the peanuts are caramelized, which brings out their flavor and gives the cookies a nice crunch.

2⅓   *cups all-purpose or unbleached white flour*
¾   *teaspoon baking powder*
1   *cup (2 sticks) unsalted butter, slightly softened*
1   *cup packed dark brown sugar*
1   *large egg*
1   *large egg yolk*

TOPPING
3   *tablespoons granulated sugar*
1   *cup finely chopped, unsalted, skinless peanuts*
¼   *cup (½ stick) unsalted butter, slightly softened*
2   *tablespoons packed dark brown sugar*
1¼   *cups powdered sugar*

Thoroughly stir together the flour and baking powder.

In a large mixing bowl, beat the butter until light and fluffy. Add 1 cup brown sugar and beat until well blended and smooth. Beat in the egg and egg yolk. Gradually beat in the dry ingredients; if the mixer motor labors, stir in the last of the dry ingredients using a large wooden spoon.

Place dough between 2 long sheets of waxed paper and roll out into a ¼-inch-thick rectangle, checking the underside and smoothing out any wrinkles in the paper. Slide the dough onto a large tray or baking sheet and refrigerate for 15 to 20 minutes, or until cool and firm but not hard.

Preheat the oven to 350 degrees F. Grease several baking sheets and set aside.

Remove dough from the refrigerator and carefully peel off bottom sheet of waxed paper, then replace it loosely. Turn dough right side up and peel off and discard top sheet of waxed paper. Cut dough crosswise at 1½-inch intervals using a pastry wheel or a large sharp knife. Then cut the dough lengthwise at 2½-inch intervals to yield 1½-inch by 2½-inch rectangles. Transfer cookies to baking sheets, spacing about 1¼ inches apart. Gather and re-roll dough scraps between waxed paper sheets and continue forming cookies until all dough is used. (If the dough is too soft to transfer to baking sheets, refrigerate it briefly first.)

Place in the center of the oven and bake cookies for 8 to 10 minutes, or until lightly tinged with brown on the edges. Remove baking sheets from the oven and let cookies stand for about 3 minutes. Transfer them to wire racks and let stand until cooled completely before adding topping.

To prepare topping, sprinkle 3 tablespoons granulated sugar in a large heavy skillet over medium heat. When the sugar begins to melt, stir in peanuts. Continue melting the sugar and heating the peanuts, lifting the pan from the heat to cool slightly if mixture starts to overheat and smoke, until the peanuts are browned, fragrant, and slightly crispy. Immediately turn out the peanuts into a heatproof bowl and let stand until cooled completely. If they have clumped together, place mixture in a heavy plastic bag and break up the pieces by pounding them with a wooden mallet or large, heavy spoon.

Combine butter and 2 tablespoons brown sugar in a mixing bowl and beat until well blended and smooth. Gradually add the powdered sugar and continue beating until completely smooth. Spread icing lightly over cooled bars with a blunt knife. Immediately sprinkle each bar with some of the peanuts, patting them down lightly.

Store bars in airtight containers in a single layer for up to a week. Freeze for longer storage.

Makes about 30 2¼- by 3-inch cookies.

Brown Sugar Cookies
(Polvorones)

Cuba

This simple, crisp sugar cookie is made with brown sugar, which gives it a particularly nice flavor.

2¼   *cups all-purpose or unbleached white flour*
¾   *teaspoon baking powder*
¼   *teaspoon salt*
⅔   *cup solid vegetable shortening or lard (see Note), at room temperature*
7   *tablespoons unsalted butter, slightly softened*
¾   *cup packed light or dark brown sugar*
1   *large egg*
2   *teaspoons vanilla extract*

Thoroughly stir together the flour, baking powder, and salt.

In a large mixing bowl, combine solid shortening and butter and beat until light and fluffy. Add sugar and beat until well blended and smooth. Beat in egg and vanilla. Gradually beat in about half the dry ingredients. Stir in remaining dry ingredients with a large wooden spoon.

Divide dough in half and place each half between two large sheets of waxed paper. Roll each half out to ¼-inch thick. Check the underside of the dough frequently and smooth out any creases. Place dough on a tray or baking sheet and refrigerate for 15 minutes, or until the dough is chilled and slightly stiff, but not hard.

Preheat the oven to 375 degrees F. Grease several baking sheets and set aside. Working with one half of dough at a time (leave the second half refrigerated), peel off bottom sheet of waxed paper, then replace it loosely. Turn dough right side up and peel off and discard top sheet of waxed paper. Cut out cookies using a 2½- to 2¾-inch round or scalloped cookie cutter. Transfer cookies to baking sheets, spacing about 1¼ inches apart. Gather dough scraps, re-roll between waxed paper sheets, and refrigerate until chilled. Cut out cookies and transfer to baking sheets. Repeat process with second half of dough.

Place in the oven and bake for 9 to 11 minutes or until cookies are tinged with brown at the edges. Remove baking sheets from the oven and let stand for about 3 minutes. Then transfer cookies to wire racks and let cool completely.

Store in an airtight container for up to a week. Freeze for longer storage.

Makes about 30 2½-inch cookies.

Note: Lard is traditionally used in this recipe by Cuban cooks. However, as it is not always easy to find fresh, good-quality lard here, you may want to substitute solid shortening.

HOLIDAY ANISE COOKIES
(BISCOCHITOS)

Mexico

Biscochitos are rolled anise-flavored cookies traditionally prepared for Christmas throughout Mexico and the American Southwest. In this version, the anise flavor is enhanced with lemon and vanilla.

2	cups all-purpose or unbleached white flour
2	teaspoons ground anise seed (see Note)
1/2	teaspoon baking powder
1/8	teaspoon salt
1	large lemon
2/3	cup granulated sugar
1/2	cup solid vegetable shortening or lard (see Note), at room temperature
5 1/2	tablespoons unsalted butter, slightly softened
1	egg yolk
1	teaspoon vanilla extract

DECORATION

1	tablespoon granulated sugar
1	teaspoon ground cinnamon

Thoroughly stir together flour, anise, baking powder, and salt and set aside. Using a small sharp knife or vegetable peeler, peel thin layer of zest (without white membrane) from the entire lemon. Combine lemon zest and sugar in a food processor fitted with a steel blade. Process until zest is very finely minced. Add shortening and butter to the processor and process about 1 minute or until well blended. Add egg yolk and vanilla and process for 20 seconds longer. Add dry ingredients and continue processing just until they are incorporated, being careful not to overprocess.

Divide dough in half. Place each portion between large sheets of waxed paper and roll out to 1/8 inch thick. Check the underside of the dough frequently and smooth out any creases. Slide dough onto a large tray or baking sheet and refrigerate for about 15 minutes or until the dough is chilled and slightly firm.

Preheat the oven to 375 degrees F. Lightly grease several baking sheets.

Working with one half of dough at a time (leave the other refrigerated), turn over dough and peel off bottom sheet of waxed paper. Replace the paper loosely, then turn dough right side up. Peel off and discard top sheet of paper. Using assorted 2 1/4- to 3-inch cookie cutters, cut out cookies. Place on baking sheets about 1 1/4 inches apart. Gather and re-roll any dough scraps and continue cutting out cookies until all the dough is used. (If cookies are too soft to transfer to baking sheets, refrigerate dough briefly.) Repeat process with second half of dough.

Place in the oven and bake for 8 to 10 minutes or until just tinged with brown at the edges. Remove baking sheets from oven and let cookies stand for about 3 minutes. Transfer them to wire racks and let stand until cooled completely. Combine remaining tablespoon sugar and the cinnamon in a small bowl. Sprinkle cookies lightly with the sugar-cinnamon mixture.

Store in an airtight container for up to 10 days. Freeze for longer storage.

Makes 35 to 40 assorted 2 1/2- to 3 1/4-inch cookies.

Note: If ground anise is unavailable, substitute 1 teaspoon anise extract. Add it along with the vanilla.

Use only very fresh, top-quality lard.

Clockwise from top: *Holiday Anise Cookies, Little Sugar Dusties (recipe on page 77), and Ladies' Rings (recipe on page 76).*

LADIES' RINGS
(ROSQUITAS DE DAMAS)

Mexico

T he combination of hazelnuts and almonds adds a rich, intriguing flavor to these traditional Mexican cookies. They are the color of eggnog, and are garnished with a light sprinkling of toasted nuts. As the name suggests, the cookies are ring shaped.

¾   cup whole hazelnuts
¾   cup slivered blanched almonds
½   cup plus 2 tablespoons (1 stick plus 2 tablespoons) unsalted butter, slightly softened
1   cup powdered sugar
3   large egg yolks
2   teaspoons vanilla extract
1¾ cups all-purpose or unbleached white flour
1   egg white

Preheat the oven to 325 degrees F. Spread hazelnuts in an even layer in a baking pan. Place in the oven and toast, stirring occasionally, for 17 to 18 minutes. Spread almonds in a separate baking pan and toast, stirring occasionally, for 6 to 7 minutes. Set nuts aside to cool.

When hazelnuts are cool enough to handle, remove the dark hulls as follows: Vigorously rub nuts, a handful at a time, between the fingers or in a clean kitchen towel, discarding the bits of hull as you work. (It isn't necessary to remove every bit of hull sticking to the nuts, but they should be relatively clean.) Chop hazelnuts and almonds moderately fine in a food processor, blender, or nut grater. Remove ¼ cup of the chopped nuts and set aside for garnish. Continue processing or grating the remaining nuts until they are ground very fine.

Place butter in a large mixing bowl and beat until light and fluffy. Add powdered sugar, egg yolks, and vanilla and beat until well-blended and smooth. Add about half the flour and the ground nuts and beat until distributed throughout. Using a large wooden spoon, stir in remaining flour until dough is well mixed. Wrap dough in plastic wrap and refrigerate for at least 2½ to 3 hours or overnight.

Preheat the oven to 350 degrees F. Lightly grease several baking sheets. Working with small amounts of dough at a time, shape into 1-inch balls. Roll each ball back and forth on a clean work surface between palms to form a 4½- to 5-inch-long rope. Lay each rope in a circle on a baking sheet and pinch ends together to form a ring. Repeat procedure, continuing to form ropes and rings until all dough is used.

Place egg white in a small bowl with 2 teaspoons water and beat well. Using a pastry brush or paper towel, brush the tops of two or three rings lightly with egg mixture. Then lightly sprinkle the tops with the reserved chopped nuts. Repeat until all rings are decorated.

Place in the center of the oven and bake for 12 to 14 minutes, or until edges are just barely tinged with brown; reverse baking sheets from front to back about halfway through baking to ensure even baking. Remove baking sheets from the oven and let stand for 3 or 4 minutes. Using a spatula, transfer cookies to wire racks to cool.

Store the cookies in airtight containers for 4 or 5 days. Freeze for longer storage.

Makes about 35 2¼-inch rings.

LITTLE SUGAR DUSTIES
(POLVORONES)

Mexico

The Spaniards brought polvorones—which roughly translated means "dusties"—with them when they came to Mexico. Over time, New World cooks modified these recipes to suit their own tastes, and now, many of their polvorones are decidedly Mexican.

In both countries the cookies are usually small and dusted with sugar, which probably accounts for their name. However, while Spanish polvorones are usually coated with powdered sugar, a number of their Mexican cousins are dusted with granulated sugar mixed with cinnamon.

I've run across several similar polvorone recipes, but this tender, cinnamony version is especially good. It comes from a New Mexican family that brought it with them when they immigrated to the United States forty years ago. They make the cookies every Christmas.

2   cups all-purpose or unbleached white
     flour
½   cup (1 stick) unsalted butter, slightly
     softened
¼   cup solid vegetable shortening or lard
     (see Note), at room temperature
⅓   cup granulated sugar
1   large egg yolk
1   teaspoon ground cinnamon
⅛   teaspoon very finely grated lemon
     zest

DUSTING
¼   cup granulated sugar
½   teaspoon ground cinnamon

Preheat the oven to 350 degrees F. Set out several baking sheets. Sift the flour and set aside.

Place butter and shortening in a large mixing bowl and beat with an electric mixer on medium speed until light and fluffy. Add sugar and continue beating until thoroughly incorporated and smooth. Beat in egg yolk, cinnamon, and lemon zest. Gradually beat in flour; if the mixer motor begins to labor, stir in remaining flour with a wooden spoon.

Pull off small dough pieces and roll between palms to form 1-inch balls. Space about 1 inch apart on baking sheets.

Place in the upper third of the oven and bake for 15 to 17 minutes or until just barely brown at the edges. Remove baking sheets from the oven and let stand about 5 minutes. Using a spatula, gently transfer cookies to wire racks and let stand until cool but not cold.

In a small, shallow bowl, stir together the remaining ¼ cup granulated sugar and ½ teaspoon cinnamon until well mixed. Handling cookies gently, as they are fragile, dredge in the sugar-cinnamon mixture to thoroughly coat.

Store cookies in an airtight container for up to a week. For longer storage, freeze cookies before dusting them. Thaw and then dredge in sugar-cinnamon mixture before serving.

Makes about 35 1¼-inch cookies.

Note: Lard is traditionally used by Mexican cooks. However, as it is not always easy to find fresh, good-quality lard here, you may want to substitute solid shortening.

PIGLETS
(COCHINITOS)

Mexico

The recipe for these whimsical, pig-shaped sugar cookies is from Arizonan Norma Guevara, who enjoyed these cookies while growing up in Mexico City.

The tan-colored piglets are decorated with a sprinkling of cinnamon sugar, which gives them a very realistic "dusty" appearance. They have a light orange-spice taste and a pleasant crispness.

Grated zest of 1 large orange
2   *4-inch cinnamon sticks*
¼   *cup orange juice*
¾   *cup packed light brown sugar*
2⅓ *cups all-purpose or unbleached white flour*
½   *teaspoon baking powder*
½   *teaspoon baking soda*
¾   *cup solid vegetable shortening or lard (see Note), at room temperature*
1   *teaspoon vanilla extract*

DECORATION
2   *tablespoons granulated sugar*
½   *teaspoon ground cinnamon*

Combine orange zest, cinnamon sticks, orange juice, and brown sugar in a small saucepan. Bring mixture to a boil, stirring, until sugar dissolves. Remove pan from heat and let stand until cool. Strain mixture through a fine sieve set over a small bowl, reserving syrup and discarding the cinnamon sticks and orange zest.

Thoroughly stir together the flour, baking powder, and baking soda.

Place shortening in a large mixing bowl and beat with an electric mixer until light and fluffy. Beat in cooled syrup and vanilla until blended. Gradually beat in flour mixture. If the mixer motor labors, stir in remaining dry ingredients with a large wooden spoon. Divide dough in half and wrap each half in waxed paper or plastic wrap. Refrigerate for about 1½ hours. (If refrigerated longer, let the dough warm up again slightly before rolling.)

To prepare for baking, preheat the oven to 375 degrees F. Grease several baking sheets. Working with one dough half at a time, roll out on a lightly floured surface to a ¼ inch thickness. Lift dough and dust rolling pin with flour several times to prevent sticking. Cut out piglets using a pig-shaped cutter. Using a spatula, transfer the cookies to baking sheets, spacing about 1¼ inches apart. Gather and re-roll any dough scraps and continue cutting out cookies until all the dough is used. Repeat process with second half of dough.

In a small bowl, combine granulated sugar and ground cinnamon and mix well. Sprinkle cookies lightly with cinnamon sugar. Place in the center of the oven and bake for 9 to 10 minutes or until light brown all over and slightly darker at the edges. Remove baking sheets from oven and let stand for about 3 minutes. Then transfer cookies to wire racks and let stand until cooled completely.

Store in an airtight container for up to a week. Freeze for longer storage.

Makes about 35 3½-inch piglets.

Note: Lard is traditionally used by Mexican cooks. However, as it is not always easy to find fresh, good-quality lard here, you may want to substitute solid shortening.

Seville Cookies
(Sevillanas)

Mexico

In this festive recipe, the cookie dough is divided into several parts, each of which is flavored and tinted differently.

In the following version, one dough portion is flavored with pineapple (or lemon) extract and tinted yellow; a second is flavored with lime zest and tinted green; and a third is flavored with orange peel and tinted orange. Other combinations—cherry-flavored dough colored red or mint cookies tinted green, for example—can be substituted.

2¾ cups all-purpose or unbleached white flour
1¼ teaspoons baking powder
⅛ teaspoon salt
1 cup solid vegetable shortening or lard (see Note), at room temperature
1 cup granulated sugar
1 large egg
Finely grated zest of 1 large lemon
¼ teaspoon pineapple extract (if unavailable, substitute ⅛ teaspoon lemon extract)
Yellow, green, and red food coloring
Finely grated zest of 1 large lime
Finely grated zest of 1 medium orange

Thoroughly stir together flour, baking powder, and salt and set aside.

In a large mixing bowl, beat shortening until light and fluffy. Add sugar and beat until well blended. Beat in egg and lemon peel. Gradually beat in about half of dry ingredients. Stir in remaining dry ingredients with a large wooden spoon.

Divide dough into thirds. Beat or knead pineapple extract and 4 drops of yellow food coloring into one portion; lime zest and 3 drops of green food coloring and 1 drop of yellow into another; and orange zest, 3 drops of yellow food coloring, and 2 drops of red into the third. Wrap each portion in plastic wrap and refrigerate for about 1½ hours, or until cold and slightly firm but not stiff.

To prepare for baking, preheat the oven to 350 degrees F. Grease several baking sheets. Working with one portion at a time, roll dough between sheets of waxed paper to ¼-inch thick. Check underside, smoothing out any wrinkles in the paper. Peel off paper from bottom of dough. Turn dough right side up again. Cut out 2¼- to 2¾-inch cookies with cookie cutters in simple shapes such as squares, diamonds, triangles, circles, or scalloped rounds. Using a spatula, transfer cookies to baking sheets, spacing about 1¼ inches apart. Gather dough scraps, re-roll, and continue cutting out until all dough is used. Repeat the process with the other two portions until all dough is used.

Place in the center of the oven and bake for 8 to 10 minutes or until *just barely brown at the edges*; don't overbake or the colorful appearance of the cookies will be spoiled. Remove baking sheets from oven and let cookies stand for about 3 minutes. Then transfer cookies to wire racks and let stand until completely cooled.

Store in an airtight container for up to a week. Freeze for longer storage.

Makes 35 to 45 2¼- to 2¾-inch cookies.

Note: Lard is traditionally used by Mexican cooks. However, as it is not always easy to find fresh, good-quality lard here, you may want to substitute solid shortening.

Brazilian Coconut Chews
(Brasileiras)

Brazil

Coconut palms are not indigenous to Brazil, but they flourish there and the meat of the large hard-shelled seeds is widely used in Brazilian cookery. These small, golden colored coconut chews are a special favorite. They are fragrant, pleasantly chewy, and have a wonderful coconut flavor.

¼	cup all-purpose or unbleached white flour
1	large egg
2	large egg yolks
½	cup granulated sugar
⅓	cup light brown sugar
	Pinch of salt
2	cups flaked or shredded sweetened coconut
¼	teaspoon vanilla extract

Preheat the oven to 350 degrees F. Grease several baking sheets and set aside. Combine flour, egg, and egg yolks in a small bowl and beat with a fork until well blended. Set aside.

Combine granulated sugar, brown sugar, salt, and ⅓ cup water in a heavy, medium saucepan over medium heat. Heat, lifting the pan and swirling the mixture several times but without stirring, until the mixture boils and reaches 230 degrees F. when tested with a candy thermometer (or forms a stiff thread when dripped into ice water). Immediately remove saucepan from the heat. Slowly pour about 2 tablespoons of the hot syrup into the flour-egg mixture, stirring vigorously, until thoroughly incorporated. Stir the coconut into the remaining syrup. Then, stirring vigorously, pour the flour-egg mixture back into the syrup-coconut mixture.

Return the saucepan to the heat and cook the mixture over medium heat, stirring constantly, until it stiffens, being careful it doesn't stick to the bottom of the pan. Stir in the vanilla until thoroughly incorporated. Remove from the heat and set aside until the mixture cools to lukewarm.

Drop mixture by heaping teaspoonfuls onto the baking sheets, spacing about 1½ inches apart. Using the fingertips, pat and smooth edges of the mounds to make them rounded and evenly shaped.

Place in the center of the oven and bake for 12 to 14 minutes, or until they are golden brown all over and tinged with darker brown on top. Remove from oven and let cookies stand on the baking sheets for 2 minutes. Then, using a spatula, transfer them to wire racks and let stand until cooled completely.

Store the cookies in an airtight container for 4 or 5 days. Freeze for longer storage.

Makes about 24 1½- to 1¾-inch cookies.

CORNMEAL COOKIES
(MOLLETES)

Mexico

Molletes are small, round cookies with pine nuts imbedded in the center to form a decorative design. (Sometimes in Mexico, biscuits or yeast rolls are also called molletes.)

These unusual, and very good cookies are made with a Mexican staple, cornmeal. It adds a pleasant "sandy" texture as well as a tantalizing sweet aroma and taste. White cornmeal is traditionally used in this recipe, but yellow cornmeal may be substituted.

¾   cup (1½ sticks) unsalted butter,
     slightly softened
⅔   cup granulated sugar
2   large egg yolks
1¼   teaspoons vanilla extract
½   cup white cornmeal
1¾   to 2 cups all-purpose or unbleached
     white flour, approximately
3   tablespoons pine nuts

Preheat the oven to 350 degrees F. Grease several baking sheets and set aside.

Place butter in a large mixing bowl and beat with the mixer on medium speed until lightened. Add sugar and beat until fluffy and well blended. Beat in egg yolks and vanilla. Add cornmeal and beat until thoroughly incorporated. Let mixture stand for 1 to 2 minutes. Using a large wooden spoon, stir in 1¾ cups flour until the mixture is well-blended and smooth. Let stand for 5 minutes. If dough seems too soft to shape with the hands, stir in a few tablespoons more flour; however, be careful not to add too much as dough will continue to stiffen and dry out slightly as the cornmeal absorbs moisture.

Pull off small portions of dough and roll between palms to form 1-inch balls. Space on baking sheets about 1½ inches apart. Gently press each ball into a 1¾-inch disc with the heel of the hand. Imbed three pine nuts in a spoke-like pattern (with narrow ends toward center) on top of each cookie.

Place in the center of the oven and bake for 14 to 16 minutes or until pale gold on top and lightly browned at edges. Turn baking sheets from front to back about halfway through baking to ensure even browning. Remove baking sheets from the oven and let stand for 3 to 4 minutes. Then transfer cookies to wire racks and let cool completely.

Store in an airtight container for up to a week. Freeze for longer storage.

Makes about 35 2-inch cookies.

Wedding Cookies
(Pastelitos de Boda)

Mexico

Even those who know very little about Mexican food and traditions are often familiar with and fond of these scrumptious pecan shortbread cookies. No doubt it's the meltingly tender texture and tantalizing pecan taste that accounts for their popularity. Very similar cookies known as pecan butter balls are popular across the American South, which may mean that we in the United States borrowed the recipe from our neighbors across the border.

As the name suggests, these cookies are traditional at Mexican wedding feasts.

1½   cups coarsely chopped pecans
1½   cups (3 sticks) unsalted butter, slightly softened
¼   teaspoon salt
⅔   cup powdered sugar
2   teaspoons vanilla extract
3   cups all-purpose or unbleached white flour

      DECORATION
½   to ⅔ cup powdered sugar

Preheat the oven to 325 degrees F. Spread the pecans in a large baking pan. Place in the oven and toast, stirring frequently, for 8 to 10 minutes, or until fragrant and very lightly tinged with brown. Remove from the oven and set aside until cooled completely. Grind the pecans to a powder using a nut grinder, food processor, or blender. Reset oven temperature to 350 degrees F. Grease several baking sheets and set aside.

Place the butter and salt in a large mixing bowl and beat with electric mixer on medium speed until light and fluffy. Add ⅔ cup powdered sugar and vanilla and continue beating until very fluffy and smooth. Beat in cooled ground pecans. Gradually beat in flour. If the mixer motor begins to labor, stir in last of the flour by hand.

Pull off dough pieces and roll between the palms into 1¼-inch balls. Space them about 2 inches apart on baking sheets. Flatten balls slightly with the heel of the hand to form 1½-inch discs.

Place in the upper third of the oven and bake 10 to 12 minutes, or until cookies are just faintly tinged with brown at the edges and still pale in the centers. Remove baking sheets from the oven and let stand about 5 minutes. Using a spatula, gently transfer cookies to wire racks and let stand until cooled slightly. Sift powdered sugar generously over the cookies and let them stand until cooled completely.

Store cookies in an airtight container for up to a week. For best appearance, add an additional light sifting of powdered sugar shortly before serving. The cookies may also be frozen before sprinkling with powdered sugar, then thawed completely and decorated before serving.

Makes 50 to 55 1¾-inch cookies.

COCONUT-PEANUT COOKIES
(GALLETAS MARIA)

Costa Rica

Maryland resident Selvin Martinez gave me this authentic Costa Rican recipe, which I've adapted for the American kitchen. Selvin, originally from Costa Rica, says these cookies are among the most popular in her native land. They are made at home and can also be bought in grocery stores there.

These cookies are a good crispy-crunchy mix of peanuts, oats, and coconut.

1½ cups all-purpose or unbleached white
    flour
1   teaspoon baking powder
¼   teaspoon baking soda
¾   cup (1½ sticks) unsalted butter,
    slightly softened
¾   cup packed light brown sugar
1   large egg
1   cup flaked or shredded sweetened
    coconut
1   cup quick-cooking oats
¾   cup unsalted roasted, skinless
    peanuts, chopped moderately fine

Preheat the oven to 350 degrees F. Grease several baking sheets and set aside. In a medium bowl, thoroughly stir together the flour, baking powder, and baking soda.

Place butter in a mixing bowl and beat with a mixer on medium speed until lightened. Add brown sugar and egg and beat until fluffy and smooth. Beat in flour mixture until incorporated. Using a large wooden spoon, stir in coconut, oats, and peanuts until distributed throughout. Set aside for 3 or 4 minutes.

Pull off pieces of dough and roll between the palms into 1¼-inch balls. Arrange them on the baking sheets about 2½ inches apart. Press each ball down with the heel of the hand to form 2-inch rounds.

Place in the center of the oven and bake for 13 to 15 minutes, or until cookies are light gold and tinged with brown at the edges. Remove baking sheets from the oven and let the cookies stand on the baking sheets for 2 minutes. Using a spatula, transfer them to wire racks and let stand until cooled completely.

Store the cookies in airtight containers for up to a week. Freeze for longer storage.

Makes about 35 2¾-inch cookies.

CHAPTER 4

BRITISH ISLES
COOKIES

SWEETS OF ALL SORTS ARE MUCH LOVED IN THE British Isles. In many homes, a tin of cookies, or "biscuits" as the British call them, is always kept on hand to serve with stewed fruit or a cup of tea or coffee.

British biscuits tend to be simple, yet gratifying. Most are firm, dry-crisp, and without icing or elaborate decorations (fancy treatments are generally reserved for cakes). However, particularly at afternoon tea, plain wafers may be dressed up by sandwiching them around jam, buttercream filling, or a lovely lemon spread known as lemon curd. Several delicious biscuits in this category are Jam-Filled Almond Shorties, Orange-Ginger Creams, and Lemon-Filled Sandwich Cookies, all of which appear in this chapter.

Without doubt, the most famous British biscuits are the shortbreads. They are traditional at Christmas and popular the rest of the year as well. Considering that these meltingly rich biscuits are normally made from only butter, sugar, flour, and perhaps salt, it's remarkable how many different variations exist. Some are thick, bar-like, and crunchy, others thinnish, wedge-shaped, and fragile. Shortbreads likewise vary in degree of sweetness. Usually, a buttery taste predominates, but in some recipes, such as Almond Petticoat Tails, an almond flavor also

comes through. Occasionally, versions are even spiced with ginger, though I feel it overwhelms the characteristic but subtle shortbread taste and is best omitted.

Surprising as it might seem, many traditional British cookies contain ginger. From at least the Middle Ages, British cooks were captivated with the spice, adding it to a wide range of sauces, minced meats, medicinals, and baked goods and providing it as a table condiment along with salt and pepper. By the eighteenth century, its wholesale use in British cookery declined, but the tradition of ginger cookies has endured. The Parlies (so named for the early Scottish Parliament members who ate them), Brandy Snaps, and Anthea's Ginger Biscuits presented in this chapter are only a few of the fine ginger-flavored cookies in the British repertoire. Gingerbread "husbands," a Scottish equivalent of American gingerbread people, continue to be popular, particularly at "nursery tea," the afternoon tea served to children.

Aside from ginger cookies, most of the other favorite British biscuits are comfortingly mild. For example, Melting Moments, Shrewsbury Biscuits, Golden Oat Cookies, and Coconut Crunchies are all understated, quintessentially go-with-something-else sweets. But enough talk. It's time to put the kettle on for tea!

Foreground: *Golden Oat Cookies (recipe on page 93).*
On plate, left to right: *Ginger Parliament Cookies*
(recipe on page 90) and Shortbread (recipe on page 88).

SHORTBREAD

Scotland and Ireland

This is an adaptation of a recipe from Orkney, a beautiful chain of islands off the northern coast of Scotland. Even in summer, days there can be cool and blustery, and a bracing cup of tea and a plate of shortbread by the fire is a wonderful afternoon treat.

Shortbreads can be found all over Scotland and the rest of the British Isles, and I tested many recipes before settling on this particular one. It produces a cookie that tastes exceptionally buttery and is crunchy-crisp. As is typical of British biscuits, this shortbread is not too sweet. If you prefer a slightly sweeter cookie, sprinkle the finished round lightly with granulated sugar after baking.

Although shortbreads contain only a few ingredients, they must be in just the right proportion so be sure to measure carefully.

½ cup plus 1½ tablespoons (1 stick plus 1½ tablespoons) unsalted butter
⅔ cup powdered sugar
Pinch of salt
1⅓ cups all-purpose or unbleached white flour

DECORATION

1 to 2 teaspoons granulated sugar (optional)

Place butter in a heavy, medium saucepan over medium heat and bring to a boil. Lower heat so the butter gently bubbles. Simmer it, uncovered and stirring frequently, for 4 to 5 minutes, until butter turns slightly golden; watch carefully to prevent browning or burning. Remove pan immediately from the heat. Cover and refrigerate until the butter resolidifies, about 1 hour. (To speed up the cooling process, place butter in the freezer for about 25 minutes, being careful not to let it become hard.)

Combine cooled butter, powdered sugar, and salt in a small mixing bowl and beat with an electric mixer on medium speed until very light and smooth. Add flour and beat until blended but not overmixed. Stir in 2 teaspoons cold water. Press dough into a smooth, evenly shaped ball. If dough still seems slightly crumbly, stir in up to another teaspoon water, but be careful not to overmoisten. Flatten the ball into a smooth disc and place between sheets of waxed paper. Using a rolling pin, roll dough out to form an evenly thick round 6½ to 7 inches in diameter. Remove the top sheet of waxed paper. Using the edge of a saucer or bowl that is about ⅛ inch smaller than the dough round as a cutting guide, trim off and discard the uneven edges of the dough with a pastry wheel or sharp knife. Replace the top sheet of waxed paper. Slide the dough onto a baking sheet and refrigerate for 20 to 25 minutes, or until it firms up slightly. Meanwhile, preheat the oven to 325 degrees F.

Remove dough from the refrigerator and carefully peel off and then loosely replace bottom sheet of waxed paper. Turn the dough over and peel off and discard top sheet of waxed paper. Form a decorative edge around the shortbread by pressing the tines of a fork into the surface. Decoratively prick the dough surface all over with a fork. Using a wide spatula, carefully transfer the dough to a baking sheet. Cut the round into quarters and then eighths using a pastry wheel or knife. (If smaller shortbread pieces are desired, cut the circle into quarters and then cut each quarter into three equal wedges to yield 12 portions.)

Place in the center of the oven and bake for 26 to 30 minutes, or until the shortbread is light tan but not brown. Remove from the oven and let shortbread stand on baking sheet for 10 minutes. Using a large, sharp knife, retrace the cuts previously made. Lightly sprinkle the wedges with granulated sugar, if desired. Transfer shortbread to a wire rack and let stand until cooled completely. Serve the wedges reassembled to form a round on a round plate.

Store shortbread in an airtight container for up to a week. Freeze for longer storage.

Makes 8 (or 12) shortbread wedges.

SHREWSBURY BISCUITS

England and Scotland

Shrewsbury biscuits are large, mild, not-too-sweet sugar cookies that go well with tea. Many British cookery books contain versions of this cookie. They are all somewhat similar, but this is the best I've found.

1½ cups all-purpose or unbleached white flour
1   teaspoon baking powder
½   teaspoon baking soda
¼   teaspoon salt
½   cup (1 stick) unsalted butter, slightly softened
½   cup granulated sugar
2   egg yolks
1   teaspoon vanilla extract
2   drops almond extract (optional)
     Finely grated zest of 1 small lemon
1½   to 2 teaspoons milk, approximately

Thoroughly stir together flour, baking powder, baking soda, and salt. Place butter in a large mixing bowl and beat with electric mixer on medium speed until light. Add sugar and egg yolks and beat until light and fluffy. Beat in vanilla, almond extract, and lemon zest. Gradually mix in dry ingredients. Add 1½ teaspoons milk, or just enough more to form a smooth, manageable dough. Press dough into a ball. Wrap in waxed paper and refrigerate for 15 minutes. Preheat the oven to 375 degrees F. Grease several baking sheets.

Place dough between sheets of waxed paper. Roll dough out to ⅜-inch thick, checking the underside of the dough and smoothing out any creases that form. Turn over the dough and peel off bottom sheet of waxed paper. Replace the paper loosely and turn dough right side up again. Remove top sheet of waxed paper. Using a fluted or plain round 2¼-inch cutter, or the rim of a 2¼-inch diameter drinking glass, cut out cookies. Using a spatula, carefully transfer cookies to baking sheets, spacing about 1½ inches apart. Gather and re-roll any dough scraps and continue cutting out cookies until all dough is used.

Place cookies in the center of the oven and bake for 11 to 13 minutes or until just barely browned. Remove baking sheets from oven and let stand for about 3 minutes. Transfer cookies to wire racks and let stand until completely cooled.

Store in an airtight container for up to 10 days. Freeze for longer storage.

Makes about 24 2¾- to 3-inch cookies.

GINGER PARLIAMENT COOKIES
(PARLIES)

Scotland

I learned of parlies during a trip to the charming old city of Edinburgh. A traditional form of crisp Scottish gingerbread, these cookies were once hawked by vendors along the streets of Edinburgh. Since the best customers were said to be the members of the Scottish Parliament hurrying back and forth on government business, the cookies were dubbed parlies.

Because the dough is simply cut into rectangles and baked, parlies are fast and easy to make. The cookies have a nice zippy flavor and an appealing crispness.

3½   cups all-purpose or unbleached white
     flour
1   tablespoon plus 1 teaspoon ground
     ginger
¾   teaspoon ground allspice
¾   teaspoon ground cinnamon
½   teaspoon baking soda
¾   cup plus 2 tablespoons (1¾ sticks)
     unsalted butter, slightly softened
½   cup dark molasses
1   cup packed light brown sugar
1   large egg

Thoroughly stir together flour, ginger, allspice, cinnamon, and baking soda in a large bowl. Place butter, molasses, and sugar in a large mixing bowl and beat until lightened and smooth. Beat in the egg.

Gradually beat in dry ingredients. If the mixer motor labors, stir in the last of the dry ingredients using a large wooden spoon. Divide the dough in half. Wrap each half in plastic wrap and refrigerate for about 1½ hours, or until cold and slightly firm but not stiff.

Preheat the oven to 375 degrees F. Grease several baking sheets and set aside.

Working with half the dough at a time and leaving the other half refrigerated, roll the dough out on a lightly floured surface into a scant ⅛-inch-thick rectangle. Lift dough and dust rolling pin and work surface with flour occasionally to prevent dough from sticking, but for best appearance of cookies be careful not to overflour.

Using a pastry wheel or large knife, cut the dough into rectangles about 2½ by 3 inches. The size does not have to be exact, but if you want the cookies to be completely uniform, measure and mark the dough before cutting. Using a spatula, transfer rectangles to baking sheets, spacing about 1 inch apart. Repeat the rolling and cutting out process with the second dough half. Gather and re-roll all dough scraps and continue preparing cookies until all dough is used. (If dough becomes too warm and soft to handle easily, refrigerate it again before re-rolling.)

Place in the center of the oven and bake for 6 to 9 minutes, or until cookies are slightly darker around the edges. Baking time will vary somewhat depending on the size of the rectangles. Remove baking sheets from the oven and let stand for 30 seconds. Using a spatula, immediately transfer cookies to wire racks. Let stand until completely cooled.

Store the cookies in an airtight container for up to 10 days. Freeze for longer storage.

Makes 50 to 55 2½- by 3-inch cookies.

Almond "Petticoat Tails" Shortbread

Scotland and Ireland

Some sources suggest that the whimsical name given this particular form of traditional shortbread is a corruption of the French "petites galettes," or little cakes. Others think the name refers to the shape: a large ring of dough is divided into eighths to make wedge-shaped pieces resembling the bell-hoop petticoats of early court ladies.

In any case, this is a fine, very fragile shortbread with a lovely almond-butter flavor. The petticoat tails are a handsome golden color and are attractive when arranged and served on a large round platter.

10	tablespoons (1 stick plus 2 tablespoons) unsalted butter
1/3	cup slivered blanched almonds
1/4	cup granulated sugar
2 1/2	tablespoons powdered sugar
1/4	teaspoon salt
1/4	teaspoon almond extract
1 1/3	cups all-purpose or unbleached white flour

DECORATION

1	egg white
1/4	cup coarsely chopped slivered blanched almonds

Place butter in a heavy, medium saucepan and heat over medium heat until it melts and bubbles. Adjust heat so that the butter bubbles and foams but does not burn, and simmer, uncovered, stirring frequently, for 4 to 5 minutes or until the butter is golden but not browned. Remove saucepan from heat and stir for 30 seconds. Cover and refrigerate for 40 to 50 minutes or until butter resolidifies, but is not extremely cold or hard. (If desired, speed up the cooling process by placing butter in freezer for about 20 minutes, but do not let it become too cold.)

Meanwhile, preheat the oven to 325 degrees F. Spread 1/3 cup slivered almonds in a baking pan. Place in the oven to toast for 7 to 8 minutes, or until tinged with brown, being careful not to let almonds burn. Remove from the oven and set aside to cool. Then place almonds in a food processor or blender and process until finely ground.

Combine resolidified butter, granulated and powdered sugars, and salt in a small mixing bowl and beat with an electric mixer on medium speed for 2 to 3 minutes, or until very light and fluffy. Beat in ground almonds and almond extract. Using a large wooden spoon, add flour and stir until incorporated and the mixture holds together. Shape dough into a ball and place between sheets of waxed paper. Using a rolling pin, roll dough out to form a round *just slightly larger* than 8 inches in diameter. Turn over dough so the underside is facing up and peel off the waxed paper; replace paper loosely. Turn dough right side up, and peel off and remove top sheet of waxed paper. Using the edge of an 8-inch round cake pan or plate as a cutting guide, trim off and discard any uneven edges of dough with a pastry wheel or a sharp knife. Then, using a 2 1/4- to 2 1/2-inch round cutter (or drinking glass) cut a circle out of the center of the round. Leaving the cut out round in place, replace top sheet of waxed paper and slide dough onto a tray or baking sheet. Refrigerate for 20 minutes, or chill in the freezer for 8 to 9 minutes, until dough firms slightly. Meanwhile, preheat the oven to 325 degrees F.

Remove bottom sheet of waxed paper from dough and place round, right side up, on a baking sheet. Remove top sheet of waxed paper. Form a decorative edge around dough with the tines of a fork. Using the point of a table knife or narrow spatula, lift the center round from dough to form a ring. Place center dough round separately on baking sheet. Mark and cut dough ring into quarters, and then eighths using a pastry wheel, pizza wheel, or knife, *leaving the wedges in place in the ring.* (If smaller shortbread pieces are desired, cut ring into quarters and then cut each quarter into three parts to yield 12 wedges.)

Combine egg white with 2 teaspoons water in a small bowl and beat well. Lightly brush ring and center round with egg white mixture, being careful not to drip it onto the baking sheet, or the shortbread may stick. Immediately sprinkle shortbread pieces with ¼ cup chopped almonds.

Place in center of the oven and bake for 25 to 29 minutes, or until shortbread is tinged with gold all over but is not brown. (If almonds begin to brown too rapidly, lower oven temperature to 300 degrees during the last 5 minutes of baking.) Remove from the oven and let shortbread stand on baking sheet for 15 to 20 minutes until cool. Then using a sharp knife, gently retrace the cuts previously made. Let the shortbread stand on baking sheet until completely cooled; it will be crumbly when warm and should not be moved. Separate wedges and serve petticoat tails on a large round plate with wedges radiating from center and with or without the center round inserted.

Store the shortbread in an airtight container for up to 10 days. Freeze for longer storage.

Makes 8 (or 12) petticoat tail wedges and one center round.

MELTING MOMENTS

Scotland and England

Melting moments are so named for their delightfully crisp-dry, melt-in-the-mouth texture. Whoever first devised this cookie must have created it specifically to go with tea.

I was first served melting moments at a bed and breakfast establishment in the Orkneys, a beautiful island chain off the northern coast of Scotland. My hostess served a plate of these cookies along with a pot of tea, and I ate nearly all of them as I sat warming my toes in front of a glowing peat fire. This recipe is from Birsay, an island near the center of the chain.

1⅔   cups all-purpose or unbleached white
       flour
⅔   cup corn starch
¾   teaspoon baking powder
1   cup (2 sticks) unsalted butter, slightly
       softened
1½   cups powdered sugar
1   large egg yolk
¼   teaspoon almond extract

COATING
⅓   cup quick-cooking oats

Preheat the oven to 350 degrees F. Grease several baking sheets and set aside. Thoroughly stir together flour, corn starch, and baking powder.

Place butter in a large mixing bowl and beat with an electric mixer on medium speed until very light. Add sugar and beat until very fluffy and smooth. Beat in egg yolk and almond extract. Gradually beat in dry ingredients until thoroughly incorporated. If mixer motor labors, gradually beat in remaining dry ingredients with a large wooden spoon.

Pull off small portions of dough and roll between palms to form 1-inch balls. Lightly roll each ball in the oats. Place balls on baking sheets about 2 inches apart. Using the heel of the hand, slightly flatten each ball into a 1½-inch round.

Place cookies in the center of the oven and bake for 13 to 16 minutes, or until pale gold on top and lightly browned at the edges. Reverse baking sheets from the front to back about halfway through baking to ensure even browning. Remove baking sheets from the oven and let stand for 3 to 4 minutes. Then transfer cookies to wire racks and let cool completely.

Store in an airtight container for up to a week. Freeze for longer storage.

Makes about 40 2½-inch cookies.

GOLDEN OAT COOKIES
(OAT BISCUITS)

Scotland

Each time I make these homey, hearty oat cookies I'm reminded of the meals I enjoyed while traveling in the Scottish Highlands. Oats are used in many traditional dishes there; cooks frequently serve up porridge for breakfast and plump oat cakes and butter with afternoon tea or supper. Simple, chewy-crisp oatmeal "biscuits," as the British call cookies, are also popular with tea.

1	cup all-purpose or unbleached white flour
¾	teaspoon baking powder
¼	teaspoon baking soda
7	tablespoons unsalted butter, slightly softened
⅓	cup granulated sugar
⅓	cup packed light brown sugar
1	large egg
3	tablespoons golden syrup (see Note)
1¾	cups rolled oats

Preheat the oven to 350 degrees F. Grease several baking sheets and set aside. Thoroughly stir together flour, baking powder, and baking soda.

In a large mixing bowl, beat butter with an electric mixer on medium speed until light. Add granulated and brown sugars, and beat until fluffy and smooth. Add egg and golden syrup, and continue beating until thoroughly blended. Beat in dry ingredients. Stir in oats using a large wooden spoon. Let mixture stand for 5 minutes to allow oats to absorb some of the moisture in the dough. Drop cookies onto baking sheets by heaping rounded teaspoonfuls, spacing them about 2½ inches apart.

Place in upper third of preheated oven and bake for 9 to 12 minutes, or until cookies are golden brown all over and slightly darker around edges. Let stand for 2 to 3 minutes before transferring to wire racks to cool.

Store cookies in an airtight container for up to a week. Freeze for longer storage.

Makes about 30 2½- to 2¾-inch cookies.

Note: Golden syrup is a cane sugar syrup widely used in Britain. It can be purchased in some American gourmet shops and large supermarkets. If golden syrup is unavailable, dark corn syrup can be substituted, though it lends a different flavor and color to the cookies.

Jam-Filled Almond Shorties

Scotland and England

Shorties are rolled Scottish cookies. As the name suggests, they are very "short" and buttery. In fact, shorties are just thinly rolled and cut out shortbread. These pretty shorties are sandwich cookies put together with tart jam. Sometimes, the cookies and jam are presented separately, and diners make their own "sandwiches" right at the tea table.

1½   *cups (3 sticks) unsalted butter, slightly softened*
1   *cup powdered sugar*
½   *teaspoon salt*
½   *teaspoon almond extract*
    Finely grated zest of 1 small lemon
⅓   *cup finely ground, blanched almonds*
3   *cups all-purpose or unbleached white flour*
½   *to ⅔ cup blackberry, apricot, gooseberry, currant, or other not-too-sweet, seedless preserves*

Place the butter in a large mixing bowl, sift in powdered sugar, and beat with an electric mixer on medium speed for 2 minutes or until very light and fluffy. Add salt, almond extract, lemon zest, and almonds, and beat about 30 seconds longer. Using a large wooden spoon, gradually add flour and stir until it is fully incorporated and the mixture begins to hold together. (For the tenderest cookies, mix dough just enough to evenly distribute flour; don't overwork.)

Divide dough in half, lay each half between large sheets of waxed paper, and roll out ¼ inch thick. Check the underside frequently and smooth out any creases. Place rolled dough sheets on a tray or baking sheet and refrigerate for 15 to 20 minutes, or until cool and somewhat firm. Meanwhile, preheat the oven to 350 degrees F. Set out several baking sheets.

To make shortie tops, remove one dough portion from the refrigerator and carefully peel waxed paper from the bottom of dough. Then replace paper loosely and turn dough right side up. Carefully peel off top sheet of waxed paper. Working quickly so that dough does not become too warm and soft, cut out rounds using a 2¼-inch or slightly larger round cutter or drinking glass. (Dip the cutter lightly in powdered sugar, if needed, to prevent dough from sticking.) Cut out the centers using a thimble, small bottle cap, or other small, round cutter. Remove centers using the point of a small knife. Using a spatula, immediately transfer cookies to baking sheets, spacing about 1 inch apart. (If the dough becomes too warm or soft to handle, return the sheet to the refrigerator briefly.) Gather centers and dough scraps, press into a ball, and re-roll between waxed paper. Chill and repeat cutting out process. Continue until all of first dough half is used.

To prepare the shortie bottoms, repeat cutting out process with second dough half, except omit cutting out center holes. Gather, re-roll, chill, and cut out scraps as before until all dough is used.

Place the cookies in the center of preheated oven and bake for 10 to 12 minutes, or until edges are just tinged with brown; the tops may take slightly less time than the bottoms. (Exact baking time will vary considerably depending on the temperature of the dough when cookies are put in the oven.) Turn baking sheets about halfway through baking to ensure even browning.

Remove baking sheets from the oven and

let cookies stand on sheets for 5 minutes. Transfer cookies to wire racks and let stand until completely cooled.

Cookies can be assembled and removed immediately or tops and bottoms can be stored as is for up to 4 days. (They may also be frozen, unassembled, for up to 10 days.) Since the moisture in the preserves will cause cookie sandwiches to gradually lose their crispness, they should be served within 3 or 4 hours of being assembled. To assemble, spread about 1½ teaspoons preserves over each cookie bottom. Center and gently press a top over each bottom.

Makes about 24 2½-inch sandwich cookies.

ORANGE MELTAWAYS

England and Scotland

Meltaways are elegant little tea cookies prepared with a pastry bag fitted with a large star tip. Their tops are brushed with an apricot jam-orange zest mixture and sprinkled with granulated sugar during baking, which gives them a lovely orange glaze and flavor. The cookies are called meltaways because of their melt-in-the-mouth texture.

1½   cups all-purpose or unbleached white
       flour
¼   cup cornstarch
¼   teaspoon baking powder
¾   cup plus 1 tablespoon (1 stick plus 5
       tablespoons) unsalted butter, slightly
       softened
⅔   cup powdered sugar
1   large egg yolk
       Finely grated zest of 1 small lemon
       Finely grated zest of 1 large orange
2   teaspoons fresh lemon juice
2   to 4 teaspoons orange juice,
       approximately

       GLAZE
¼   cup strained apricot preserves
½   teaspoon fresh lemon juice
¼   teaspoon very finely grated orange
       zest
1½   to 2½ tablespoons granulated sugar

Preheat the oven to 350 degrees F. Grease several baking sheets and set aside. Sift together flour, cornstarch, and baking powder.

In a large mixing bowl, beat the butter with an electric mixer on medium speed for 3 minutes, until very light. Add the powdered sugar and beat until very fluffy and smooth. Beat in egg yolk, lemon zest, orange zest, lemon juice, and 2 teaspoons orange juice until mixture is well blended. Add dry ingredients and beat until thoroughly incorporated. Let stand for 2 or 3 minutes. If the mixture seems too stiff to pipe through a pastry tube, beat in a bit more orange juice to soften it just slightly.

Fit a pastry bag with a ½-inch-diameter or slightly larger star tip. Stand the bag, tip down, in a tall glass and turn down a wide cuff at the top. Spoon mixture into the bag until two-thirds full. Turn the cuff up and twist the top tightly to close. Pipe 1½-inch shell shapes onto baking sheets, spacing them about 1½ inches apart. Let stand for about 5 minutes.

Meanwhile, prepare the glaze by stirring together strained apricot preserves, lemon juice, and orange zest in a small bowl.

Place cookies in the center of the oven and bake for 12 to 14 minutes, or until the edges are lightly browned. Remove baking sheets from the oven and lightly brush tops of cookies with the glaze. Generously sprinkle the glazed cookies with granulated sugar. Return baking sheets to the oven and continue baking for 4 to 5 minutes longer, or until glaze starts to bubble and caramelize and cookies are browned at the edges. Remove baking sheets from the oven and let cookies stand for about 2 minutes. Then transfer them to wire racks and let stand until cooled completely.

Store the cookies in an airtight container in a single layer for up to a week. Freeze for longer storage.

Makes about 40 1¾- to 2-inch cookies.

Brandy Snaps

England

Almost every English cookbook includes a recipe for these special brittle-crisp ginger wafers. They are rolled up into cylinders around wooden spoon handles while still warm and when cooled are served with decorative swirls of whipped cream piped into the cylinder ends.

Originally, brandy snaps were made with treacle. Today, however, British brandy snap recipes usually call for a cane sugar syrup known as golden syrup. This product, which is widely used in Great Britain, can sometimes be purchased in American gourmet shops or the international sections of large supermarkets. Dark corn syrup can be substituted, although the taste and color of the cookies will not be quite the same.

7   *tablespoons unsalted butter*
½   *cup granulated sugar*
⅓   *cup golden syrup, or dark corn syrup*
¾   *cup all-purpose or unbleached white flour, sifted after measuring*
1½ *teaspoons ground ginger*
1½ *teaspoons brandy*
    Finely grated zest of half a medium-sized lemon

Filling
1   *cup heavy cream*
1   *tablespoon brandy*
3   *to 4 tablespoons powdered sugar (optional)*

Preheat the oven to 350 degrees F. Cover several baking sheets with aluminum foil cut to fit. Generously grease foil. Lay out 3 or 4 long-handled wooden spoons to use for rolling up warm wafers.

Combine butter, sugar, and golden syrup in a small saucepan. Warm over medium-low heat, stirring, just until butter melts but mixture has not become hot. Immediately remove saucepan from heat. Stir in flour, ginger, brandy, and lemon zest until mixture is well blended and very smooth.

Drop 5 or 6 very small, evenly shaped teaspoonfuls of batter onto each foil-lined baking sheet, spacing about 3 inches apart. Don't crowd cookies or make them too large, as they will spread a great deal. Bake no more than 5 or 6 wafers at once, as they cool rapidly and must be rolled into cylinders while still warm.

Place in upper third of preheated oven and bake for 8 to 10 minutes, or until brandy snaps have bubbled and turned deep golden brown; turn baking sheet from front to back about half way through baking to ensure even browning. Immediately remove baking sheet from oven and let wafers stand for 1 to 2 minutes. As soon as the cookies have cooled just enough to be handled and lifted without tearing, begin loosening them from the foil and rolling each *loosely* around a spoon handle. (The first several wafers will be very pliable, but the last will have cooled enough to be fairly stiff. If the last ones are too stiff to roll, they may be softened by re-warming briefly in the oven.) As soon as the rolled cookies have cooled enough to hold their shape, slip them off the spoon handles and transfer to wire racks to cool.

Continue baking and shaping cookies until all batter is used. If batter begins to cool and stiffen, rewarm slightly over low heat. The foil-lined baking sheets may be used over and over, if desired, but should be regreased several times.

When all the cookies have been baked, shaped, and cooled, they may be stored in an airtight container for up to a week or frozen for several weeks.

Just before serving time, prepare filling by combining cream, brandy, and sugar (if used) in a small, chilled mixing bowl and beating until firm peaks form. Spoon filling into a pastry bag fitted with a large star tip, and pipe a decorative swirl of cream into each end of rolled cookies. Serve immediately.

Makes 25 to 30 2½- to 3-inch long cylinders.

Note: American cookie recipes usually call for sweetened whipped cream, but traditional British brandy snap recipes use unsweetened cream. Use whichever one you prefer.

Coconut Crunchies

England

Acoconut tea biscuit prepared by a commercial bakery in Derbyshire, England inspired this recipe. These simple but delicious cookies have a crunchy-crisp texture, golden color, and a light yet satisfying coconut flavor.

1¾ cups all-purpose or unbleached white
    flour
½ teaspoon baking soda
½ teaspoon baking powder

½ cup plus 2 tablespoons (1¼ sticks)
    unsalted butter, slightly softened
⅔ cup packed light brown sugar
½ cup granulated sugar
1 large egg
¾ cup quick-cooking (not instant) oats
½ cup shredded or flaked coconut

Preheat the oven to 400 degrees F. Generously grease several baking sheets and set aside.

Thoroughly stir together flour, baking soda, and baking powder. Place butter in a large mixing bowl and beat with an electric mixer set on medium speed until lightened. Add brown and granulated sugars and beat until fluffy and smooth. Beat in the egg. Place oats and coconut in a food processor and process until very finely ground. Turn the oat-coconut mixture into the mixing bowl with butter-sugar mixture and stir with a wooden spoon. Add the flour mixture and stir until thoroughly incorporated.

Shape dough into generous 1-inch balls and place on baking sheets, spacing about 2½ inches apart. Flatten cookies into 2-inch rounds using the heel of the hand.

Place in the upper third of the oven and bake for 8 to 10 minutes, or until golden brown. Remove from the oven and let cookies stand on baking sheets for 1 to 2 minutes. Using a spatula, transfer the cookies to wire racks and let stand until cooled completely.

Store in an airtight container for up to a week. Freeze for longer storage.

Makes 45 to 50 2½-inch cookies.

Overleaf: *Lemon-Filled Sandwich Cookies (recipe on page 102).*

LEMON-FILLED SANDWICH COOKIES
(LEMON TEA BISCUITS WITH LEMON CURD)

England and Scotland

I find the taste and texture combination of these fine tea cookies irresistible. Crisp and buttery wafers enclose a zingy yet silky-smooth lemon filling. Called lemon curd by the British, this filling is the consistency of seedless jam and tastes like the lemony layer of a really good lemon meringue pie. Lemon curd is so popular in the United Kingdom that it is available commercially in jars. It is used as a spread for scones, tea biscuits, and breads just as jams and jellies are.

Some gourmet shops in the United States carry imported lemon curd, which can be substituted for the filling included in this recipe, if desired. (In this case, you will need a generous ¾ cup.) However, the homemade product is much better.

Both the cookies and the filling can be made ahead and stored for several days, but for best texture don't combine the two until just before serving time.

Since these cookies are incredibly rich and served in pairs, it's a good idea to keep them small. I like to use a 2 inch cutter.

Although this makes rounds that look tiny when cut out, the finished sandwiches aren't a skimpy serving at all.

1¼ cups (2½ sticks) unsalted butter, slightly softened
½ cup granulated sugar
⅛ teaspoon salt
Very finely grated zest of 2 large lemons
2⅔ cups all-purpose or unbleached white flour

FILLING
⅓ cup plus 2 tablespoons fresh lemon juice
Finely grated zest of 2 large lemons
1 large egg
2 large egg yolks
1½ cups powdered sugar
2 tablespoons (¼ stick) cold unsalted butter, cut into small pieces

DECORATION
1 to 2 tablespoons powdered sugar

Combine the butter, granulated sugar, salt, and lemon zest in a large mixing bowl. Beat on medium speed for 2 minutes or until very light and fluffy. Using a large wooden spoon, vigorously stir in the flour until it is incorporated and the mixture just becomes cohesive. (For the tenderest cookies, mix the dough just enough to evenly distribute the flour.)

Divide the dough in half and lay each half between large sheets of waxed paper. Using a rolling pin, roll out each half a scant ¼-inch thick, checking the undersides several times as you work and smoothing out any creases that form in the paper. Stack the rolled dough sheets on a tray or baking sheet. Refrigerate for 17 to 18 minutes, or until cool and fairly firm. (To speed up the chilling process place dough in the freezer for 9 or 10 minutes, but don't allow it to become too cold and hard.)

Preheat the oven to 350 degrees F. Set out several baking sheets.

Working with one chilled dough sheet at a time and leaving the other refrigerated, peel off the bottom sheet of waxed paper, and then replace it loosely. Turn the dough over and peel off and discard the top sheet of waxed paper. Working quickly so that the dough doesn't become too warm and soft, cut out 2- to 2⅛-inch rounds using a scalloped or fluted cutter or the rim of a small juice or sherry glass. Dip the cutter lightly in powdered sugar if needed to prevent the dough from sticking to it. Using a spatula, immediately transfer the rounds to the ungreased baking sheets, spacing about 1 inch apart. Gather dough scraps and roll out again between sheets of waxed paper. (If necessary, return the dough to the refrigerator and chill again.) Then cut out rounds until all the dough is used. Repeat the cutting out process with the second dough sheet.

Place in the center of the oven and bake for 9 to 12 minutes, or until edges are just barely tinged with brown; the tops should not be colored. Reverse baking sheets from front to back about halfway through baking to ensure even browning. Remove baking sheets from the oven and let stand for 1 minute. Carefully transfer cookies to wire racks and let stand until cooled completely. The cookies can be assembled and served immediately or stored as is for up to 3 days.

To prepare filling, beat or whisk together lemon juice, lemon zest, egg, egg yolks, and powdered sugar in the top of a double boiler until light and frothy. Cook over simmering water, stirring frequently, for 12 to 15 minutes, or until the mixture thickens almost to thin pudding consistency and coats the spoon. Strain the mixture through a fine sieve. Gradually stir the butter into the mixture until it is melted and the filling is smooth. Cover and refrigerate filling until cool. Filling may be stored in a non-metallic container for up to 48 hours.

To assemble cookies, spread a generous 1 teaspoon cooled filling over the underside of a cookie round. Gently press a second round over the filling to make a sandwich. Continue until all the sandwiches are formed. Decorate the sandwiches by lightly sifting powdered sugar over the tops.

Store the sandwiches in an airtight container perfectly flat (to prevent the tops from sliding off), and preferably in one layer. The cookies may also be frozen, unassembled, for up to 10 days. Since the moisture in the filling will cause the cookie sandwiches to gradually lose their crispness, they should not be assembled more than an hour or two before they are served.

Makes 22 to 24 2¼-inch sandwich cookies.

ANTHEA'S GINGER BISCUITS

England and Scotland

This is a splendid cookie with a light, crisp texture and pleasant gingery taste. It is a little like an American ginger snap, but the flavor and texture are more delicate and the color is a beautiful golden brown.

The English acquaintance who gave me this recipe, Jo Simons, says she obtained it from a friend, who in turn got it from her Scottish grandmother.

1⅔   cups all-purpose or unbleached white flour
2   teaspoons baking powder
1   teaspoon baking soda
1¼   to 1½ teaspoons ground ginger (see Note)
      Pinch of salt
½   cup (1 stick) unsalted butter, slightly softened
1   cup granulated sugar
1   large egg
2   teaspoons golden syrup (see Note)

COATING
1   to 2 tablespoons granulated sugar

Preheat the oven to 375 degrees F. Grease several baking sheets and set aside. Thoroughly stir together flour, baking powder, baking soda, ginger, and salt.

Place butter and sugar in a large mixing bowl and beat with mixer on medium speed, until light and smooth. Add egg and golden syrup and continue beating until thoroughly blended and smooth. Gradually beat in about half the dry ingredients. As dough stiffens, stir in remaining dry ingredients with a large wooden spoon.

To form biscuits, pull off small dough portions and roll between palms into 1-inch balls. Space about 2½ inches apart on baking sheets. Lightly grease the bottom of a flat drinking glass and dip surface lightly into granulated sugar. Flatten each dough ball with glass bottom to form biscuits about ¼-inch thick and 1¾ inches in diameter; dip glass bottom into sugar after each biscuit to prevent dough from sticking to glass.

Place biscuits in upper third of the oven for 8 to 10 minutes or until they are a rich golden brown in the center and just slightly darker around edges. (The longer baking time will yield crisper cookies.) Remove baking sheet from the oven and let stand for 30 seconds. Then, using a spatula, transfer biscuits to wire racks and let stand until completely cooled. Let baking sheets cool thoroughly between batches, to prevent dough from becoming overheated and spreading too much.

Store biscuits in airtight containers for up to a week. Freeze for longer storage.

Makes 40 to 45 2¾-inch biscuits.

Note: If ginger is very fresh and pungent use the smaller amount; otherwise, use the larger amount.

Golden syrup is a cane sugar syrup widely used in Britain. It can be purchased in some American gourmet shops and large supermarkets. If golden syrup is unavailable, dark corn syrup can be substituted, though it lends a different flavor and color to the cookies.

ORANGE-GINGER CREAMS

England and Scotland

When cookies are called "creams" in Britain it usually means they are sandwiched around a buttercream filling. In this recipe delicious ginger and orange-flavored cookies are paired with a rich, not-too-sweet orange buttercream.

3½	cups all-purpose or unbleached white flour
1¼	teaspoons baking powder
¼	teaspoon baking soda
1¼	teaspoons ground ginger
¾	teaspoon ground cinnamon
½	teaspoon ground nutmeg
1	cup (2 sticks) unsalted butter, slightly softened
¾	cup plus 3 tablespoons granulated sugar
¾	cup light brown sugar
3	large egg yolks
2	tablespoons dark molasses
	Very finely grated zest of 1 large orange
	Very finely grated zest of 1 large lemon

FILLING

½	cup (1 stick) unsalted butter, slightly softened
2	cups powdered sugar
	Very finely grated zest of 2 large oranges

Preheat the oven to 375 degrees F. Grease several baking sheets and set aside. Thoroughly stir together flour, baking powder, baking soda, ginger, cinnamon, and nutmeg in a large bowl.

In a large mixing bowl, combine butter, ¾ cup of the granulated sugar, and brown sugar and beat with an electric mixer on medium speed until light and smooth. Add egg yolks, molasses, orange zest, and lemon zest and continue beating until thoroughly blended and smooth. Gradually beat in dry ingredients. If mixer motor begins to labor, stir in the last of the dry ingredients, using a large wooden spoon.

To form the cookies, pull off pieces of dough and roll between the palms to form generous 1-inch balls. Space them about 2½ inches apart on baking sheets. Lightly grease the bottom of a flat-bottomed drinking glass and very lightly dip the bottom into the remaining 3 tablespoons granulated sugar. Use the glass to flatten dough balls until they are about ¼-inch thick and 1¾ inches in diameter. Continue very lightly dipping the bottom of the glass into the sugar before flattening each cookie to prevent the dough from sticking.

Place in the upper third of the oven and bake for 8 to 10 minutes, or until cookies are just slightly darker around the edges. Remove baking sheets from the oven and let stand for 30 seconds. Using a spatula, transfer the cookies to wire racks to cool completely. Allow baking sheets to cool completely between batches.

To prepare the filling, combine butter, powdered sugar, and orange zest in a large bowl and beat until very light and fluffy.

To assemble cookies, spread a heaping teaspoon of filling over the flat side of one cookie round. Gently press the flat side of a similarly sized round over the filling. Continue until all the cookie sandwiches are prepared.

Store cookies in an airtight container, refrigerated, for 3 or 4 days. If desired, freeze the cookies for up to a week, and allow to thaw in the refrigerator before serving.

Makes about 30 2½-inch sandwich cookies.

COUNTRY FAIR COOKIES
(TEISENNAU FFAIR LLANDDAROG)

Wales

One summer vacation my family traveled the ruggedly beautiful countryside of Wales, and I collected recipes and small, regional cookery booklets as we went. The following is an adaptation of a number of similar recipes—one provided by a bed and breakfast hostess, and several others garnered from little printed recipe collections. These are crisp, lightly spiced, and good.

"Tea cakes" of this sort are said to have been sold at the fair in Llanddarog, a small town near the southwestern coast of Wales. They are typical of Welsh cakes and breads in that they combine currants and candied fruit with a bit of cinnamon and cloves. Unlike many of the oldest Welsh recipes, however, these are baked in the oven rather than cooked on a griddle. (Griddle cakes and biscuits were commonplace because Wales has always been a poor country, and in the past, most homes didn't have ovens.)

¾   cup dried currants
1½   tablespoons warm brandy or rum
2⅓   cups all-purpose or unbleached white flour
1¼   teaspoons baking powder
½   teaspoon baking soda
¼   teaspoon ground cinnamon
¼   teaspoon ground cloves
1   cup (2 sticks) unsalted butter, slightly softened
¾   cup granulated sugar
1   large egg yolk

Finely grated zest of 1 small lemon
½   cup finely chopped mixed candied fruit

Preheat the oven to 375 degrees F. Grease several baking sheets and set aside.

In a small bowl, combine ½ cup of the currants with the brandy, reserving remaining currants for garnish. Thoroughly stir together flour, baking powder, baking soda, cinnamon, and cloves and set aside. Place butter in a large mixing bowl and beat with an electric mixer on medium speed until light. Add sugar, egg yolk, and lemon zest, and beat until light and fluffy. Stir in the ½ cup currants along with any unabsorbed liquid, and ¼ cup of the candied fruit. Gradually add dry ingredients, stirring until thoroughly incorporated.

Divide dough in half. Place each half between sheets of waxed paper. Using a rolling pin, roll dough to a ⅜-inch thickness. Working with one dough sheet at a time, peel off bottom sheet of waxed paper, replace loosely and turn dough right side up. Remove and discard top sheet of waxed paper. Cut out cookies using a plain round 2¼-inch cutter or the rim of a 2¼-inch diameter drinking glass. Using a spatula, carefully transfer cookies to baking sheets, spacing them about 1½ inches apart. Re-roll any dough scraps and continue cutting out cookies until all dough is used. Sprinkle a few currants and candied fruit pieces over each cookie, patting down to imbed slightly in the dough.

Place in the center of preheated oven and bake for 11 to 13 minutes, or until just lightly browned. Remove baking sheets from the oven and let stand for about 3 minutes. Then transfer cookies to wire racks and let stand until cooled completely.

Store in an airtight container for up to a week. Freeze for longer storage.

Makes 25 to 28 3-inch cookies.

CORNISH FAIRINGS

England

With such a picturesque name, the traditional English spice cookies known as Cornish fairings almost have to be good! Cornish refers to the cookie's place of origin in Cornwall, southwestern England, and a fairing is a sweet that is bought at a fair.

These Cornish fairings have a nice, light blend of spices and a pleasant chewy-crispness. They also have a golden, crinkly top.

2   cups all-purpose or unbleached white flour
1¼   teaspoons baking powder
1   teaspoon baking soda
1¼   teaspoons ground cinnamon
¾   teaspoon ground ginger
½   teaspoon ground nutmeg
½   teaspoon ground cloves
½   cup (1 stick) unsalted butter, slightly softened
1   cup granulated sugar
1   large egg
¼   teaspoon finely grated lemon zest
2   tablespoons golden syrup (see Note)

Preheat the oven to 375 degrees F. Generously grease several baking sheets and set aside. Thoroughly stir together flour, baking powder, baking soda, cinnamon, ginger, nutmeg, and cloves.

In a large mixing bowl, combine butter and sugar and beat with an electric mixer on medium speed until light and smooth. Add egg, lemon zest, and golden syrup and continue beating until thoroughly blended and smooth. Gradually beat in about half the dry ingredients. As dough stiffens, stir in remaining dry ingredients using a large wooden spoon.

To form cookies, pull off small pieces of dough and roll between the palms to form 1-inch balls. Space about 2½ inches apart on baking sheets. Press down balls with the heel of the hand to flatten them *just slightly*.

Place in the upper third of the oven and bake for 9 to 11 minutes, or until cookies are a rich brown and slightly darker around edges. (The cookies will puff up and then "fall" as they bake, which gives them a crackled surface.) Remove baking sheets from oven and let stand for 1 to 2 minutes. Then, use a spatula to transfer cookies to wire racks and let stand until cooled completely.

Store cookies in an airtight container for up to a week. Freeze for longer storage.

Makes 45 to 50 2¾-inch cookies.

Note: Golden syrup is a cane sugar syrup widely used in Britain. It can be purchased in some American shops and large supermarkets. If golden syrup is unavailable, dark corn syrup can be substituted, though it lends a different flavor and color to the cookies.

EMBOSSED CARDAMOM WAFERS
(KRUMKAKE)

Norway

Norwegian cookie collections always include at least one recipe for the thin, waffle-like wafers known as krumkake, and often, there are several different versions to choose from. Like Italian pizzelle, these wafers are prepared by heating batter in a special iron. But instead of being left flat like pizzelle, krumkake are quickly rolled into a cone after cooking. The cooled cones are often served filled with whipped cream and decorated with fruit.

The following recipe produces lightly spiced, fragile, and crispy wafers. Cardamom, an extremely popular ingredient with Scandinavian cooks, is the predominant flavor.

Experienced krumkake bakers know exactly how much batter to spoon onto krumkake irons to cover the surface without oozing out the edges. Some authentic recipe booklets even caution against using too much batter on the iron. However, I've found that for the beginner it's much easier to obtain fully formed, even wafers if a little excess batter is used. It will spatter a bit as the plates close, but it can be quickly scraped off and does not harm the iron.

Krumkake irons can be mail ordered from the Minneapolis firm, Maid of Scandinavia. (For more details, see page 13.)

6   tablespoons (¾ stick) unsalted butter, very soft but not melted
2   large eggs
1   cup granulated sugar
     Finely grated zest of 2 large lemons
1½   teaspoons ground cardamom
½   teaspoon ground ginger
⅔   cup light cream
1⅓   to 1½ cups all-purpose or unbleached white flour, approximately
     Flavorless vegetable oil for oiling krumkake iron

TO SERVE
1½   cups lightly sweetened whipped cream (optional)

Combine butter, eggs, sugar, lemon zest, cardamom, and ginger in a large bowl and beat lightly with a wire whisk until well mixed. Gradually beat in cream. Sift 1⅓ cups flour over the mixture, then whisk until flour is thoroughly incorporated.

Lightly brush the plates of a seasoned krumkake iron (see Note) with vegetable oil, being sure to coat all indentations. Place the krumkake burner ring over a large burner and place the iron in the ring. Heat the iron on one side over *medium heat* for 6 to 7 minutes. Then turn iron over and heat the other side for 5 minutes. When a drop of water sizzles as it hits the interior surfaces, the iron is ready.

Prepare a test wafer by spooning about 2 generous teaspoons batter into the center of one plate. Using the handles, lift the iron off the burner ring and hold it over a sheet of waxed paper. *Carefully hold the iron away from you to avoid any splatters and steam*; close the iron. Immediately, use a knife to scrape off any batter that oozes out the edges. Return the iron, still closed, to the burner ring, and heat the wafer for about 30 seconds. Then open the iron and check wafer for doneness; it should be light gold but not at all burned.

If the wafer is too brown, turn down the heat a bit before proceeding with more wafers; if still pale, raise the heat. Turn the iron over to heat the other side. Begin frequently opening the iron and checking the wafer. It is done when golden and nicely tinged with brown, but not dark brown all over. Using a fork, immediately remove the wafer from the iron and lay it flat on a wire rack. Let it stand for about 5 seconds, or until just cool enough to handle. Then immediately roll it into a cone, by either rolling it around a wooden krumkake shaper or forming it into a cone by hand. Lay the cone, seam side down, on the rack and let stand until cool. If the test wafer is so thin that there are tiny holes in the surface, thicken the batter slightly by sifting a tablespoon or two more flour over it. Stir until incorporated. Then continue cooking and rolling wafers as described until all the batter is used. If wafers stick to the iron, lightly brush the plates with flavorless vegetable oil between each use.

Store wafers in an airtight container for up to a week. Freeze for longer storage. If desired, spoon or pipe unsweetened or very lightly sweetened whipped cream into the cones just before serving.

Makes about 35 4-inch long cones.

Note: Season a new krumkake iron according to the manufacturer's directions. If no directions are provided, generously coat the plates of the iron with flavorless vegetable oil and heat the iron directly over medium heat. Heat on one side for 6 minutes, and then the other side for about 6 minutes. Let the iron cool to warm and then wipe off any excess oil.

To maintain the finish of a seasoned iron, whisk through warm soapy water, then rinse and pat dry. If necessary, clean the surfaces with a soft-bristled scrub brush, but do not scrub the plates with abrasives or harsh detergents or they will need to be reseasoned.

SAND TARTS
(SANDKAGER)

Denmark

A number of countries have cookies called sand tarts. This delicious Danish version is almost paper thin and buttery—just as many American sand tarts are. However, while American sand tarts are often sprinkled with a little cinnamon sugar, this Danish version is decorated with plain sugar and almond slivers. This recipe also calls for cardamom, a favorite spice in Scandinavia, but one that is hard to find in some parts of the United States. Even if you can't locate cardamom and have to omit it from the recipe, the cookies are still well worth making.

Making good sand tarts requires rolling the dough out extremely thin without over-flouring it. While this can be difficult using conventional methods, the following recipe includes a special technique that makes it much easier. The dough is rolled out between large sheets of waxed paper and chilled on a metal tray. Then the cookies are cut out while still on the cold tray. This keeps them from softening, and they can be easily lifted from the nearly transparent yet firm layer of dough. People always marvel at the crisp, papery wafers that result from this process and wonder how it's done. Now you know and can do it too!

$1\frac{3}{4}$ cups all-purpose or unbleached white flour
$1\frac{1}{2}$ teaspoons baking powder

1/8	teaspoon salt
1/2	cup (1 stick) unsalted butter, slightly softened (see Note)
3/4	cup granulated sugar
1	large egg
1/4	teaspoon ground cardamom (optional)
2	drops almond extract

DECORATION

1	large egg white
2/3	to 3/4 cup slivered blanched almonds for garnishing cookies
2	tablespoons granulated sugar

Thoroughly stir together flour, baking powder, and salt in a bowl. In a larger bowl, beat the butter until fluffy. Add sugar and beat until blended. Add egg, cardamom, and almond extract and continue beating until smooth and well blended. Add dry ingredients and beat until incorporated.

Divide the dough into quarters. Roll out each quarter between sheets of waxed paper as thinly as possible (about 1/16-inch thick) and until dough is slightly translucent. Check underside of dough frequently and smooth out any wrinkles that form in the paper. Stack dough sheets on a large *metal* tray or baking sheet. Refrigerate for about 10 minutes until cold and firm but not hard. Chill a second tray or baking sheet at the same time. (To speed up the chilling, place the trays in the freezer for about 5 minutes, being careful not to let the dough become too cold and hard.)

Preheat the oven to 375 degrees F. Grease several baking sheets. Remove one dough sheet and the chilled metal tray from the refrigerator; the cold tray will keep the very thin dough layer from warming up too quickly. Working on the tray, turn dough over and very gently peel off bottom sheet of waxed paper, then replace it loosely. Turn dough right side up on the tray and gently peel off and discard the top sheet of waxed paper. Cut out the cookies using a 2¼- to 2½-inch round cutter. Using a spatula, transfer cookies to baking sheets, spacing about 1 inch apart. (If dough begins to soften and the cookies become difficult to transfer to the baking sheets, return the dough and tray to the refrigerator or freezer for 3 to 4 minutes.)

In a small bowl, beat the egg white with 1 tablespoon water. Lightly and carefully brush cookie tops with the egg-white mixture, using a pastry brush or paper towel. Press three or four almond slivers into each cookie top, arranging them so they radiate like spokes from the center. Very lightly sprinkle some sugar over the cookies. Repeat the cutting out process with the other dough sheets, remembering to re-chill the tray so you will have the necessary cold work surface. Gather dough scraps and re-roll between sheets of waxed paper. Chill again until firm. Then repeat the cutting out and decorating process until all dough is used.

Place in the center of the oven and bake for 4 to 6 minutes, or until cookies are just barely brown around the edges, watching carefully to prevent them from burning. Remove baking sheets from the oven and let stand for 1 minute. Using a spatula, carefully transfer the cookies to wire racks and let stand until completely cooled. Handle carefully, as they are very crisp and fragile.

Store the cookies in airtight containers for up to a week. Freeze for longer storage.

Makes 75 to 85 2½- to 2¾-inch cookies.

Note: Do not substitute margarine in this recipe. It will not firm up during chilling as much as butter does, and the wafers will be extremely difficult to transfer to baking sheets.

JELLY ROUNDS
(SYLTBOLLAR)

Sweden and Norway

Light and pretty, syltbollar look a lot like ordinary thumbprint cookies but are airier, more delicate, and spread more during baking. They have a smooth, crisp-dry texture and a slightly lemony flavor.

1½   cups all-purpose or unbleached white flour
¼   cup potato flour or cornstarch (see Note)
1   teaspoon baking powder
¾   cup (1½ sticks) unsalted butter, slightly softened
¾   cup powdered sugar
1   large egg yolk
1½   teaspoons vanilla extract
    Finely grated zest of 1 large lemon
½   to ¾ cup apricot, peach, berry, or cherry jelly or seedless preserves (or a combination of several varieties)

Preheat the oven to 350 degrees F. Grease several baking sheets and set aside. Sift together flour, potato flour, and baking powder.

Place butter in a large mixing bowl and beat until very light. Sift in powdered sugar and beat until very fluffy and smooth. Beat in egg yolk, vanilla, and lemon zest. Gradually beat in dry ingredients until blended. If dough is too soft and warm, refrigerate it for a few minutes until firm enough to shape into balls. When dough is firm enough to handle, pull off small portions and roll between palms to form 1-inch balls. Space about 2½ inches apart on baking sheets. Press your knuckle or thumb into the center of each cookie to make a deep well. Spoon about ¾ teaspoon jelly into each indentation.

Place in the oven and bake for 10 to 11 minutes or until cookies are slightly firm on top and jelly is beginning to melt; cookies will not be browned. Remove baking sheets from the oven and let stand for 3 to 4 minutes. Then carefully transfer cookies to wire racks and let stand until completely cooled.

Store in an airtight container for up to a week. Freeze for longer storage.

Makes about 30 2¼-inch cookies.

Note: Potato flour, sometimes called potato starch, is a very fine, powdery potato product sold in Scandinavian grocery and gourmet stores. Many health food stores also stock potato flour, though some brands are unsuitable because the product is coarse rather than powdery.

LITTLE SUGAR CAKES
(SYKUR KAKA)

Iceland

These are light, almond-flavored sugar cookies popular in Iceland. The dough is often tinted pastel colors and the tops are decorated with designs from traditional carved molds. Sugar cakes can also be decorated with colored sugar sprinkles.

2⅓ *cups all-purpose or unbleached white flour*
½ *teaspoon baking powder*
¼ *teaspoon baking soda*
¾ *cup (1½ sticks) unsalted butter, slightly softened*
¾ *cup granulated sugar*
1 *large egg*
1¼ *teaspoons almond extract*
  Several drops food coloring (optional)

  DECORATION
  Colored decorating sugar (optional)

Grease several baking sheets and set aside. Thoroughly stir together flour, baking powder, and baking soda in a large bowl.

In a large mixing bowl, beat butter with an electric mixer on medium speed until very light. Add the sugar and beat until well blended and smooth. Beat in the egg and almond extract. If desired, tint the dough with several drops of food coloring. Gradually beat in the dry ingredients until thoroughly incorporated but not over-mixed.

Divide dough in half. Place each portion between large sheets of waxed paper and roll out to ⅛-inch thick, checking the underside of the dough frequently and smoothing out any creases. Stack dough sheets on a tray or baking sheet and refrigerate for about 20 minutes, or until cold and slightly stiff. (The chilling process can be speeded up by placing the dough in the freezer instead of the refrigerator for about 12 minutes, but make sure the dough doesn't become too cold and hard.)

Preheat the oven to 350 degrees F. Working with one portion of dough at a time and keeping the other refrigerated, peel off the bottom sheet of waxed paper, then replace it loosely. Turn dough over and peel off and discard the top sheet of paper. Cut out the cookies using assorted 2- to 3-inch cutters. Using a spatula, transfer cookies to baking sheets, spacing them about 1½ inches apart. Gather dough scraps and re-roll between sheets of waxed paper. Repeat the chilling and cutting out process. Lightly sprinkle the cookies with colored sugar, if desired. Repeat the cutting out and decorating process with the second half of dough.

Place in the center of the oven and bake the cookies for 6 to 8 minutes, or until they are just barely beginning to brown at the edges. The time will vary depending on their size. Remove baking sheets from the oven and allow cookies to firm for 2 minutes. Using a spatula, immediately transfer them to wire racks to cool.

Store the cookies in an airtight container for up to a week. Freeze for longer storage.

Makes 40 to 50 cookies depending on the size of the cutters used.

Overleaf, clockwise from top: *Ginger Thins (recipe on page 123), Napoleon's Hats (recipe on page 121), Iced Spiced Christmas Cookies (recipe on page 128), Butter "S" Cookies (recipe on page 129), and Scandinavian Sugar Pretzels (recipe on page 120).*

SCANDINAVIAN SUGAR PRETZELS
(KRINGLOR)

Sweden and Denmark

Like the Germans, Scandinavians enjoy making cookies in pretzel shapes and garnishing them with coarse crystal sugar (called pearl sugar) to suggest coarse salt. However, Scandinavian pretzels, or kringlor, are shaped a little differently from German ones, and do not have a twist at the point where the dough crosses. In addition, kringlor often look more like plump, curvy "B's" than pretzels as Americans know them. This plump pretzel shape is, in fact, the Scandinavian professional baker's symbol.

These golden-colored kringlor have a mild, pleasant sugar flavor and aroma and are topped with a generous sprinkling of crunchy sugar crystals.

½   cup slivered blanched almonds
2¼   cups all-purpose or unbleached white
     flour
¾   teaspoon baking soda
⅛   teaspoon salt
½   cup (1 stick) unsalted butter, slightly
     softened
⅔   cup granulated sugar
1   large egg

1   large egg yolk
1¼   teaspoons vanilla extract
½   teaspoon almond extract
¼   teaspoon finely grated lemon zest

DECORATION
1   egg yolk
¼   cup uncolored coarse sugar crystals
     or turbinado sugar crystals (see
     Note)

Preheat the oven to 325 degrees F. Spread almonds in a large baking pan. Place in the oven and toast, stirring occasionally, for 5 to 6 minutes. Remove from the oven and let stand until completely cooled. Place almonds in a food processor, nut grinder, or blender, process until finely ground, and set aside. Combine flour, baking soda, and salt.

Place butter and sugar in a mixing bowl and beat with an electric mixer on medium speed until light and fluffy. Add egg and egg yolk and beat until well blended. Add vanilla and almond extracts and grated lemon zest. Add ground almonds and about half the dry ingredients and beat until thoroughly incorporated. Very vigorously stir in remaining dry ingredients with a large wooden spoon. Divide the dough in half and place each half on a sheet of plastic wrap. (Don't use waxed paper, as the dough may stick to it.) Shape each portion into an evenly thick 7-inch log. Wrap up tightly and refrigerate at least 4 hours and as long as overnight, if desired.

To prepare for baking, remove dough from refrigerator and allow it to warm up slightly. Preheat the oven to 400 degrees F. Grease and set aside several baking sheets. Working with one dough portion at a time, carefully mark and then cut log into 14 equal sections. To form a pretzel, knead a dough section briefly to soften it slightly. Using the fingers, roll dough back and forth on a clean work surface into a 7- or 8-inch-long rope, keeping the rope as evenly thick as possible. (The dough is fairly pliable, but if it breaks piece it back together or roll it out again.) Place rope on a baking sheet crossing the ends over one another. Then lift the ends up and curve them back over the other side of the loop (see illustration on page 252). Repeat process until all 14 pretzels are formed, spacing them about 2 inches apart on baking sheets. Repeat with the second half of dough.

In a small bowl, beat egg yolk with 1 tablespoon water. Using a pastry brush (or a paper towel) and working with a few pretzels at a time, lightly brush their tops with the egg yolk-water mixture. Try not to drip egg mixture onto baking sheet, as it may cause cookies to stick. Sprinkle each pretzel generously with coarse sugar crystals.

Place in the center of the oven and bake for 8 to 10 minutes or until tops are a light golden brown. Reverse baking sheets halfway through baking to ensure even browning and watch carefully to avoid burning cookies. Remove baking sheets from the oven and let stand for 1 to 2 minutes. Then transfer pretzels to wire racks, using a spatula. Let stand until completely cooled.

Store pretzels in an airtight container for 3 or 4 days. Freeze for longer storage.

Makes 28 2¾- to 3-inch pretzels.

Note: Coarse crystal sugar can be purchased in some German and Scandinavian import shops, or from shops and mail order firms that carry specialty baking and cake decorating supplies (see page 13).

NAPOLEON'S HATS
(NAPOLEONHATTAR)

Sweden

The most famous and traditional tricorne cookies are the Jewish hamantaschen, but the pretty Swedish cookies called Napoleon's hats deserve to be known as well. Smooth and aromatic marzipan (often tinted a pastel shade for visual appeal) is tucked into tricorner hat-shaped pockets of almond-flavored dough. The cookies are then finished with a dusting of powdered sugar.

DOUGH
½ cup chopped blanched almond slivers
2½ cups all-purpose or unbleached white flour
1 teaspoon baking powder
⅛ teaspoon salt
¾ cup (1½ sticks) cold unsalted butter, cut into small pieces
½ cup granulated sugar
1 large egg
1 large egg white
2 teaspoons fresh lemon juice
¼ teaspoon almond extract
⅛ teaspoon very finely grated lemon zest

FILLING
7 to 8 ounces marzipan or almond paste (see Note)
1 teaspoon egg white
½ teaspoon fresh lemon juice
1 to 2 drops food coloring (optional)

DECORATION
1½ to 2 tablespoons powdered sugar

To prepare dough, place almonds in a food processor fitted with a steel blade and process until finely ground. Add flour, baking powder, and salt. Process in on/off pulses for about 15 seconds longer, or until the ingredients are well blended. Sprinkle the butter over the dry ingredients. Process in on/off pulses until the butter is incorporated and the mixture resembles coarse crumbs. In a small bowl, beat together sugar, egg, egg white, lemon juice, almond extract, and lemon zest using a fork. Add egg mixture to the processor and process for about 30 seconds, or until ingredients are incorporated and dough begins to mass around the blade, being careful not to overprocess.

Turn dough out of the processor and divide in half. Roll out each half to a scant ¼-inch thick between sheets of waxed paper, being sure to smooth out any creases in the underside of the dough. Stack dough sheets on a large tray or baking sheet and refrigerate for about 15 minutes, or until cool but not cold or stiff.

To prepare filling, combine marzipan, egg white, lemon juice, and food coloring (if used) in the food processor. Add 1 teaspoon water and process until the mixture is smooth and well blended. If mixture is still too dry to hold together, add enough additional water (1 to 2 teaspoons) to soften and smooth it. Cover the mixture and set aside.

Preheat the oven to 350 degrees F. Generously grease several baking sheets and set aside. Remove one sheet of dough from the refrigerator and carefully peel off the bottom sheet of waxed paper, then replace it loosely. Turn dough over and peel off top sheet of paper. Cut dough into rounds using a 2½-inch round cutter or the rim of a drinking glass. Working with one dough round at a time, place a small, rounded ½ teaspoon marzipan filling in the center. To form a tricorner hat, lift up about a third of the edge of the round, fold it back against the almond filling, and press gently to form one side of the brim. Lift up and fold back another third of the edge to form the second side of the brim. Finally, fold the last third of the edge over the center to complete the third side of the brim (see the illustration on page 252). The marzipan should mound just slightly in the center of the "hat." Repeat with each round, spacing the cookies about 2 inches apart on greased baking sheets. If the rounds become soft and difficult to handle at any point, simply slide the cookies and waxed paper onto a tray or baking sheet and refrigerate until they firm up again. Gather dough scraps and roll out between sheets of waxed paper again. Cut out the cookies, transfer to baking sheets, and fill and shape until all dough is used. Repeat the process with the second half of the dough.

Place in the center of the oven and bake for 10 to 12 minutes, or until the cookies are just barely tinged with brown at the edges. Remove from the oven and allow cookies to firm on baking sheets for 1 to 2 minutes. Using a spatula, transfer cookies to wire racks and let stand until cooled completely. Sprinkle the tops of cookies with a generous sifting of powdered sugar.

Store cookies in an airtight container for up to 1 week. Freeze for longer storage.

Makes 36 to 38 2½-inch filled cookies.

Note: Almond paste is usually slightly softer and moister than marzipan. It is likely to require less liquid, but otherwise can be handled in the same manner.

GINGER THINS
(PIPARKAKUT)

Finland

The Finns make these delicious, spicy rolled cookies all year round. Often, the cookies are cut out with a round or scalloped cutter and served plain. At Christmas they are cut into animal, people, or heart shapes and may be accented with a piped powdered sugar icing.

The finished cookies ought to be very thin—no more than about ⅛ inch—which makes them wonderfully crisp and slightly fragile. To decorate them, combine 1 cup powdered sugar with enough water to yield a spreadable icing and pipe it through a pastry bag fitted with a very fine writing tip.

2⅔	cups all-purpose or unbleached white flour
2¼	teaspoons ground cinnamon
1¼	teaspoons ground cloves
1¼	teaspoons ground allspice
¾	teaspoon ground cardamom
½	teaspoon ground ginger
½	teaspoon baking soda
¾	cup (1½ sticks) unsalted butter, slightly softened (see Note)
½	cup dark corn syrup
¾	cup granulated sugar
1	large egg
	Finely grated zest of 1 small lemon

Sift together flour, cinnamon, cloves, allspice, cardamom, ginger, and baking soda. Place butter, corn syrup, and sugar in a large mixing bowl and beat until lightened and smooth. Beat in egg and lemon zest. Beat in about half the dry ingredients. Stir in remaining dry ingredients with a large wooden spoon. The dough will be fairly stiff. Divide the dough in thirds. Place each between sheets of waxed paper and roll out each third to ⅛-inch thick, working carefully and smoothing out any creases in the paper. Slide dough portions onto a large baking sheet. Refrigerate for about 20 minutes until cold and firm but not hard.

Preheat the oven to 375 degrees F. Grease several baking sheets. Working with one dough sheet at a time, and leaving the others refrigerated, turn over dough. Peel off bottom sheet of waxed paper, and then replace it loosely. Turn dough right side up and peel off and discard top sheet of waxed paper. Cut out cookies using assorted 2- to 3-inch cutters. Using a spatula, quickly transfer cookies to baking sheets, spacing about 1 inch apart. (If dough begins to soften and cookies become difficult to transfer to baking sheets, slide dough onto a baking sheet again and chill briefly in the refrigerator until firm.) Repeat the cutting out process with the second and third dough sheets. Gather scraps and re-roll between sheets of waxed paper. Chill dough, then repeat cutting out process until all dough is used.

Place in the center of the oven and bake for 6 to 8 minutes, or until cookies are just slightly darker around the edges. Remove baking sheets from the oven and let stand for about 2 minutes. Using a spatula, transfer cookies to wire racks and let stand until completely cooled. Decorate with icing if desired and let stand until the icing is completely set.

Store the cookies in an airtight container for up to 2 weeks. Freeze for longer storage.

Makes 70 to 85 2¼- to 3-inch cookies.

Note: Do not substitute margarine as the recipe will not work. The dough will not firm up enough during chilling to allow cookies to be transferred to baking sheets.

Butter Spritz Cookies
(Spritskakor)

Sweden and Denmark

These delicious cookies are almost as well known in the United States as they are in Scandinavia. This particular version has an appealing vanilla and almond flavor, buttery texture, and handsome appearance. Butter spritz are also fairly quick and easy to make. You will need a pastry bag and a large star tip for this recipe.

1	cup (2 sticks) unsalted butter, slightly softened
2/3	cup powdered sugar
1	large egg yolk
1¼	teaspoons vanilla extract
½	teaspoon almond extract
½	cup finely ground blanched almonds
2	cups all-purpose or unbleached white flour

DECORATION
Candied cherry halves (optional)

Preheat the oven to 375 degrees F. Grease several baking sheets and set aside.

Place butter in a large mixing bowl and beat with an electric mixer on medium speed until very light. Add the sugar and egg yolk and beat until very fluffy and smooth. Beat in vanilla and almond extracts and almonds. Gradually beat in flour until thoroughly incorporated but not overmixed.

Fit a pastry bag with a ⅜-inch diameter star tip. Stand the bag, tip down, in a tall glass and turn down a deep cuff at the top. Spoon the dough into it until the bag is no more than two-thirds full. Unfold the cuff and tightly twist the bag closed at the top. Pipe 1¼-inch diameter rosettes onto a baking sheet, spacing about 1½ inches apart. Press a cherry half, cut side down, into the center of each cookie, if desired.

Place in the center of the oven and bake the cookies for 7 to 10 minutes, or until slightly browned at the edges. Remove baking sheets from the oven and let cookies stand for 2 to 3 minutes. Then transfer them to wire racks and let stand until cooled completely.

Store in an airtight container for up to a week. Freeze for longer storage.

Makes 50 to 60 1¾-inch rosette cookies.

Chocolate Spritz Cookies

(Lekebergskakor)

Sweden and Denmark

The Scandinavians use chocolate in cakes and fancy pastries, and they produce some wonderful chocolate candy, but for some reason, chocolate cookies are a rarity. Although nearly every family has a favorite recipe for plain spritz cookies, recipes for chocolate spritz are much harder to find. This particular version was inspired by a recipe I discovered in a popular Swedish baking book, *Sju Sorters Kakor*.

The cookies are rich, and have a nice chocolate flavor.

1   large egg yolk
⅛   teaspoon instant coffee powder, preferably fine granules, not crystals
1   cup (2 sticks) unsalted butter, slightly softened
¾   cup powdered sugar
1½ tablespoons unsweetened cocoa powder
1¾ cups all-purpose or unbleached white flour
1½ ounces bittersweet or semisweet chocolate, very finely grated

DECORATION
1   tablespoon powdered sugar (optional)

Preheat the oven to 350 degrees F. Grease several baking sheets and set aside.

In a small bowl, stir together the egg yolk and coffee powder. Let stand for about 5 minutes, or until the coffee dissolves. In a large mixing bowl, beat the butter with an electric mixer on medium speed until very light. Add sugar, cocoa powder, and egg yolk-coffee mixture and beat until very fluffy and smooth. Gradually beat in flour until thoroughly incorporated but not overmixed. Stir in grated chocolate until evenly distributed throughout.

Fit a large pastry bag with a large (⅜-inch diameter) star tip. Stand the bag, tip down, in a tall glass and fold down the top of the bag about 3½ inches. Spoon in enough dough to fill it two-thirds full. Unfold the cuff and tightly twist the top to close it. Pipe 1¼-inch diameter rosettes onto a baking sheet, spacing about 1½ inches apart.

Place in the center of the oven and bake the cookies for 8 to 10 minutes, or until slightly firm on top. Remove baking sheets from the oven and let the cookies stand for 2 to 3 minutes. Then transfer them to wire racks and let stand until cooled completely. Lightly dust the cookies with powdered sugar just before serving, if desired.

Store in an airtight container for up to a week. Freeze for longer storage.

Makes 50 to 60 1¾-inch rosette cookies.

HOLIDAY PRUNE-FILLED PINWHEELS
(JOULUTORTUT)

Finland

These pretty pinwheel cookies are a Christmas favorite in Finland, and just about every Finnish baking book has at least one recipe for them. Some versions call for a yeast-dough base and others for a puff pastry. This version uses a buttery yet easy-to-handle cookie dough.

Traditionally, these cookies are made with a delicious prune filling, but if prunes don't appeal to you, dried apricots may be substituted.

If you've never made pinwheel-shaped cookies and think they look tricky, they really aren't. And they don't take a lot of time. Just follow the recipe directions.

2¾ cups all-purpose or unbleached white flour
¼ teaspoon baking soda
¼ teaspoon salt
1 cup (2 sticks) unsalted butter, slightly softened
⅔ cup granulated sugar
1 large egg
½ teaspoon finely grated orange zest

FILLING
1¼ cups (about 7 ounces) chopped pitted prunes (or substitute dried chopped apricots, if desired; see Note)
½ cup granulated sugar
½ cup orange juice
Finely grated zest of 1 small orange
⅛ teaspoon ground cinnamon

Thoroughly stir together flour, baking soda, and salt and set aside. Place butter in a mixing bowl and beat with an electric mixer on medium speed until light. Add sugar and continue beating until mixture is very light and fluffy. Beat in egg and orange zest. Gradually beat in dry ingredients until thoroughly incorporated.

Divide dough in half and place each half between large sheets of waxed paper. Using a rolling pin, roll each half out into a ⅛-inch thick rectangle, checking the underside of dough and smoothing out any wrinkles in the paper. Slide rolled dough sheets onto a tray or baking sheet and refrigerate for 15 to 20 minutes, or until chilled and firm but *not stiff*. Grease several baking sheets and set aside. Preheat the oven to 375 degrees F.

To prepare the filling, combine prunes, sugar, orange juice, orange zest, and cinnamon in a medium saucepan. Bring to a simmer over low heat and gently cook, uncovered, stirring occasionally, for about 10 minutes or until softened and fairly smooth. If mixture still seems lumpy, mash prunes with the back of a spoon, or transfer filling to a processor and purée briefly.

Working with one chilled portion at a time and leaving the other refrigerated, carefully peel off top sheet of waxed paper. Replace the paper loosely. Turn dough over and gently peel off and discard bottom sheet of waxed paper. Using a pastry wheel or large sharp knife, cut dough rectangle into 2½-inch squares. Immediately transfer squares to baking sheets, spacing about 2 inches apart.

Using a sharp knife or pastry wheel, make a 1-inch cut from the four corners of each square toward its center. Using your thumb, press down the center of each square to make a shallow well. Spoon a generous ¾ teaspoon filling into each indentation. Lift up every other corner tip of dough and fold tip into the center to make a pinwheel, pressing tips firmly

together to hold them in place. (If the dough softens too much to work with, slide baking sheet into the refrigerator or freezer for a few minutes to chill.) Combine dough scraps and re-roll between sheets of waxed paper. Refrigerate dough until firm, then cut out and form pinwheels. Repeat procedure with the second half of dough.

Place in the center of the oven and bake for 7 to 10 minutes or until just slightly colored on top and golden brown at the edges. Reverse baking sheets from front to back about halfway through baking to ensure even browning. Remove sheets from the oven and let stand for about 2 minutes. Transfer cookies to wire racks until cooled completely.

Store in an airtight container for up to a week. Freeze for longer storage.

Makes about 30 3-inch cookies.

Note: If apricots are substituted, taste the filling for sweetness and add a bit more sugar if needed.

ICED SPICED CHRISTMAS COOKIES
(JULEKAKER)

Norway

Decorated with candied fruit and a thin lemon glaze, these lightly spiced, rolled sugar cookies look beautiful and taste delicious. Like many Scandinavian baked goods, they are flavored with cardamom.

2   cups all-purpose or unbleached white flour
1   teaspoon baking powder
1/2   teaspoon ground cinnamon
1/2   teaspoon ground ginger
1/4   teaspoon ground cardamom
1/8   teaspoon ground allspice
10   tablespoons (1 1/4 sticks) unsalted butter, slightly softened
1/3   cup granulated sugar
1/4   cup light corn syrup
1   large egg yolk
1   teaspoon vanilla extract
1   teaspoon fresh lemon juice
1/4   teaspoon very finely grated lemon zest

LEMON ROYAL ICING
1   large egg white, at room temperature
     Pinch of salt
1   tablespoon fresh lemon juice
1 1/2   cups sifted powdered sugar

DECORATION
Candied red cherries and candied orange peel, cut into small pieces
Candied yellow and green pineapple wedges, cut into thin slivers

Thoroughly stir together flour, baking powder, cinnamon, ginger, cardamom, and allspice.

Place butter in a mixing bowl and beat with an electric mixer on medium speed until light. Add sugar and corn syrup and continue beating until mixture is very light and fluffy. Beat in egg yolk, vanilla, lemon juice, and lemon zest. Gradually add dry ingredients and beat until thoroughly incorporated and dough is smooth.

Divide dough in half and place each portion between large sheets of waxed paper. Using a rolling pin, roll each portion out to 1/8-inch thick. Check the underside frequently and smooth out any creases. Slide rolled dough portions onto a tray or baking sheet. Refrigerate for 15 to 20 minutes or until cold and slightly firm.

Preheat the oven to 375 degrees F. Grease several baking sheets and set aside.

Working with one chilled portion at a time, carefully turn over dough so underside is facing up and gently peel away bottom sheet of waxed paper; then replace it loosely. Turn dough right side up and peel off and discard top sheet of waxed paper. Using a petal shaped, scalloped, or plain round 2 1/4- to 2 1/2-inch cutter (or the rim of a 2 1/2-inch-diameter drinking glass), cut out the cookies. Carefully lift them from the waxed paper, using a spatula, and space about 1 inch apart on baking sheets. Gather and re-roll dough scraps between waxed paper sheets and chill. Continue cutting out cookies. Repeat process with second half of dough.

Place in the center of the oven and bake for 6 to 9 minutes, or until just slightly colored on top and lightly browned at the edges. Reverse baking sheets from front to back about halfway through baking to ensure even browning. Remove from the oven and let stand for about 2 minutes. Ice and decorate cookies while slightly warm.

To prepare the icing, place egg white in a completely grease-free mixing bowl and beat with an electric mixer on medium speed until frothy. Beat in salt and 1/2 teaspoon of the lemon juice. Increase mixer speed to high and beat until fluffy. Continue beating, gradually adding remaining lemon juice, powdered sugar, and 1½ teaspoons water. Beat until sugar is incorporated and icing is stiff and glossy.

Using a blunt knife, neatly spread a thin layer of icing over the top of each cookie. Immediately press a small piece of candied cherry or orange peel into cookie center. Arrange three or four thin slivers of candied pineapple, in a spoke pattern radiating from the center. Let cookies stand on wire racks for at least 45 minutes or until icing sets. (If the icing becomes too stiff to spread easily, stir in several drops of water or lemon juice.)

Store in an airtight container for up to a week. Freeze for longer storage.

Makes 35 to 40 2¼-inch cookies.

BUTTER "S" COOKIES
(ÄSSÄT)

Finland

Making butter cookies in an S-shape seems to be popular all across Europe. I have seen recipes for S-shaped cookies not only in Scandinavian collections, but in German, Greek, and Eastern European cookbooks, although the cookies do not always taste alike.

This particular "S" cookie is an excellent one—buttery and crisp, with a great almond flavor. The dough is also malleable and smooth, which makes forming the S-shapes a fairly simple matter.

1	large egg, separated
1	3½-ounce package almond paste, cut into small pieces
½	cup granulated sugar
¼	teaspoon almond extract
¾	cup (1½ sticks) unsalted butter, slightly softened
2	cups all-purpose or unbleached white flour
½	to ⅔ cup finely chopped blanched almonds

Preheat the oven to 375 degrees F. Grease several baking sheets and set aside.

In a large mixing bowl, combine egg yolk, almond paste, sugar, and almond extract. (Reserve egg white for garnishing cookies.) Beat egg yolk mixture with an electric mixer on medium speed for about 3 minutes, or until almond paste is thoroughly incorporated and smooth. Add butter and continue beating until very fluffy and smooth. Gradually add flour and beat until thoroughly incorporated but not overmixed. If the mixer motor labors, stir in last of flour using a large wooden spoon.

Pull off dough pieces and shape into 1¼-inch balls. Lay each ball on a clean work surface and roll back and forth to form a smooth, evenly thick 4½- to 5-inch rope. Place ropes on baking sheets, shaping each into an "S" and spacing about 1¼ inches apart. Using a fork, beat egg white until frothy. Using a pastry brush or a paper towel, lightly brush tops of three or four cookies at a time with the egg white. Be careful not to drip, as egg white may cause cookies to stick. Immediately sprinkle cookies with chopped almonds.

Place in the center of the oven and bake for 10 to 12 minutes, or until cookies are just slightly colored on top and barely tinged with brown at the edges. Remove baking sheets from the oven and let stand for 3 to 4 minutes. Carefully transfer cookies to wire racks and let stand until cooled.

Store in an airtight container for up to 10 days. Freeze for longer storage.

Makes 40 to 45 2½- to 3-inch cookies.

ALMOND COOKIE RING CAKE
(KRANSEKAKE)

Denmark, Norway, and Sweden

The tall, many-tiered cookie ring cake known as kransekake is one of the most impressive and delicious creations in the Scandinavian cookie repertoire. Scandinavian friends tell me that these "cakes" are served on special occasions, particularly weddings, where guests break off and eat pieces of the almond-flavored cookie rings to wish the newlyweds well. Sometimes the graduated tiers of large ring cakes are fitted over a bottle of champagne, which the celebrants enjoy once the rings are gone. These ring cakes are traditionally decorated with little paper Scandinavian flags.

The following recipe was created by home economist Jene Springrose, a friend of Scandinavian descent. The dough she developed makes excellent-tasting cookies and is easy to work with. To make an 18-ring kransekake (like the one shown) using a standard-size food processor, you will need to prepare the dough recipe which follows in two batches.

DOUGH
2   cups (4 sticks) unsalted butter, slightly softened
2   cups powdered sugar
14   to 16 ounces almond paste, cut into small pieces
2   large eggs
2   large egg yolks
2   teaspoons almond extract

5   cups all-purpose or unbleached white flour

ICING
1   large egg white, at room temperature
1/4   teaspoon fresh lemon juice
    Pinch of salt
1/2   teaspoon almond extract
1¼   cups powdered sugar

DECORATION
Silver dragées (optional)
Novelty paper flags (optional)

Preheat the oven to 350 degrees F. Generously grease kransekake pans. Lightly dust the pans with powdered sugar. (Even if non-stick pans are used, it is best to grease them and dust with powdered sugar.)

To prepare a batch of dough, combine 1 cup butter and 1 cup powdered sugar in a food processor and process for about 30 seconds, or until creamy and well-mixed. Add 7 or 8 ounces of almond paste through the feed tube and continue processing until the mixture is very smooth. Add 1 egg, 1 egg yolk, and 1 teaspoon almond extract and process until blended. Add 2½ cups flour, about ¾ cup at a time, and process until thoroughly incorporated but not overmixed. At this point, the dough should be fairly firm, but still soft enough to pipe through a pastry tube. If it is too firm, add a few drops of water.

Spoon dough into a large pastry bag fitted with a plain ½-inch tip. (Don't use a larger tip or the cookie rings may expand beyond their grooves and bake together.) A slightly smaller pastry tip may be used, but some dough will be left over and the cookie ring cake will not be quite as large as the one shown. Pipe dough out in a long rope into the ring-shaped grooves of the kransekake pans. Press together rope "ends" or any breaks in the dough to form smooth, unbroken rings. When all the dough is used, use remaining dough ingredients to prepare a second batch in the

same manner as the first. Refill pastry bag and continue piping rings until all the kransekake pans have been filled.

Place in the oven and bake for 16 to 18 minutes, or until rings are lightly tinged with brown. Transfer pans to wire racks and immediately run a knife around the edge of each ring to loosen the cookie. Let stand until cooled completely. Leave the cookie rings in their pans until ready to assemble the "cake," as this is the easiest way to determine the correct order of placement.

To prepare the icing, combine the egg white, lemon juice, salt, and almond extract in a large mixing bowl and beat with an electric mixer on medium speed until frothy. Increase mixer speed to high and, continuing to beat, gradually add powdered sugar until thoroughly incorporated and the icing is glossy and smooth. Icing should be fairly stiff but still runny enough to pipe through a pastry bag fitted with a fine tip. If too stiff, stir in a few drops of water.

Spoon the icing into a pastry bag fitted with a fine writing tip. Pipe a thick ring of icing around the center top of the largest cookie ring in the largest pan. Then gently turn the ring over onto a large serving plate so the iced top surface becomes the bottom and the icing anchors this base to the plate.

Using the photograph as a guide, pipe a decorative line of icing loops all the way around the upper edge of the bottom ring. Carefully invert the largest ring from the second largest pan so the smooth bottom becomes the top, and center it over the first ring. Repeat the inverting and stacking process, adding icing loops and then the largest ring from the third largest pan, followed by the largest ring from the fourth largest pan, and so on. Continue stacking the middle-sized rings and then the smallest rings in the pans according to size, being careful to center each over the next, until all are used. (If any rings happen to break during construction, use a bit of icing to "glue" them back together again.) To decorate with silver dragées, pipe small dots of icing onto the rings and press dragées into place, spacing them attractively above the loops as shown in the photograph. Add Scandinavian flags, if desired. Let the kransekake stand for at least 1 hour, until the icing completely sets.

Store the cookie ring cake, lightly covered with foil or plastic wrap, for up to a week. If desired, the unassembled cookie rings can also be wrapped airtight and frozen for longer storage, and then thawed and assembled when needed. To avoid confusion, pack the largest rings from all the pans together, the middle-sized rings together, and the smallest rings together.

An 18-ring kransekake pan set makes 1 10½- to 12-inch-high cookie ring cake.

SWEDISH LACE COOKIES
(HAVREFLARN)

Sweden

This recipe yields thin, golden-brown cardamom- and ginger-flavored wafers that are brittle and lacy. They look similar to the old-fashioned lace cookies prepared in the United States, but have a spicy rather than a mild flavor.

10	*tablespoons (1¼ sticks) unsalted butter*
¾	*cup granulated sugar*
⅓	*cup light corn syrup*
1	*cup quick-cooking oats*
⅔	*cup all-purpose or unbleached white flour, sifted after measuring*
1	*teaspoon ground cardamom*
¾	*teaspoon ground ginger*
¼	*teaspoon baking soda*
¼	*teaspoon baking powder*
¼	*teaspoon finely grated lemon zest*
1	*teaspoon vanilla extract*

Preheat the oven to 375 degrees F. Line several baking sheets with aluminum foil, allowing foil to overlap two ends. Lightly grease the foil.

Place butter in a medium saucepan and melt over medium heat. Stir in sugar, corn syrup, and 2½ tablespoons water and remove pan from heat. Stir in oats, flour, cardamom, ginger, baking soda, baking powder, and lemon zest until well mixed. Let mixture stand for 10 minutes. Add vanilla and stir until well blended.

Drop dough by very small rounded teaspoonfuls about 3 inches apart on foil. (Do not crowd the cookies, as they spread a great deal.)

Place in the upper third of the oven and bake for 6 to 8 minutes or until cookies are light brown all over, turning baking sheets from front to back about halfway through baking to ensure even browning. Remove from the oven and let cookies stand on baking sheets for about 1½ minutes. Then, using overlapping foil ends as handles, transfer cookies to a flat surface and let stand on foil until completely cooled. Carefully peel cookies from foil. (The foil may be reused, if it is not too rumpled, but it must be regreased first.) Allow baking sheets to cool completely between batches.

The cookies may be stored in an airtight container for up to a week. Freeze for longer storage.

Makes 35 to 40 3¼- to 3½-inch cookies.

MOLASSES SPICE COOKIES
(PEPPARKAKAR)

Sweden

Ohio resident Anne Dietrich gave me this recipe, which she obtained from a friend whose Swedish grandmother always made these cookies.

While some pepparkaker are light and mild-tasting, these have a full-bodied molasses and spice flavor.

4   cups all-purpose or unbleached white flour

2   teaspoons ground cinnamon
1   teaspoon ground ginger
1   teaspoon ground cardamom
1¾   teaspoons baking soda
1   cup light molasses
1   cup granulated sugar
1   cup (2 sticks) unsalted butter, slightly softened
2   large eggs
½   teaspoon finely grated lemon zest

    DECORATION
¼   cup plump dark seedless raisins

Grease several baking sheets and set aside. Thoroughly stir together flour, cinnamon, ginger, cardamom, and baking soda in a large bowl. Set aside.

Combine the molasses, sugar, and butter in a medium saucepan and warm over medium heat, stirring, until butter melts. Immediately remove saucepan from heat and allow mixture to cool to tepid. Using a large wooden spoon, beat eggs into molasses mixture until thoroughly blended and smooth. Stir in lemon zest.

Pour the molasses mixture over dry ingredients and stir until well mixed and smooth. Cover dough and refrigerate for 30 to 40 minutes, or until cool and slightly stiffened.

Preheat the oven to 375 degrees F. Roll pieces of dough into scant 1¼-inch balls. Space about 2½ inches apart on baking sheets.

Place in center of the oven and bake for 9 to 11 minutes, or until cookies are tinged with brown around edges. (The longer the baking time the firmer the cookies.) Remove baking sheets from oven and immediately press a raisin into the center of each cookie. Let the cookies cool on baking sheets for 1 minute. Using a spatula, transfer cookies to wire racks and let stand until completely cooled.

Store in an airtight container for up to 10 days. Freeze for longer storage.

Makes 45 to 50 2¾-inch cookies.

no good

ICED HONEY COOKIES
(HONNINGKAGER)

Denmark

These attractive honey-brown spice cookies are easy to make and keep well. They are topped with a shiny white icing and, for a festive touch, can be decorated with colored sugar or nonpareils.

1½   cups all-purpose or unbleached white flour
2   teaspoons ground cinnamon
2   teaspoons ground ginger
2   teaspoons ground cardamom
¼   teaspoon baking powder
¼   teaspoon baking soda
⅛   teaspoon salt
½   cup (1 stick) unsalted butter, slightly softened
⅓   cup granulated sugar
⅓   cup mild honey
2   large egg yolks

ROYAL ICING AND DECORATION
1   large egg white, at room temperature
¼   teaspoon fresh lemon juice
       Pinch of salt
1¼   cups powdered sugar
       Colored sugar or nonpareils (optional)

Preheat the oven to 375 degrees F. Generously grease several baking sheets. Thoroughly stir together the flour, cinnamon, ginger, cardamom, baking powder, baking soda, and salt.

Combine butter, sugar, and honey in a small mixing bowl and beat with an electric mixer on medium speed until light and fluffy. Add egg yolks and beat until blended. Gradually beat in dry ingredients. If mixer motor begins to labor, stir in remaining dry ingredients with a large wooden spoon.

To form cookies, roll dough between palms to form scant 1-inch balls. Space about 2 inches apart on baking sheets. Using the bottom of a large, flat glass dipped in cold water, flatten each ball to form a disc about 2 inches in diameter.

Place in the center of preheated oven and bake for 9 to 11 minutes, or until cookies are brown at the edges. Immediately remove baking sheets from the oven, and let cool for 2 to 3 minutes. Using a spatula, transfer cookies to wire racks and let cool completely.

Meanwhile, prepare icing. Place egg white in a completely grease-free mixing bowl and beat with an electric mixer on medium speed until frothy. Beat in lemon juice and salt. Raise mixer speed to high and beat until well mixed and fluffy. Continue beating, gradually sifting in powdered sugar. Beat until sugar is completely incorporated and icing is stiff and glossy.

Using a blunt knife, neatly top each cookie with icing. Immediately sprinkle colored sugar or nonpareils, if using, very lightly over icing before it sets. Let cookies stand on wire racks until icing sets. (If icing becomes too stiff while decorating cookies, stir in several drops of water to thin.)

These cookies are best if allowed to mellow overnight before serving. Store in an airtight container for up to 2 weeks. Freeze for longer storage.

Makes 35 to 40 2¼-inch cookies.

SWEDISH GINGERSNAPS
(INGEFÄRSPEPPARKAKOR)

Sweden

Zippy, crunchy-crisp, and aromatic, these attractive cookies taste somewhat like American gingersnaps, but are not crinkly on top.

2⅓ cups all-purpose or unbleached white
     flour
2¾ teaspoons ground ginger
1½ teaspoons ground cinnamon
½   teaspoon ground cloves
½   teaspoon ground allspice
     Pinch of salt
1   teaspoon baking powder
¾   teaspoon baking soda
2   teaspoons unsweetened cocoa powder
½   cup (1 stick) unsalted butter, slightly
     softened
½   cup dark molasses
½   cup packed light brown sugar
1   large egg
1   teaspoon vanilla extract
2½ tablespoons granulated sugar

Sift together flour, ginger, cinnamon, cloves, allspice, salt, baking powder, baking soda, and cocoa powder and set aside. Combine butter, molasses, and sugar in a large mixing bowl and beat until lightened and smooth. Beat in egg and vanilla. Stir in dry ingredients until mixture is well blended and smooth. Wrap dough in waxed paper and refrigerate for at least 1½ hours or up to 24 hours, if desired.

To bake cookies, preheat the oven to 350 degrees F. Grease several baking sheets. Working with half of dough at a time and keeping remaining half chilled, pull off pieces and shape into 1-inch balls. Place balls about 1½ inches apart on baking sheets. Lightly grease the bottom of a flat-bottomed drinking glass and dip bottom into granulated sugar. Flatten each ball to about ¼-inch thick and 1¾ inches in diameter, dipping glass bottom into sugar after each cookie to prevent dough from sticking.

Place in the center of the oven and bake for 10 to 11 minutes or until cookies are just tinged with brown around edges and almost firm on top. Remove baking sheets from oven and let stand for 1½ minutes. Using a spatula, transfer cookies to wire racks and let stand until completely cooled. They will firm as they cool.

Store the cookies in an airtight container for up to 2 weeks.

Makes 40 to 45 2¼-inch cookies.

Buttercream Sandwich Cookies
(Pariservåfflor)

Sweden

Simple but elegant butter wafers sandwiched together with a smooth buttercream icing, these very small, dainty, sinfully rich cookies are a handsome addition to a tea or coffee table. The buttercream icing can be tinted a pastel shade to give these fragile, melt-in-the-mouth treats a very festive look.

Be careful not to roll the dough too thin, or the cookies may be so fragile that they break apart.

1½   cups all-purpose or unbleached white flour
⅔   cup cornstarch
⅛   teaspoon salt
1   cup (2 sticks) unsalted butter, slightly softened
⅓   cup plus 1 tablespoon granulated sugar
1   teaspoon vanilla extract

Buttercream Icing
1¼   cups powdered sugar
½   cup (1 stick) unsalted butter, slightly softened
1   teaspoon fresh lemon juice
¾   teaspoon vanilla extract
3   or 4 drops almond extract
    Drops of food coloring, if desired

Sift together the flour, cornstarch, and salt. Place butter in a mixing bowl and beat until light and fluffy. Beat in sugar and vanilla until blended and very smooth.

Add dry ingredients and beat until incorporated but not overmixed. Cover the mixture and refrigerate for 5 to 10 minutes, or until it firms slightly.

Divide dough in half and place each half between large sheets of waxed paper. Roll each out to ⅜-inch thick, checking the undersides of the dough, smoothing out any creases, and working carefully so that *each layer is evenly thick*. Slide dough sheets onto a tray or baking sheet. Refrigerate for about 20 minutes, or until cold and slightly firm. (To speed up chilling process, place dough in the freezer for 10 minutes instead, being careful not to allow it to become too cold and hard.)

Preheat the oven to 375 degrees F. Grease several baking sheets and set aside.

Working with one half of dough at a time and leaving the other half refrigerated, gently peel off bottom sheet of waxed paper, and replace it loosely. Turn dough over and peel off and discard top sheet of waxed paper. Using a 1¼-inch plain or scalloped cutter (or the rim of a liqueur glass or other small round) cut out the cookies, dipping the cutter in powdered sugar before each use to prevent dough from sticking. Using a spatula, transfer cookies to baking sheets, spacing them about 1 inch apart. Gather and re-roll dough scraps between waxed paper sheets, chill until firm, then continue cutting out cookies. Repeat the process with the second half of dough until all dough is used. Using a fork dipped in powdered sugar before each use, decoratively prick each round across the top three times to produce three parallel lines.

Place in the center of the oven and bake for 7 to 9 minutes, or until cookies just begin to brown at the edges. Remove baking sheets from the oven and let cookies stand for about 2 minutes. Very gently transfer to wire racks and let stand until cooled completely.

To prepare icing, sift powdered sugar into a small mixing bowl. Add butter, lemon juice, and vanilla and almond extracts and beat until well blended. Add a few more drops lemon juice if needed to make a smooth and slightly soft buttercream. Beat in a drop or two of food coloring, if desired. (If you wish, divide the icing into several different portions and tint each a different color.) Using a blunt knife, spread icing in an even ⅛-inch layer over the flat side of one cookie. Then *very lightly press* the flat side of a second wafer over the icing, handling gently as the cookies are quite fragile. Repeat until all sandwich cookies are prepared. Let stand until the icing firms up slightly.

Store the cookies in an airtight container for up to a week. Freeze for longer storage.

Makes 40 to 50 1½-inch sandwich cookies.

DREAMS
(DRÖMMAR)

Norway and Sweden

Dreams" seems a fitting name for these extremely light and fragile cookies. They have a melt-in-the-mouth texture, a delicate buttery flavor, and a pale color. They are easy to make.

1¼ *cups all-purpose or unbleached white flour*
½ *cup potato flour (see Note)*
1 *teaspoon baking powder*
½ *cup (1 stick) unsalted butter, slightly softened*
1 *cup powdered sugar*
2 *large egg yolks*
2 *teaspoons vanilla extract*
⅛ *teaspoon almond extract*
18 *to 20 blanched almonds, halved lengthwise, or about ¼ cup blanched almond slivers*

Preheat the oven to 350 degrees F. Grease several baking sheets and set aside. Sift together flour, potato flour, and baking powder.

Place butter in a large mixing bowl and beat with an electric mixer on medium speed until very light. Add sugar and beat until very fluffy and smooth. Beat in egg yolks and vanilla and almond extracts. Gradually add dry ingredients and beat until thoroughly incorporated but not overmixed. Pull off small portions of dough, roll between palms to form 1-inch balls, and space about 2 inches apart on baking sheets. Press an almond half or sliver into the center of each cookie, taking care not to flatten balls too much.

Place in the oven and bake for 9 to 10 minutes or until slightly firm on top; cookies will not be browned. Remove baking sheets from the oven and let cookies stand for 3 to 4 minutes. Then transfer them to wire racks and let stand until completely cooled.

Store in an airtight container for up to a week. Freeze for longer storage.

Makes 30 to 35 2-inch cookies.

Note: Potato flour, sometimes called potato starch, is a very fine, powdery potato product sold in Scandinavian grocery and gourmet stores. Many health food stores also stock potato flour, though some brands are unsuitable because the product is coarse rather than powdery.

CHAPTER 6

WESTERN EUROPEAN
COOKIES

I N THE HEART OF WESTERN EUROPE, COOKIES ARE a treasured part of the culinary heritage. The custom of cookie baking has flourished for hundreds of years in Germany, Austria, Switzerland, and neighboring countries. Cooks in the region continue to produce these sweets in extraordinary variety.

The earliest cookies made here were simple honey cakes, honey being the only sweetener readily available before the 1600s. As trade increased, recipes incorporated spices from the East Indies and cane sugar from the New World, and gradually, a variety of appealing "gingerbread" cookies evolved. Today, rolled, molded, and bar cookie versions abound, particularly in the German speaking countries. In most modern recipes, including the Honey Lebkuchen and the German Cookie House in this chapter, honey is used more as a flavoring than a sweetener.

While many early doughs were simple mixtures, the cookies themselves often looked grand. Then, as now, cookies were considered special treats for festive occasions, and presentation was raised to an art. Some of the best loved and oldest varieties, such as lightly spiced Speculaas in Belgium and the Netherlands and anise-scented embossed Springerle in Germany and Austria, are traditionally created using finely detailed molds and seem almost too beautiful to eat. Other favorites, like lemon-iced Sweet Pretzels in Alsace and Chocolate Pretzels in Germany, are carefully hand-formed and glazed for an enticing visual effect. Several other amusing trompe l'oeil creations include German chocolate cookies resembling sausage rounds and dark bread slices, and French meringue sweets shaped like button mushrooms.

Beyond this interesting assortment, the region produces a wealth of exceptional butter cookies—from Viennese Almond Crescents and Chocolate-Glazed Apricot Sandwich Cookies to German Hazelnut Spritz and French Sablés. As a contrast to these, there are also numerous delicious butter-free, egg white-based cookies, including spicy Cinnamon Stars, classic Almond and Chocolate Macaroons, and chewy-chocolatey Basel "Brown" Cookies.

Cookies are always popular in Western Europe, but during Christmas a kind of cookie madness takes hold. Grocery shelves sag with nuts, dried fruit, spices, chocolate blocks, glittery nonpareils, and the myriad other baking supplies. Magazines—even those not devoted to food—feature dazzling cookie photographs and collections to entice and set a festive mood. At home, cooks draw out heirloom recipes, and, following the custom of countless generations before them, set to baking. For most families, Christmas just wouldn't be Christmas without the traditional holiday cookie store.

Little Rascals (recipe on page 140).

LITTLE RASCALS
(SPITZBUBEN)

Germany, Switzerland, and Austria

Spitzbuben are buttery almond cookies sandwiched together with raspberry or currant jelly. These pretty cookies have a star, heart, or other decorative shape cut out of the top to reveal the brightly colored jelly filling. The tops are also decorated with a light sprinkling of powdered sugar.

This attractive, delicious cookie is very popular throughout Central Europe.

1   cup (about 4½ ounces) slivered
      blanched almonds
1¾   cups plus 2 tablespoons all-purpose
      or unbleached white flour
⅛   teaspoon salt
¾   cup (1½ sticks) unsalted butter,
      slightly softened
½   cup granulated sugar
1   teaspoon vanilla extract
2   to 3 drops almond extract

TO ASSEMBLE
¼   cup red raspberry or red currant jelly
2   to 3 tablespoons powdered sugar

Place almonds in a food processor or blender and process until finely ground. Stir together flour and salt and set aside. Place butter in a mixing bowl and beat with an electric mixer set on medium speed until lightened. Add sugar and beat until light and fluffy. Beat in vanilla and almond extracts. Gradually add dry ingredients, beating until smooth. Fold or knead in ground almonds. Form dough into a ball and divide in half. Roll each half out between sheets of waxed paper to ⅛ inch thick. Slide dough sheets onto a large tray or baking sheet and refrigerate for 15 minutes.

Preheat the oven to 350 degrees F. Grease several baking sheets.

Working with one dough sheet at a time and leaving the other refrigerated, turn over dough and peel off bottom sheet of waxed paper. Replace paper loosely. Turn dough right side up and peel off the top sheet of paper. Cut out cookies using a 1¾- to 2-inch scalloped, saw-edged, or plain round cutter. Transfer to baking sheets, spacing rounds about 1½ inches apart.

To make cookie tops, remove second dough sheet from the refrigerator. Turn over dough and peel off bottom sheet of waxed paper. Replace paper loosely. Turn dough right side up and peel off and discard top sheet of paper. Cut out 1¾- to 2-inch rounds as before. Then cut out the center of each circle using a miniature star or heart-shaped cutter, a thimble, or the cap of a vanilla extract bottle. Lift out the center dough trimming with the point of paring knife.

Place in the center of the oven and bake cookies until pale gold, 8 to 10 minutes. Remove from the oven and let stand on baking sheets for 1 to 2 minutes. Transfer to wire racks to cool completely.

Store plain unassembled cookies in an airtight container for 5 to 6 days. Assemble the cookies shortly before serving time. (The cookies will still taste fine if assembled in advance, but they will lose their crispness.)

To assemble cookies, melt jelly in the top of a double boiler set over hot water until slightly liquefied, stirring occasionally. Meanwhile, lightly sift powdered sugar over cut-out cookie tops. Place about ½ teaspoon jelly onto center of each plain cookie bottom, then center a top over each bottom and firmly but gently press it onto jelly to form a sandwich. Cookies are best eaten within 8 hours of assembling.

Makes about 25 1¾-inch sandwich cookies.

MADELEINES

France

Madeleines are eaten as cookies, but in fact these shell-shaped little sweets are delicately delicious morsels of sponge cake. Sometimes, a bit of fruit brandy or liqueur is added to the batter, lending a tantalizing aroma as well as flavor. The following recipe, which I obtained in Alsace, includes kirsch. The Alsatians seem partial to this cherry brandy; their famous kougelhopf yeast bread is often laced with it, and other sweets include it too. It is wonderful in madeleines.

Madeleines are said to have been invented in the town of Commercy for Stanislas, the Duke of Lorraine. The creator was a servant girl helping with the pastry making, named—what else?—Madeleine.

½	cup (1 stick) unsalted butter
1¼	cups all-purpose or unbleached white flour
¼	teaspoon baking powder
1	large egg
3	large egg yolks
1	cup powdered sugar
1	teaspoon fresh lemon juice
¼	teaspoon very finely grated lemon zest
	Pinch of salt
1	tablespoon plus 1½ teaspoons kirsch, or other cherry brandy

DECORATION
Powdered sugar

Preheat the oven to 400 degrees F. Very generously grease the shell-shaped molds of two madeleine pans with butter (see Note). Carefully dust the molds with flour, then tap off excess. Warm butter in a small saucepan over low heat until melted. Set aside to cool. Sift together flour and baking powder.

In a large mixing bowl, beat together the egg and egg yolks with an electric mixer on medium speed. Sift in powdered sugar and add lemon juice, lemon zest, and salt, beating. Gradually raise speed to high and continue beating for 5 to 7 minutes, or until the mixture is thickened and light-colored, and falls in wide ribbon-like streams from the beater. Lightly beat in kirsch. Using a rubber spatula, gently fold in the flour mixture. Then, fold in melted butter until thoroughly incorporated but not overmixed.

Divide the batter among the 24 molds in madeleine pans, spreading batter out evenly with a blunt knife.

Place in the center of the oven and bake for 9 to 11 minutes, or until madeleines are tinged with brown and slightly darker at the edges. Remove from the oven and let the madeleines stand for 1 minute. Then gently loosen them from the pans with the point of a paring knife. Turn madeleines out onto a wire rack and let stand for a minute or two. Then turn them ridged-side-up and let stand until cooled completely. Dust them with powdered sugar just before serving.

Madeleines are best when very fresh, but may be stored in an airtight container for up to 24 hours. Freeze for longer storage.

Makes 24 3-inch madeleines.

Note: If only one madeleine pan is available, use it to prepare half the madeleines. Then, after cleaning and drying the pan, regrease and flour it again, and prepare the second 12 cakes.

Chocolate-Glazed Hazelnut Spritz Wafers
(Haselnuß-Spritzgebäck)

Germany

Another European cookie that makes the most of the natural affinity between chocolate and hazelnuts.

These wafers are elegant and relatively easy to make if you have a pastry bag and a large plain or star tip. They are thin, tender-crisp, and richly flavored with toasted nuts and butter. A bittersweet chocolate glaze drizzled back and forth across the wafers goes well with the hazelnuts, and gives the cookies a professional-looking finish.

½   cup whole hazelnuts
¾   cup (1½ sticks) unsalted butter, slightly softened
½   cup granulated sugar
1   large egg
1¼   teaspoons vanilla extract
⅛   teaspoon salt
1¼   cups all-purpose or unbleached white flour

     CHOCOLATE GLAZE
1   ounce unsweetened chocolate
1   ounce semisweet chocolate
¼   teaspoon solid shortening

Preheat the oven to 325 degrees F. Spread the hazelnuts in a large baking pan. Toast in the oven, stirring occasionally, for 16 to 18 minutes, or until the hulls begin to loosen and the nuts are tinged with brown.

Remove from the oven and set aside until cool. To remove hulls from the nuts, rub a handful at a time back and forth between palms or in a clean kitchen towel, discarding dark skins as you work. (It isn't necessary to remove every dark particle, but the nuts should be fairly clean of hull.) Place nuts in a food processor or blender and process until finely ground.

Reset oven temperature to 350 degrees F. Lightly grease several baking sheets. Place butter in a mixing bowl and beat until light. Add sugar and beat until smooth and fluffy. Beat in egg, vanilla, and salt until blended. Gradually add flour and beat until thoroughly incorporated. Fold in ground nuts.

Spoon dough into a pastry bag fitted with a star or plain tip ⅜ inch in diameter. Pipe 2¼-inch-long strips of dough onto baking sheets, spacing about 1½ inches apart. Place in the center of the oven and bake for 9 to 11 minutes or until edges just begin to brown. Remove from the oven and let stand for 1 to 2 minutes. Then, before cookies become brittle, quickly transfer to wire racks set over waxed paper, lining them up in even rows with sides almost touching. Let the wafers cool slightly.

To prepare glaze, place unsweetened and semisweet chocolates and solid shortening in the top of a double boiler over barely simmering water and warm, stirring occasionally, until mixture is melted and smooth.

Using a spoon, drizzle thin lines of glaze back and forth *crosswise* over the wafers until all have been decorated. Let wafers stand until the glaze is completely set, about 45 minutes. To speed up setting, place wafers in the refrigerator for about 10 minutes.

Store the wafers in an airtight container for 3 or 4 days. They may be frozen unglazed and then glazed shortly before serving, if desired.

Makes 40 to 45 3-inch-long wafers.

CHOCOLATE PRETZELS
(SCHOKOLADEN-BREZELN)

Germany and Austria

The pretzel shape has been in use at least a thousand years and may be an early astronomical symbol relating to the sun's path. Americans may associate the shape with crisp, salty, unsweetened bread snacks, but Europeans also use this form for certain cookies. Glazed chocolate pretzels are particularly popular in Germany, and a recipe for them can be found in nearly every German baking book. Shaping the dough into pretzels takes a little practice, but it's relatively easy to master if the directions are followed.

2¹⁄₃   cups all-purpose or unbleached white flour
¹⁄₄   cup plus 3 tablespoons unsweetened cocoa powder
¹⁄₂   teaspoon baking powder
¹⁄₈   teaspoon salt
5¹⁄₂   tablespoons unsalted butter, slightly softened
¹⁄₃   cup granulated sugar
3   tablespoons light corn syrup
2   large eggs
1¹⁄₂   teaspoons vanilla extract
¹⁄₂   cup finely ground walnuts
2   ounces bittersweet or semisweet chocolate, finely grated

GLAZE
1   cup powdered sugar
¹⁄₃   cup plus 1 tablespoon coffee or water
1   teaspoon solid vegetable shortening
1   teaspoon light corn syrup
6   ounces bittersweet (not unsweetened) or semisweet chocolate, broken or chopped into small pieces

DECORATION
1   to 2 tablespoons coarse crystal sugar (optional)
1¹⁄₂   ounces white chocolate, melted (optional)

Thoroughly stir together flour, cocoa powder, baking powder, and salt and set aside.

Place the butter in a mixing bowl and beat with an electric mixer on medium speed until light and fluffy. Add sugar and corn syrup and beat until well blended and light. Add eggs and vanilla and continue beating until thoroughly blended and smooth. Gradually beat in about half the dry ingredients until thoroughly incorporated. Beat in the ground walnuts and chocolate. Using a large wooden spoon, vigorously stir in remaining dry ingredients.

Divide dough in half and place each half in a sheet of plastic wrap. (Do not use waxed paper, as the dough may stick to it.) Shape each half into an evenly thick 6-inch log. Wrap logs up tightly and refrigerate for about 1 hour, or until the dough is chilled, but not hard and stiff.

Preheat the oven to 350 degrees F. Grease several baking sheets.

Working with one dough portion at a time, carefully mark and then cut the log into 12 equal sections. Working with one section at a time, knead briefly to soften it slightly, then roll it back and forth on a clean work surface with the fingers to produce an evenly thick rope slightly thicker than a pencil and 10 to 12 inches long. (The dough is fairly easy to handle if you take care to keep the rope evenly thick. If rope breaks, simply piece it back together.) Gently lift rope and transfer to

baking sheet. Cross rope ends over one another pretzel-fashion (see illustration on page 252) and twist the rope at the crossing point. Then lift up ends from baking sheet and press them firmly over the loop. Repeat the process until all 12 pretzels are formed, spacing them about 1½ inches apart on baking sheets. Repeat with the second half of dough.

Place in the center of the oven and bake for 9 to 11 minutes, or until edges are just beginning to brown. Remove from the oven and let stand for a minute or two. Then, using a spatula, transfer pretzels to wire racks set over waxed paper. Let pretzels cool to room temperature, then glaze and decorate.

To prepare the glaze, sift powdered sugar into a medium, heavy saucepan. Add coffee, shortening, and corn syrup, place over medium heat, and bring to a boil, stirring. Remove from the heat, add chocolate, and stir until melted and smooth.

Using tongs, dip the pretzels, one at a time, into the glaze to coat all over. (They should be completely but not thickly coated with glaze. If glaze seems too thick, or if it begins to dry out as you are dipping pretzels, thin it with a few drops of water or coffee.) Shake off excess glaze and place the pretzels, right side up, on wire rack to drain, being sure they don't touch one another. Sprinkle a few coarse sugar crystals over each pretzel, if desired. Or let the pretzels stand until glaze sets and then drizzle them lightly with white chocolate.

Let the pretzels stand for 5 minutes. Then carefully lift and reposition them so they don't stick to the rack. Let stand until the glaze is completely set, about 30 minutes longer.

The pretzels are best the day they are made, but may be stored in an airtight container for 2 or 3 days. They may be frozen unglazed, then thawed completely and glazed prior to serving, if desired.

Makes 24 3-inch pretzels.

RASPBERRY-CHOCOLATE BARS
(HIMBEER-SCHOKOLADEN STÄNGERL)

Germany and Austria

I don't know whether the Germans or Austrians deserve credit for originally coming up with the extraordinary flavor combination of chocolate, raspberry, hazelnuts, and almonds, but they can both take credit for using these ingredients to great advantage in a wide variety of baked goods.

These sumptuous bar cookies—which feature a short dough crust covered with raspberry jelly and toasted nuts and then topped with a drizzling of dark chocolate—are just one irresistible example. Though they take time, the bars are not difficult to prepare.

¼   cup whole hazelnuts
¼   cup slivered blanched almonds
2½ cups all-purpose or unbleached white flour
½   teaspoon baking powder
¼   teaspoon salt
½   cup (1 stick) unsalted butter, slightly softened
⅓   cup plus 2 tablespoons granulated sugar
3   large eggs
1   tablespoon kirsch, or orange juice
½   cup red raspberry jelly
2   ounces bittersweet or semisweet chocolate
½   ounce unsweetened chocolate (see Note)
½   teaspoon solid vegetable shortening

Preheat the oven to 325 degrees F.

Spread the hazelnuts in a baking pan and place in the oven. Toast, stirring occasionally, for 16 to 18 minutes, or until hulls begin to loosen and the nuts color slightly. Spread almonds in a separate baking pan and toast, stirring occasionally, for 5 minutes. Set nuts aside to cool.

Reset the oven temperature to 350 degrees F. Grease a large baking sheet and set aside.

When the hazelnuts are cool enough to handle, remove the dark hulls by rubbing a handful of nuts at a time vigorously between the palms or in a clean kitchen towel, discarding bits of skin as you work. (It is usually difficult to remove all bits sticking to the nuts, but they should be relatively free of hull.) Combine the hazelnuts and almonds in a food processor or blender and chop moderately fine.

Thoroughly stir together flour, baking powder, and salt. Combine butter and granulated sugar in a large mixing bowl. Beat with an electric mixer on medium speed until light and fluffy. Add 2 of the eggs and the kirsch, and beat until well blended. Beat in about half the dry ingredients. Stir in ⅓ cup of the chopped hazelnuts and almonds. (Reserve remaining nuts to decorate cookies.) Using a large wooden spoon, stir in the remaining dry ingredients until the dough is well mixed and begins to hold together.

Divide dough into thirds. Place each third on a large sheet of waxed paper and roll back and forth in the paper to form a smooth, evenly thick 11-inch log. Transfer logs to the baking sheet, spacing them as far from one another as possible. Form a deep trough about 1½ inches wide down the center along the entire length of each log using the side of the hand. (Be sure the trough has a rim all the way around as it will be needed to keep the melted jelly from running out.) Place the remaining egg in a small bowl and beat with 1 tablespoon water until well combined.

Evenly brush the top and sides of each log with the egg-water mixture, being careful not to drip on the baking sheet.

Place in the center of the oven and bake the logs for 9 minutes. Remove from the oven. Lightly brush logs again with the egg-water mixture. Spoon about 2½ tablespoons of the raspberry jelly evenly along the indentation in each log. Lightly sprinkle logs with some chopped nuts, reserving a few for decoration. Return logs to the oven and bake for 11 to 13 minutes longer, or until they are browned and the jelly is bubbly. Remove baking sheet from the oven and let stand for at least 15 minutes.

Combine the bittersweet and unsweetened chocolates and the shortening in a small heavy saucepan and melt over lowest heat, stirring occasionally, until well blended and smooth. Remove from the heat. Very carefully transfer the logs to wire racks set over waxed paper. Decoratively drizzle the chocolate back and forth over the logs. Sprinkle the remaining chopped nuts over the logs. Let the logs stand until they are completely cooled and the chocolate is set. Carefully transfer logs to a cutting board. Using a large sharp knife and cutting on a diagonal, trim off and discard the ends. Then, still cutting on a diagonal, slice each log crosswise into 12 or 13 slices. Transfer slices to wire racks and let stand until chocolate sets.

The bars are best when served fresh but may be stored in an airtight container for 3 or 4 days. The logs may also be frozen whole, thawed, and then cut into slices before serving.

Makes about 40 3-inch-long bars.

Note: For a slightly sweeter taste, omit the unsweetened chocolate and substitute another ½ ounce of bittersweet chocolate.

Overleaf, clockwise from top right: *Honey Lebkuchen (recipe on page 150), Cinnamon Stars (recipe on page 155), Springerle (recipe on page 152), and Speculaas (recipe on page 153).*

HONEY LEBKUCHEN
(HONIGLEBKUCHEN)

Germany

This is a classic German rolled cookie featuring a fragrant blend of spices, honey, and a decorative piped powdered-sugar icing. The cookies are crunchy and taste a bit like ginger snaps, though ginger is not the predominate spice. Honey lebkuchen are a nice golden brown and when decorated in the traditional manner look festive and colorful. Often, the dough is cut out in heart shapes of varying sizes and the cookies are edged with a lacy-looking white or red icing trim. During Advent and Christmas, the cookies are frequently cut out with a St. Nicholas cutter and left out to reward "good" children when St. Nicholas secretly visits them each December 6. Other popular shapes include angels, Christmas trees, and stars.

This recipe includes directions for preparing the icing and decorating the cookies using a pastry bag fitted with a fine tip. However, if you wish, opaque commercial icing that comes in a squeeze-out tube with a writing tip may be substituted.

$4\frac{1}{3}$ cups all-purpose or unbleached white flour
$1\frac{1}{2}$ tablespoons unsweetened cocoa powder
4 teaspoons ground cinnamon
2 teaspoons ground cloves
$1\frac{3}{4}$ teaspoons ground mace
$1\frac{1}{2}$ teaspoons ground ginger
$\frac{1}{4}$ teaspoon ground cardamom (optional)
$\frac{1}{4}$ teaspoon baking powder
$\frac{1}{4}$ teaspoon baking soda
1 cup (2 sticks) unsalted butter, slightly softened
$\frac{3}{4}$ cup clover or other mild honey
1 cup granulated sugar
1 large egg
Finely grated zest of 1 large lemon

ICING AND DECORATION
$1\frac{1}{4}$ cups powdered sugar
1 tablespoon lemon juice, preferably fresh
Silver dragées, cinnamon red hot candies, and assorted nonpareils (optional)
1 to 2 drops red food coloring (optional)

Thoroughly stir together flour, cocoa powder, cinnamon, cloves, mace, ginger, cardamom, baking powder, and baking soda and set aside.

Combine butter, honey, and sugar in a mixing bowl and beat until very light and smooth. Beat in egg and lemon zest until well mixed. Gradually beat in dry ingredients, stirring in the last bit by hand if the mixer motor begins to labor. Divide dough in thirds. Place each third between long sheets of waxed paper and roll each out to ¼-inch thick. Check the underside frequently and smooth out any creases that form. Slide dough sheets onto a large tray or baking sheet and refrigerate for at least 1½ hours or until cold and firm. (To speed up chilling, place dough in freezer for 30 to 40 minutes instead.)

Preheat the oven to 350 degrees F. Generously grease several baking sheets.

Remove one dough sheet from the refrigerator (leave the others refrigerated), and carefully peel off the bottom sheet of waxed paper, then replace it loosely. Turn dough over and carefully peel off and discard top sheet of waxed paper. Cut out dough using cutters in the shape of hearts, St. Nicholas, or other forms. Transfer cookies to baking sheets, spacing about ¾ inch apart. (If some of the shapes are much larger than others, group like-sized shapes together on separate baking sheets.) Gather dough scraps and re-roll dough between waxed paper. Return it to the refrigerator to chill until cold and firm before continuing to cut out cookies. Repeat the process until all the dough is used. Then repeat with second and third dough sheets until all dough is used.

Place in the center of the oven and bake cookies until almost firm and just barely browned at edges, 10 to 13 minutes, depending on the size of the cookies. Remove from the oven and immediately transfer cookies to wire racks using a spatula. Let stand until cooled completely.

To prepare icing, combine powdered sugar, lemon juice, and 1½ teaspoons water in a small bowl and stir until smooth. Stir in ½ to 1 teaspoon more water, a few drops at a time, until icing holds its shape but is soft enough to be piped through a pastry bag fitted with a fine-line or fine star decorator tip. Pipe an attractive edging around the heart shapes, making dots, ric-rac trim, wavy lines, braiding, or scallops. If desired, pipe additional dots of icing onto each heart to use as "glue" and top with silver dragées or cinnamon red hots. If desired, outline the boots, beard, sack, etc. of St. Nicholas cookies with icing, and add nonpareils or red hots for buttons, eyes, nose, and mouth. (If desired, reserve part of the icing and tint with red food coloring. Pipe an additional edging around cookies for more elaborate decoration.) Let the cookies stand until icing is completely set, about 1 hour.

The cookies are best if packed in airtight containers and allowed to mellow overnight before serving. They can be stored for up to 2 weeks. Freeze for longer storage.

Makes 30 to 40 2½- to 4-inch hearts or about 24 4-inch St. Nicholas cookies.

SPRINGERLE

Germany

Springerle are traditional German anise-flavored cookies made by imprinting rolled-out dough with designs from carved rolling pins, boards, and wooden or metal molds. In the past, in some families, every child was presented with a separate mold and each year during the Christmas and Easter holidays his or her "personal" cookies were made from it. Today, the imprinted designs are sometimes painted with a food color wash and the cookies are given as Christmas cards or gifts.

It is said that town bakers were frequently responsible for the early beautiful springerle molds, many of which featured birds, flowers, and heart motifs. The shop that sold the prettiest cookies was the one likely to capture the largest share of the holiday trade, so enterprising bakers engaged carvers to create elaborate molds for them. Some bakeries offered new designs each year.

Although most antique springerle molds are now in museums or private collections, there is a variety of modern metal, wooden, and ceramic ones available. All types are easy to use and yield very attractive results. There are a number of sources for springerle molds and rolling pins here in the United States, including at least one master carver producing handsomely finished basswood molds of his own design (see page 13).

Springerle are firm (sometimes even hard), fragrant cookies and keep well. Since they tend to be dry, they are often served with coffee and may even be dunked in it.

3   large eggs, at room temperature
1⅓ cups granulated sugar
    Very finely grated zest of 2 medium
    lemons
½   teaspoon vanilla extract
3   to 3⅓ cups all-purpose or unbleached
    white flour, approximately

DECORATION
3   to 4 tablespoons whole anise seeds
    Food coloring (optional)

In a large mixing bowl, beat eggs with an electric mixer on high speed for about 2 minutes, or until lightened and fluffy. Gradually beat in sugar and continue beating on high speed for 10 to 12 minutes, or until the mixture is very light and almost as thick as sour cream. Add grated lemon zest and vanilla and beat 30 seconds longer. Using a large wooden spoon, stir in 3 cups of the flour until thoroughly incorporated. If necessary, stir in a few more tablespoons flour to produce a stiff but not crumbly dough. Stir or knead the dough in the bowl for several minutes, until it is very smooth. Tightly wrap dough in plastic wrap and refrigerate for at least 2 hours, or up to 8 hours, if desired.

To form cookies, grease several baking sheets. Generously sprinkle each with anise seeds. Lightly dust a springerle rolling pin, board, or cookie molds with flour; tap off the excess. Lightly dust work surface with flour.

Roll out chilled dough a generous ¼-inch thick on work surface; lightly dust rolling pin frequently and lift dough several times to make sure it isn't sticking. Firmly roll or press springerle rolling pin, board, or molds into the dough to imprint designs. If molds are used, gently lift them off the dough. Cut the designs apart using a pastry wheel or sharp knife. Using a spatula, transfer the cookies to prepared baking sheets, spacing about ½ inch apart. Gather up dough scraps and knead briefly. Then repeat the rolling and imprinting process until all the dough is used. (Work rapidly as the dough dries out as it stands.) For best appearance, brush off any flour clinging to the tops of cookies. Set cookies aside, uncovered, for at least 18 hours and up to 24 hours to allow the designs to set.

Preheat the oven to 250 degrees F. Bake for 25 to 45 minutes, or until tops are firm but not colored; the time will vary, depending on the size of the cookies. (Very small cookies about 1½ inches square will take 25 minutes; 3- to 4-inch squares may require twice as long.) Transfer cookies to wire racks and allow to cool for at least 1 hour.

If desired, paint the cookies as follows: Dilute food colorings with a bit of water and, using a small brush, apply a light wash of color to the raised areas of the cookie designs. Let painted cookies stand until completely dry, about 2 hours.

Store the cookies in airtight containers or plastic bags for 2 weeks. For a more pronounced anise flavor, add a teaspoon or two of anise seeds to the storage container. Freeze for longer storage.

Makes 20 to 35 cookies, depending on the size of designs.

SPECULAAS

Belgium and the Netherlands

Traditional speculaas are much-loved spice cookies that are often prepared in carved wooden molds. They are a special favorite in Belgium and the Netherlands. Nearly identical cookies, called spekulatius, are also found in Germany. Throughout the region, these cookies are associated with St. Nicholas Day, December 6, when St. Nicholas visits all children as they sleep and leaves "good" youngsters a bowl or shoe full of cookies, candies, and other small treats.

If you don't have any speculaas or speculatius molds, tasty rolled and cut-out cookies can be prepared with this recipe. Simply roll the chilled dough out on a lightly floured surface ¼-inch thick and cut out cookies using assorted cutters. The dough may also be used with some of the modern clay cookie molds that are available in American kitchen boutiques, Christmas shops, and mail order firms. These produce not only interesting shapes but appealing surface details similar to those made by traditional speculaas molds. (For specific information, see page 13.)

This dough makes forming speculaas fairly easy, although it may take several tries before you can turn out perfect cookies. Of course, no harm is done because the dough can simply be smoothed out, returned to the refrigerator briefly, and used again. Children seem particularly delighted by these cookies. They are crunchy-crisp and have an appealing, mild spice flavor.

3¾ cups all-purpose or unbleached white
flour
1 tablespoon plus 1½ teaspoons ground
cinnamon
¾ teaspoon ground ginger
½ teaspoon ground cloves
½ teaspoon ground nutmeg
⅛ teaspoon baking soda
1 cup (2 sticks) unsalted butter, slightly
softened
1⅓ cups granulated sugar
2 large eggs
¼ teaspoon finely grated lemon zest
⅔ cup finely ground blanched almonds
Flavorless vegetable oil for oiling
molds
Cornstarch or flour for dusting molds

In a large bowl, thoroughly stir together
flour, cinnamon, ginger, cloves, nutmeg,
and baking soda and set aside.

Place butter and sugar in a mixing bowl
and beat until well blended and smooth.
Lightly beat in the eggs and grated lemon
zest. Beat in about half the dry ingredients
and the almonds until just incorporated.
Stir in remaining dry ingredients using a
large wooden spoon. Wrap the dough in
plastic wrap and refrigerate for at least 3
hours or up to 48 hours, if desired. (The
dough may also be frozen for up to 2
weeks. Allow it to thaw completely in the
refrigerator before using.)

Preheat the oven to 350 degrees F.
Grease several baking sheets. Prepare
wooden (or ceramic) molds by lightly
brushing vegetable oil over all interior
surfaces, being sure to reach all the
crevices and indentations. (A pastry or
basting brush works well for this task.)
Lightly sprinkle or sift cornstarch over
molds, tipping them back and forth until
all the crevices are coated, then inverting
and tapping them against a hard surface to
remove all excess cornstarch. (A thin film
works best and produces more attractive
cookies.) The molds must be redusted with
cornstarch after each cookie, but do not
need to be re-greased.

Working with a small portion of the
dough at a time and leaving the remainder
refrigerated, pull off a piece large enough
to fill the mold being used. A bit at a time,
press the dough into the shape to be
formed. (Even if the dough seems too stiff
at first, work with it; it will soften as the
cookie is formed.) When the interior of the
mold is completely filled, press down all
over to remove any air spaces. Also press
any dough protruding over the edges back
inside the mold. Using a large, sharp knife,
cut away excess dough so the cookie
surface is flush with the back of the mold.
To remove cookie from a *wooden* mold,
hold it upside down and rap it repeatedly
and sharply against a hard surface until
the cookie loosens. For a *ceramic* mold,
rap it a little more gently against a wooden
board or other slightly softer surface to
avoid chipping or breaking the form. When
the cookie is loose all over, tap or peel it
out onto the baking sheet. If one particular
section sticks, very carefully loosen it with
the point of a paring knife. Space the
cookies about 1½ inches apart.

Place in the center of the oven and bake
for 10 to 15 minutes, depending on the size
of the cookies, or until they are tinged
with brown around the edges. Remove
from the oven and let the cookies stand on
baking sheets for several minutes. Using a
spatula, transfer the cookies to wire racks
and let stand until completely cooled.

Store in an airtight container for up to 2
weeks or freeze for longer storage.

**Makes 20 to 40 cookies, depending on the
size of the molds used.**

CINNAMON STARS
(ZIMTSTERNE)

Germany

Cinnamon stars are prepared from an egg white and almond dough similar to that used for macaroons. However, the mixture is rolled and cut out to yield flat, crispy-chewy cookies rather than soft, mounded ones. The rather sweet dough is enhanced with cinnamon and lemon, and the cookie tops are decorated with an attractive shiny glaze.

Though it is not well known to Americans, this is perhaps *the* favorite cookie in Germany. It is unusual but good.

2½ cups slivered blanched almonds
⅓ cup egg whites (2 to 3 large egg whites), at room temperature
Pinch of salt
⅛ teaspoon fresh lemon juice
2 cups powdered sugar, sifted after measuring if lumpy, plus ½ to ⅔ cup for rolling out cookies
1 tablespoon ground cinnamon
1¼ teaspoons very finely grated lemon zest

DECORATION
1 to 2 teaspoons fresh lemon juice, for icing

Preheat the oven to 300 degrees F. Thoroughly grease and flour several baking sheets or line them with baking parchment. Finely grind the almonds in a food processor or blender; set aside.

Combine egg whites and salt in a large, completely grease-free bowl and beat until frothy. Add the lemon juice and gradually raise the speed to high. Beat on high speed until soft peaks form. Gradually add powdered sugar. Continue beating until whites are stiff but not dry. Remove ½ cup of egg-white mixture and set aside in a small bowl for the glaze.

Stir almonds, cinnamon, and lemon zest into the large bowl of whites until well blended. Dust a work surface with powdered sugar and turn out dough. Gradually knead enough additional powdered sugar into dough to make it very stiff.

Sprinkle the work surface with more powdered sugar. Roll out dough ¼-inch thick, dusting rolling pin frequently with powdered sugar and lifting dough several times. Using a 2¼- to 2½-inch star-shaped cutter, cut out the cookies. Transfer to baking sheets, spacing about 1¼ inches apart. Gather any scraps and continue rolling and cutting out cookies until all the dough is used.

To make icing, gradually stir enough lemon juice into the reserved egg white mixture to yield a spreadable consistency. Using a table knife, spread top of each star with enough icing to cover with a smooth, even, thin layer. Add a few extra drops of lemon juice to the icing if it begins to dry out.

Bake the cookies until just tinged with brown and crisp on the outside but still slightly chewy on the inside, 20 to 23 minutes. Using a spatula, immediately transfer cookies to wire racks and cool completely.

Store in an airtight container for up to 10 days. Freeze for longer storage. Cinnamon stars taste best if allowed to mellow for 24 hours before serving.

Makes about 35 2¾- to 3-inch cookies.

ALMOND "TILE" WAFERS
(TUILES AUX AMANDES)

France and Spain

The fragile, gently curled wafers known as tuiles (French for tiles) are among the most elegant yet simple cookies I know. They have a light almond flavor and a papery crispness that makes them crumble and almost dissolve in the mouth. The cookies are called tiles because they are draped over a rolling pin or similarly curved form when warm and take on the form of old-fashioned French roof tiles as they cool.

Tuiles are not only popular in France, but also in Spain, where they are usually made into extremely large cookies that are broken into pieces at the dining table. A tap with a tablespoon is enough to shatter them.

Because tuiles are so thin and delicate, they can be tricky to remove from the baking sheet. After trying several types of pans and techniques, I've found that plain aluminum, rather than nonstick, baking sheets work best. They should be cooled, cleaned, and heavily greased before each use. It's also helpful to use a wide spatula with a very thin blade. For best results, use quick jabbing motions to loosen wafers in just an instant or two rather than slow, gentle efforts to pry them off. Since there are only about 30 seconds to easily lift them off baking sheets in one piece before they become too brittle, I never bake more than 4 or 5 at a time. Smaller wafers, 3 to 3¼ inches in diameter, seem a little sturdier and easier to remove.

5	tablespoons unsalted butter
¼	cup (about 2 large) egg whites
	Pinch of salt
¾	cup plus 1 tablespoon powdered sugar
¼	teaspoon almond extract
⅓	cup plus 2 tablespoons all-purpose or unbleached white flour
½	to ⅔ cup sliced unblanched almonds

Preheat the oven to 350 degrees F. Very generously grease several baking sheets. Set out several rolling pins, wine bottles, or other similar-sized cylinders for shaping wafers and lightly grease them.

Warm butter in a small saucepan over lowest heat. Remove from the heat and set aside to melt and cool slightly. In a large mixing bowl, beat together the egg whites and salt with a wire whisk until frothy. Gradually sift in powdered sugar, whisking until blended and smooth. Whisk in almond extract. Gradually sift flour into mixture, whisking until very smooth and slightly thickened. Whisk in the cooled butter.

Drop 4 or 5 very small rounded teaspoonfuls of batter onto a baking sheet, spacing them at least 3¼ inches apart. (Keep the portions very small and don't crowd them as they spread a great deal.) Using the tip of a table knife, and swirling in a circular motion, spread each spoonful of batter into a 1¾-inch round. Very generously sprinkle sliced almonds all over each round.

Place on the top rack of the oven and bake for 5 to 7 minutes, or until the wafers are rimmed with ½ inch of brown. Reverse baking sheet from front to back halfway through baking to ensure even browning.

Remove baking sheet from the oven and let stand for about 20 seconds. Begin gently testing the edges of wafers with a spatula and as soon as they are firm enough to lift without tearing, quickly loosen each from the sheet using a thin-edged, wide-bladed spatula. Immediately drape wafers over rolling pins or cylinders. (If the last wafers on baking sheet cool too much while others are being removed, return baking sheet to oven for 1 or 2 minutes to rewarm. They may still be difficult to remove, however.) As soon as tuiles are stiff, transfer from rolling pins to wire racks to cool thoroughly. Cool, clean, and thoroughly regrease baking sheets before reusing. Repeat with remaining batter.

Store tuiles in an airtight container for up to a week. Freeze for longer storage. Handle wafers gently as they are extremely fragile.

Makes about 30 3- to 3½-inch wafers.

GLAZED SWEET PRETZELS
(BRETZELS SUCRES)

France

Many families in Alsace feel Christmas just wouldn't be Christmas without sweet pretzels, and nearly every holiday table contains a platter or two of these traditional sweets. The eye-catching, pretzel-shaped cookies are normally fairly large, slightly sweet, and glazed with a smooth and glossy powdered sugar glaze. Very often, they have a pronounced anise flavor, although some versions, like this recipe I obtained on a trip to Strasbourg, feature a subtle blend of lemon, vanilla, and anise.

If you don't care for or can't find anise, it can be omitted from this recipe and the results will still be good. However, most people who try these unusual cookies find the hint of anise extremely appealing.

2⅔ *cups all-purpose or unbleached white flour*
¼ *teaspoon salt*
¾ *teaspoon baking powder*
10 *tablespoons (1¼ sticks) unsalted butter, slightly softened*
½ *cup powdered sugar*
3 *large eggs*
1 *teaspoon ground anise, or ½ teaspoon anise extract (optional)*

1½ teaspoons vanilla extract
1 teaspoon fresh lemon juice
Finely grated zest of 2 medium
lemons

GLAZE
2¼ cups powdered sugar
2 teaspoons fresh lemon juice
¾ teaspoon light corn syrup

Thoroughly stir together flour, salt, and baking powder and set aside.

Combine the butter and ½ cup powdered sugar in a large mixing bowl and beat with an electric mixer on medium speed until light and fluffy. Add eggs and beat until well blended. Add anise, vanilla, lemon juice, and lemon zest. Beat in about half the dry ingredients until thoroughly incorporated. Vigorously stir in remaining dry ingredients with a large wooden spoon. The dough should be rather elastic.

Divide dough in half and wrap each half in plastic wrap. (Do not use waxed paper as dough will stick to it.) Shape each half into an even 6-inch-long log. Wrap up tightly, and refrigerate overnight, or for at least 5 hours.

Preheat the oven to 375 degrees F. Grease several baking sheets and set aside.

Working with one dough half at a time, carefully mark the log into 12 equal sections. Then, using a sharp, heavy knife, cut along markings. To shape pretzels, roll each section back and forth on a clean work surface to form a 17- or 18-inch-long rope. (The dough is fairly elastic, but if it breaks, simply piece it back together.) Transfer rope to a baking sheet, crossing the ends over one another pretzel-fashion (see illustration on page 252). Twist the rope ends together at crossing point, then lift and press ends firmly over the loop.

Repeat the process until all 12 pretzels are formed. Space them about 1½ inches apart. (If the dough becomes sticky or difficult to handle, return it to the refrigerator to cool for a few minutes.) Repeat with the second half of dough.

Place in the center of the oven and bake for 9 to 11 minutes, or until edges are just tinged with brown. Remove from the oven and let stand for 1 to 2 minutes. Then, using a spatula, transfer pretzels to wire racks set over waxed paper to cool while preparing glaze. Pretzels should be glazed while still slightly warm, but not hot.

To prepare the glaze, sift 2¼ cups powdered sugar into a small, deep bowl, and stir in 3 tablespoons hot water, the lemon juice, and corn syrup. Set the bowl in a saucepan of hot water to keep the mixture slightly warm. Using tongs, dip pretzel tops, one at a time, into the glaze. Shake off excess glaze and replace pretzels, right side up, on the wire rack to drain, being sure they don't touch each other. If glaze begins to dry out as you work, add a few drops of water to thin it to the desired consistency. Let pretzels stand for 5 minutes. Then carefully lift and reposition them so they don't stick to the rack. Let stand until glaze sets completely, about 30 minutes longer.

The pretzels are best when fresh, but they may be stored in a single layer in an airtight container for 48 hours. They may also be frozen for 3 or 4 days.

Makes 24 3¼- to 4-inch pretzels.

Viennese Chocolate-Glazed Apricot Sandwich Cookies
(Ischler-Plätzchen)

Austria and Germany

Ischler cookies are famous in Central Europe, and with good reason. Not only are these tender, buttery sandwich cookies delicious, they are also quite handsome. Two wafers are sandwiched together with apricot preserves, and then the cookie is dipped into a glossy chocolate glaze until half its surface is covered. The result, of course, is a pretty contrasting light side and dark side.

These cookies are sometimes prepared with ground almonds, sometimes with ground hazelnuts, and occasionally with a combination of the two. Almonds are easier to find, less trouble to prepare (since they don't have to be hulled), and some people prefer their milder flavor. So, in the following recipe, you may use all almonds if you wish. I like the combination of hazelnuts and almonds, feeling that the two together lend a distinctive yet mellow taste that stands up better against the dark chocolate glaze. Thus, directions are also given for using both in the recipe.

It is best to do the final assembly of the cookie sandwiches the day they will be served. Otherwise, the moisture in the apricot preserves begins to soften the wafers and they lose some of their appealing crispness.

1   cup whole blanched almonds, or ⅔ cup whole blanched almonds and ⅓ cup whole hazelnuts
1   cup (2 sticks) unsalted butter, slightly softened
1   cup powdered sugar
⅛   teaspoon salt
1½ teaspoons vanilla extract
3   to 4 drops almond extract
2   cups all-purpose or unbleached white flour
⅔   to ¾ cup apricot preserves

Chocolate Glaze
1¼ cups powdered sugar
¾   teaspoon light corn syrup
1   tablespoon kirsch, or orange juice
1½ ounces unsweetened chocolate, finely grated

Preheat the oven to 325 degrees F. Set out several baking sheets. Spread the almonds in a baking pan, place in the oven and toast, stirring occasionally, for 6 to 7 minutes, or until just beginning to color. If hazelnuts are also used, spread them in a separate baking pan. Place in the oven and toast, stirring occasionally, for 16 to 17 minutes, or until the hulls begin to loosen and the nuts are tinged with brown. When hazelnuts are cool enough to handle, remove their hulls by vigorously rubbing them, a handful at a time, between the palms or in a clean kitchen towel, discarding dark skin as you work. (It is usually difficult to remove all bits sticking to nuts, but they should be relatively clean of hulls.) Place toasted almonds and hazelnuts (if using) in a nut grinder, food processor, or blender and grind to a powder. Set aside. Reset oven temperature to 350 degrees F.

Combine butter and powdered sugar in a large mixing bowl and beat with an electric mixer on medium speed until light and smooth. Add the salt and vanilla and almond extracts and beat about 30 seconds longer. Using a large wooden spoon, vigorously stir in nuts and flour until they are incorporated and mixture just begins to hold together.

Divide dough in half and place each half between large sheets of waxed paper. Using a rolling pin, roll each half out to a scant ¼-inch thick. Check the underside of the dough frequently and smooth out any creases in the paper. Slide rolled dough sheets onto a tray or baking sheet and refrigerate for 10 to 15 minutes, or until cool and firm but not hard. (To speed up the cooling, place dough in the freezer for about 8 minutes, watching carefully to make sure it doesn't become too cold and hard.)

Remove one chilled dough sheet from the refrigerator and turn over. Peel off bottom sheet of waxed paper, replace paper loosely, and gently turn dough over. Peel off and discard top sheet of waxed paper. Cut out wafers using a 2-inch round cutter (or the rim of a small drinking glass). Using a spatula, transfer rounds to baking sheets, spacing about 1 inch apart. Gather and re-roll dough scraps between waxed paper. Then cut out rounds as before until all the dough is used. (If the dough becomes too warm to handle, return it briefly to refrigerator to chill again.) Repeat process with second dough sheet until all rounds are prepared.

Place in the oven and bake for 11 to 13 minutes, or until wafers are tinged with gold all over and edges are lightly browned. Remove baking sheets and let stand on wire racks for 5 minutes. Using a spatula, transfer wafers to wire racks and let stand until cooled completely. The wafers can be stored as is for a day or so if they won't be eaten right away, or spread with preserves and glazed immediately, if desired.

To assemble cookie sandwiches, strain enough preserves through a fine sieve to yield about ½ cup. Using a blunt knife, spread ½ to ¾ teaspoon apricot preserves over the underside of half the rounds. Gently press a plain wafer over each apricot-jam-covered wafer to form a sandwich, being careful not to press too hard, as the wafers are fairly fragile and may break.

To prepare glaze, sift powdered sugar into a small heavy saucepan. Stir in corn syrup, kirsch, and 3 tablespoons hot water until smooth and well blended. Bring the mixture to a boil over medium-high heat, stirring until very smooth. Remove from the heat. Stir in chocolate and let stand, stirring occasionally, until chocolate melts and the mixture is glossy and smooth. If necessary, add a bit more water until glaze is fairly thin and fluid. (It should be thick enough to cover cookies, but thin enough to form only a thin layer of glaze.)

Dip wafer sandwiches, one at a time, into the glaze, tipping pan so the glaze covers half the top of each cookie. Hold the dipped wafers up vertically for several seconds to allow excess chocolate to drain off. Then gently scrape bottom and glazed edge of each wafer against the pan edge to remove more excess chocolate. Return wafers to the wire rack and let stand until glaze sets, at least 45 minutes. Repeat with the remaining cookies. (Add a few more drops of hot water to glaze if it begins to dry out and thicken as you work.)

Store cookies in one layer in an airtight container until serving, preferably the same day. (They will still taste good if stored longer, but will become soft from the moisture in the preserves.) The cookie tops and bottoms may also be frozen for up to 10 days and then assembled and glazed as needed, if desired.

Makes 25 to 30 2¼-inch cookies.

VIENNESE ALMOND CRESCENTS
(KIPFERL)

Austria and Germany

I was first served these cookies one Christmas by the hostess of a small pension in the Austrian alps. On the afternoon of our arrival, she welcomed us in from the biting cold with large plates of vanilla-scented kipferl and steaming cups of dark, rich coffee. The combination was—and still is—matchless.

These are buttery, fragile, and delicately flavored. Some kipferl are rolled in granulated sugar, but I prefer the vanilla and powdered-sugar dusted type like these. In Austria and Bavaria, kipferl are practically obligatory on the home cook's Christmas cookie tray.

1	cup slivered blanched almonds
⅔	cup granulated sugar
1	cup plus 2 tablespoons (2¼ sticks) unsalted butter, slightly softened
1	large egg
1	large egg yolk
⅛	teaspoon salt
¼	teaspoon baking powder
2	teaspoons vanilla extract
½	teaspoon almond extract
2⅓	cups all-purpose or unbleached white flour

COATING
3	tablespoons granulated sugar
1½-	to 2-inch piece vanilla bean, broken or chopped into small pieces
¾	cup powdered sugar

Preheat the oven to 325 degrees F. Spread the almonds in a large baking pan. Place in the oven and toast, stirring occasionally, for 7 to 8 minutes, or until the almonds are just barely tinged with brown. Immediately remove them from the oven and set aside until completely cooled.

Combine sugar and cooled almonds in a food processor fitted with a steel blade, and process for 3 to 4 minutes, or until almonds are very finely ground, but the mixture still has a slightly granular, rather than paste-like, consistency. (If a processor isn't available, a blender may be used. In this case, place half the almonds and half the sugar in the blender and blend on medium speed until the almonds are finely ground. Stop the blender every few seconds and stir to redistribute the contents to ensure that all the almonds are ground, and to prevent clumping. Repeat with the second half of the almonds and sugar.)

Place butter in a large mixing bowl and beat with an electric mixer on medium speed until light and smooth. Add almond-sugar mixture and continue beating until thoroughly incorporated. Beat in egg, egg yolk, salt, baking powder, and vanilla and almond extracts until mixture is well blended. Gradually beat in flour. If the mixer motor begins to labor, stir in remaining flour by hand. Continue stirring until flour is evenly distributed throughout, but do not overwork dough. Cover and refrigerate for 35 to 45 minutes, or until firm but not stiff. (If storing dough for longer than 1 hour, allow it to warm up slightly before proceeding.)

Preheat the oven to 350 degrees F. Lightly grease several baking sheets and set aside.

To form crescents, remove about a third of the chilled dough from the refrigerator. Break off ¾-inch balls of dough and roll between the palms or on a flat surface to form ropes, about 3½ inches long and ⅜ inch thick, tapering ends slightly. (Don't taper the ends too much or they may break off as the cookies are handled.) Space ropes about ¾ inch apart on baking sheets, gently curving them to form crescents. Repeat the shaping process with remaining dough portions.

Place crescents in the upper third of the oven and bake for 11 to 13 minutes, or until just barely brown at the edges. Remove baking sheets from the oven and let stand for 1 minute. Using a spatula, gently transfer crescents to wire racks and let stand until cool.

Prepare coating mixture by combining the granulated sugar and vanilla bean pieces in a blender. Blend, stopping the blender and stirring to redistribute the contents several times, until the vanilla bean is completely pulverized and the mixture is smooth. Stir the mixture into the powdered sugar until well blended.

Put vanilla sugar mixture in a sturdy plastic bag. Gently drop several crescents into the plastic bag and carefully tip bag back and forth until they are lightly but thoroughly coated with the sugar. Repeat until all crescents are coated.

Store crescents in an airtight container for up to a week. Or, freeze plain crescents for longer storage, thaw, then coat with powdered-vanilla sugar shortly before serving time.

Makes 50 to 60 3-inch crescents.

NUT WREATHS
(NUßKRÄNZCHEN)

Germany and Austria

Avery typical Central European cookie, this is a crunchy-crisp, attractive little ring with a delicate yet distinctive nut flavor. For a festive look, the rings may be decorated with bits of candied cherry, cut and arranged to suggest the red bow on a holiday wreath.

¾   *cup whole hazelnuts*
¾   *cup slivered blanched almonds*
2   *cups all-purpose or unbleached white flour*
½   *teaspoon baking powder*
¼   *teaspoon salt*
¾   *cup (1½ sticks) unsalted butter, slightly softened*
⅔   *cup granulated sugar*
1   *large egg*
½   *teaspoon vanilla extract*
¼   *teaspoon almond extract*

DECORATION
1   *egg*
⅓   *to ½ cup candied cherries (optional)*

Preheat the oven to 325 degrees F. Grease several baking sheets and set aside. Spread the hazelnuts in a baking pan. Place in the oven and toast, stirring occasionally, for 16 to 17 minutes, or until the hulls begin to loosen and the nuts are tinged with brown. Spread almonds in a separate baking pan in the oven and toast, stirring occasionally, for 7 to 8 minutes. Remove from the oven and set nuts aside to cool. Reset oven temperature to 375 degrees F.

When the hazelnuts are cool enough to handle, remove hulls by vigorously rubbing between palms or in a clean kitchen towel, discarding the bits of hull as you work. (It is usually difficult to remove all bits sticking to the nuts, but they should be relatively free of hull.) Finely chop enough hazelnuts to make ⅓ cup. Finely chop enough of the almonds to make ⅓ cup and add them to the hazelnuts; reserve for decorating cookies. Combine the remaining hazelnuts and almonds in a food processor, blender, or nut grinder and grind them to a fine powder. Set aside.

Thoroughly stir together flour, baking powder, and salt. Place butter and granulated sugar in a large mixing bowl, and beat with an electric mixer on medium speed until lightened and smooth. Add egg and vanilla and almond extracts and beat until well blended. Beat in the *ground* nuts until distributed throughout. Stir the dry ingredients into creamed mixture until well mixed and cohesive.

Divide dough in half. Place each half between large sheets of waxed paper and, using a rolling pin, roll each out to a scant ¼ inch thick. Check the underside of the dough frequently and smooth out any creases in the paper. Place rolled dough sheets on a large tray or baking sheet and refrigerate for about 15 minutes, or until cold and firm.

Working with one dough sheet at a time and leaving the second sheet refrigerated, carefully peel off bottom sheet of waxed paper, then replace it loosely. Turn over dough and peel off and discard top sheet of waxed paper. Cut out rounds using a 2¼-inch round or fluted cutter, or the rim of a small drinking glass. Then using a thimble, small bottle cap, or other round about 1 inch in diameter, cut out center of each cookie to form a ring. Lift out centers with the point of a knife or, using a spatula, lift the rounds and push out centers with a finger. Transfer rings to baking sheet, spacing about 1 inch apart. Gather dough scraps into a ball, re-roll between waxed paper, and cut out rings as before until all the dough is used. (If the dough becomes too soft to handle, return it briefly to the refrigerator and chill again.) Repeat the process with the second dough sheet.

In a small bowl, beat the egg with 2 teaspoons water. Brush the tops of two or three rings at a time lightly with egg mixture, using a pastry brush or a piece of paper towel. If desired, quickly arrange four small cherry pieces on each ring in the form of a bow. Then sprinkle the tops lightly with some of the reserved nuts. Repeat until all the rings are decorated.

Place in the center of the oven and bake for 9 to 11 minutes, or until edges are just tinged with brown, reversing baking sheets from front to back about halfway through baking to ensure even browning.

Remove from the oven and let stand on wire rack for 1 minute. Using a spatula, transfer cookies to wire racks to cool.

Store the cookies in an airtight container for up to a week. Freeze for longer storage.

Makes 45 to 50 2½-inch wreaths.

SABLES

France

Sablés, which means "sandies" in French, are a classic French almond butter cookie with a slightly sandy texture. They are rich, mild in flavor, and quite attractive. They are also simple to prepare.

½ cup slivered blanched almonds
¾ cup granulated sugar
¾ cup (1½ sticks) unsalted butter, slightly softened
1 large egg
1 large egg yolk
⅛ teaspoon salt
⅛ teaspoon almond extract
2¾ cups all-purpose or unbleached white flour

DECORATION
¼ to ⅓ cup sliced unblanched almonds

Preheat the oven to 325 degrees F. Spread the slivered almonds in a large baking pan. Place in the oven and toast, stirring occasionally, for 6 to 7 minutes, or until almonds are just beginning to color. Remove pan from the oven and let almonds cool.

Place cooled almonds in a blender or food processor with the sugar, and process until completely ground and smooth. (If a blender is used, stop the motor frequently and stir to redistribute mixture.) Reset the oven temperature to 350 degrees F.

Place butter in a large mixing bowl and beat with an electric mixer on medium speed until light. Add the sugar-almond mixture, egg, egg yolk, salt, and almond extract and beat until well blended. Using a large wooden spoon, vigorously stir in flour until it is incorporated and the mixture is well blended.

Divide the dough in half. Place each half between large sheets of waxed paper and roll each out with a rolling pin to ⅜ inch thick. Slide rolled dough sheets onto a tray or baking sheet. Refrigerate for about 10 minutes, or until cold and slightly firm. Set out several baking sheets.

Working with one chilled dough sheet at a time, carefully peel off bottom sheet of waxed paper, then replace paper loosely. (This will make it easier to lift cookies from the paper later.) Turn dough right side up and peel off and discard top sheet of waxed paper. Using a fluted or plain 2-inch round cutter, or the rim of a 2-inch diameter juice glass, cut out the cookies. Carefully lift cookies from waxed paper with a spatula and place on baking sheets, spacing them about 1 inch apart. Press three almond slices into each cookie, arranging them so they radiate like spokes from the center. Gather and re-roll any dough scraps between waxed paper and continue cutting out cookies until all the dough is used. (If dough becomes too warm to handle easily, refrigerate it again briefly.) Repeat with second sheet of dough.

Place in the center of the oven and bake cookies for 14 to 16 minutes, or until just slightly colored on top and barely brown at the edges. Reverse baking sheets from front to back about halfway through baking to ensure even browning. Remove from the oven and let stand for about 3 minutes. Then transfer cookies to wire racks and let stand until completely cooled.

Store in an airtight container for up to a week. Freeze for longer storage.

Makes about 30 2¼-inch cookies.

Viennese Stamped Butter Cookies
(Wiener Butterplätzchen)

Austria

Many butter cookies are firm and fairly thick, but these are fragile and thinnish and have a nice, crisp texture. These are designed to be prepared with cookie stamps, which produce very handsome cookies with lightly embossed tops. In case you don't have any cookie stamps, directions are given for preparing these cookies without them. They will still be delicious.

2⅓ cups all-purpose or unbleached white flour
¼ teaspoon baking powder
⅛ teaspoon salt
¾ cup plus 2 tablespoons (1¾ sticks) unsalted butter, slightly softened
⅔ cup granulated sugar
1 large egg yolk
1¼ teaspoons vanilla extract
⅛ teaspoon almond extract
Powdered sugar for dusting

Preheat the oven to 350 degrees F. Generously grease several baking sheets. In a large bowl, stir together the flour, baking powder, and salt.

Place butter in a mixing bowl and beat with an electric mixer on medium speed until light and fluffy. Add sugar and beat until well-blended and smooth. Beat in egg yolk and vanilla and almond extracts. Beat in about half the dry ingredients. Stir in remaining dry ingredients using a large wooden spoon. Set dough aside for about 10 minutes to firm up slightly.

Pinch off pieces of dough and roll into ¾-inch-diameter balls between the palms. Space on baking sheets about 1¾ inches apart.

Very lightly grease the surface of each cookie stamp, then dip each stamp in powdered sugar. Carefully tap off any excess sugar from the stamp. Center the stamp over a ball and press down until the dough flattens to about ⅛-inch thick. Carefully lift the stamp from the dough. Stamps do not need to be regreased but should be dipped in powdered sugar before each use. Continue stamping the balls of dough until all the cookies are formed. (To make these cookies without stamps, lightly grease the bottom of a large glass. Dip the greased surface in powdered sugar and tap off excess. Center glass bottom over a ball of dough and press down as with stamp to form a round about ⅛-inch thick. Dip the glass bottom into powdered sugar before each use.)

Place in the center of the oven and bake the cookies for 8 to 11 minutes, or until just barely tinged with brown at the edges. Let stand on baking sheets for 1 to 2 minutes. Then carefully transfer cookies to wire racks using a spatula. Let stand until cooled completely.

Store the cookies in an airtight container for up to 3 or 4 days. Freeze for longer storage.

Makes 40 to 45 2¼-inch diameter cookies.

Overleaf: *"Sausage" Cookies and "Dark Bread" Cookies (recipes on pages 170–171).*

"DARK BREAD" COOKIES
(FALSCHES SWARTZBROT)

Germany

The Germans enjoy a wonderful variety of dark, hearty rough-textured breads, and this interesting trompe l'oeil cookie was obviously created with these in mind. Called "fake black bread" in German, it is made dark with chocolate and ground hazelnuts and is baked in loaves which are then cut into slices and briefly baked again. The technique yields a crunchy, rusk-like texture and a shape similar to that found in the better-known German-Jewish cookie, mandelbrot. The cookies may not actually be mistaken for bread slices, but there's no question about what they aim to imitate.

The combination of chocolate, hazelnuts, and orange gives these cookies a rich, exotic flavor. They are especially good served with strong black coffee.

1   cup whole hazelnuts
3⅓   cups all-purpose or unbleached white flour
1½   teaspoons baking powder
     Pinch of ground cinnamon
     Pinch of ground cloves
4   tablespoons (½ stick) unsalted butter, slightly softened
¼   cup flavorless vegetable oil
1   cup granulated sugar
2   large eggs
1   large egg white
     Finely grated zest of 2 medium oranges
6½   ounces finely grated bittersweet or semisweet chocolate

Preheat the oven to 325 degrees F. Spread the hazelnuts in a baking pan and toast in the oven, stirring occasionally, for 17 to 18 minutes, or until the hulls begin to loosen and the nuts are tinged with brown. Set the nuts aside to cool. Reset the oven temperature to 350 degrees F. Grease a large baking sheet or 2 small baking sheets and set aside.

When hazelnuts are cool enough to handle, remove the hulls by vigorously rubbing a handful of nuts at a time between the palms or in a clean kitchen towel, discarding the bits of skin as you work. (It's all right if some bits of hull remain, but the nuts should be fairly clean.) Place hazelnuts in a nut grater, food processor, or blender and grind finely. Set the nuts aside.

Thoroughly stir together the flour, baking powder, cinnamon, and cloves in a bowl.

In a large mixing bowl, beat the butter, oil, and granulated sugar until well blended. Add the eggs, egg white, and orange zest and beat until light and smooth. Gradually beat in about half the flour mixture. Stir in the hazelnuts and grated chocolate until evenly distributed. Beat or stir in the remaining flour. Let the mixture stand, uncovered, for about 5 minutes.

Divide the dough in half. Place each half on a large sheet of waxed paper and shape and roll back and forth to form a smooth, evenly thick 8½-inch-long log. Unroll logs directly from waxed paper onto the baking sheet, spacing them at least 3 inches apart.

Place in the center of the oven and bake logs for 40 minutes. Cracks will develop in their surface during baking. Remove logs from the oven and let stand on baking sheet for at least 1 hour, or until completely cooled. Then, using a wide spatula, carefully transfer the logs to a cutting board and cut crosswise into ⅜-inch-thick slices using a large sharp knife. Lay slices flat and just slightly separated on the baking sheet. Return slices to the oven to bake for 15 minutes. Remove from the oven and let slices stand on baking sheet for about 5 minutes. Transfer them to wire racks and let stand until cooled completely.

Store in an airtight container for up to 2 weeks. Freeze for longer storage.

Makes about 40 3½-inch cookies.

"SAUSAGE" COOKIES
(WURST PLÄTZCHEN)

Germany

There are a number of trompe l'œil cookies popular in Europe, but these wurst (sausage)-shaped sweets from Germany are among the most amusing. For fun, pair these on a serving tray with another trompe l'œil creation, "dark bread" cookies (opposite).

¾   cup chopped blanched almonds
⅓   cup chopped pistachio nuts
2   cups all-purpose or unbleached white flour
¼   cup plus 3 tablespoons unsweetened cocoa powder
½   teaspoon baking powder
1   cup (2 sticks) cold unsalted butter, cut into small pieces
1   cup granulated sugar
1   large egg
½   teaspoon almond extract
½   teaspoon vanilla extract
3   ounces bittersweet or semisweet chocolate, finely grated

Preheat the oven to 325 degrees F. Spread almonds and pistachios in a large baking pan and toast, stirring occasionally, for 7 to 8 minutes. Set aside until cool.

Thoroughly stir together flour, cocoa powder, and baking powder. Cut butter into dry ingredients using a pastry blender, forks, or your fingertips until mixture resembles very fine crumbs.

In a medium mixing bowl, combine sugar, egg, and almond and vanilla extracts and beat with a fork until well blended. Stir in grated chocolate and cooled chopped nuts. Stir egg mixture into the flour-butter mixture until thoroughly incorporated. Dough may seem too stiff at first, but will soften during mixing.

Spoon dough into two empty 12-ounce orange juice concentrate cans, or similar cardboard juice cans, tightly packing dough down as you work to eliminate any air spaces. Wrap filled cans in plastic wrap or place each in a plastic bag. Refrigerate for at least 3 hours or until firm. (The dough may also be frozen for up to a week, but should be allowed to thaw partially in the refrigerator before it is baked.)

Preheat the oven to 350 degrees F. Lightly grease several baking sheets and set aside.

Working with one dough cylinder at a time, cut or tear off the cardboard can from around the dough. Cut dough into ⅛-inch slices using a large sharp knife. Place rounds on baking sheets, spacing them about 1½ inches apart.

Place in the center of the oven and bake for 8 to 10 minutes, or until almost firm on top. Remove baking sheets from the oven and let stand for about 3 minutes. Transfer cookies to wire racks to cool completely.

Store in an airtight container for up to a week. Freeze for longer storage.

Makes about 45 2¾-inch rounds.

Basel "Brown" Cookies
(Basler Brunsli)

Switzerland

It's not surprising that one of Switzerland's most popular cookies contains chocolate. The Swiss have a well-deserved international reputation for producing excellent chocolate and greatly enjoy eating it themselves.

These yummy cookies have a chewy-crisp texture and a flavor similar to chocolate macaroons. In fact, except that they are lightly spiced with cinnamon and cloves, brunsli contain the same ingredients as classic chocolate macaroons.

The melted white chocolate decoration suggested in the following recipe is not traditional, but adds pizzazz to these homey-looking treats.

1¼   cups (about 7 ounces) whole
      blanched almonds
1½   cups powdered sugar
3½   tablespoons unsweetened cocoa
      powder
2½   teaspoons ground cinnamon
⅛   teaspoon ground cloves
3   ounces bittersweet or semisweet
      chocolate, chopped
¼   teaspoon almond extract
2   large egg whites

      DECORATION
2   to 4 tablespoons powdered sugar for
      rolling out cookies
1½   ounces imported white chocolate
      (optional)

Preheat the oven to 325 degrees F. Line several baking sheets with aluminum foil.

In a food processor fitted with a steel blade, process the almonds and 1 cup of the powdered sugar until almonds are ground to a powder, stopping the processor and scraping down sides several times. Add cocoa powder, cinnamon, cloves, and chocolate and continue processing until chocolate is finely ground. Add remaining ½ cup powdered sugar, almond extract, and egg whites and process until mixture is blended and forms a mass. Set dough aside for 5 minutes, or until it stiffens slightly.

Generously dust a work surface with powdered sugar. If dough seems too soft to roll out easily, dust it with additional powdered sugar and knead until the sugar is incorporated and the consistency is manageable. Roll dough out to ¼ inch thick, lifting it occasionally and redusting the surface with powdered sugar. Cut out cookies using a 2½- to 2¾-inch trefoil-shaped cutter or other 2½-inch cutter. Using a spatula, transfer cookies to foil-lined baking sheets, spacing about 1 inch apart.

Place in the center of the oven and bake for 10 to 12 minutes, or until almost firm on top and slightly puffy. Remove from the oven and let cookies stand on foil until completely cooled. Peel from the foil.

If desired, decorate cookies with white chocolate as follows: Warm chocolate in the top of a double boiler over barely simmering water until melted. Remove from the heat and set aside until cooled. Spoon chocolate into a pastry bag fitted with a very fine writing tip and pipe fine lines diagonally across the cookies at about ¼-inch intervals. Let stand until chocolate sets.

Store in an airtight container for up to a week. Freeze for longer storage.

Makes 35 to 40 2½-inch cookies.

Left to Right: *Raspberry-Chocolate Bars (recipe on page 146), Chocolate Hazelnut Crisps (recipe on page 174), and Basel "Brown" Cookies.*

CHOCOLATE HAZELNUT CRISPS
(SCHOKOHASELNUßPLÄTZCHEN)

Switzerland and Germany

The combination of chocolate and hazelnuts is much appreciated in Germany, Switzerland, and a number of other European countries. In addition to numerous cookies that feature the two ingredients, there are chocolate hazelnut tortes, candies, puddings, liqueurs, and even a popular chocolate hazelnut sandwich spread!

These cookies are crisp, rich, and flavorful. Although they are good plain, they are downright decadent when dressed up with a chocolate glaze. In this case, the rounds are dipped far enough into melted chocolate to coat a scant half of the top surface. Normally in Switzerland and Germany, bittersweet chocolate would be used for dipping, but, if you like, a good-quality imported white chocolate may be substituted. This will produce a dramatically different look as well as much sweeter cookies. White chocolate also lends a mild, smooth chocolate taste instead of the intense, bittersweet flavor that dark chocolate imparts.

Since ordinary chocolate that has not been specially handled, or tempered, tends to gradually discolor (confectioners call this "blooming") after standing awhile, for best appearance do not dip the cookies more than 24 hours before they will be served. Blooming, a harmless, if unattractive, process in which some of the whitish cocoa butter rises to the chocolate surface, can also be partially controlled by refrigerating the cookies until serving time. (Serve the cookies slightly cold and don't let them stand at room temperature for longer than about an hour.) Of course, if the cookies are decorated with white chocolate, the white-colored bloom is not as noticeable.

2/3   cup whole hazelnuts
4½   ounces bittersweet or semisweet chocolate, coarsely chopped or broken into pieces
3/4   cup powdered sugar
1/4   teaspoon instant coffee powder (use only fine granules, not crystals)
1/8   teaspoon salt
1¼   cups all-purpose or unbleached white flour
1/2   cup (1 stick) cold unsalted butter, cut into small pieces
2   teaspoons vanilla extract

DIPPING CHOCOLATE
8   ounces bittersweet or semisweet chocolate or good-quality imported white chocolate, coarsely chopped or broken into large pieces
1   tablespoon solid shortening (reduce to 1½ teaspoons if white chocolate is used)

Preheat the oven to 325 degrees F. Grease several baking sheets and set aside. Spread the hazelnuts in a baking pan and toast in the oven, stirring occasionally, for 16 to 18 minutes, until the hulls begin to loosen and the nuts are slightly colored and fragrant. Set the nuts aside until cool.

In a double boiler over barely simmering water, warm the 4½ ounces chocolate until melted and smooth. Set aside until just barely warm.

When the hazelnuts are cool enough to handle, remove the hulls by vigorously rubbing a handful of nuts at a time between the palms or in a clean kitchen towel, discarding the bits of skin as you work. (It is usually difficult to remove all bits sticking to the nuts, but they should be relatively free of hull.)

Combine the hazelnuts, powdered sugar, instant coffee, and salt in a food processor fitted with a steel blade. Process for 1½ to 2 minutes or until the hazelnuts are ground to a powder. Add the flour and process until incorporated. Sprinkle the butter over the flour mixture. Processing in on/off pulses, cut in the butter until the mixture resembles fine crumbs.

Add the cooled chocolate and vanilla to processor, and process in on/off pulses only until the ingredients are blended and hold together and almost all flecks of butter have disappeared.

Remove dough from the processor and shape into a mass. Knead briefly to ensure that chocolate is evenly distributed. Divide dough in half. Place each portion between sheets of waxed paper and, using a rolling pin, roll out ⅛-inch thick. Check underside of dough frequently and smooth out any creases that form in the paper. Stack dough sheets on a tray or baking sheet and refrigerate for about 10 minutes or until dough is firm. (To speed up the process, place dough in the freezer for about 5 minutes.)

Remove one dough sheet from the refrigerator. Carefully peel off the bottom sheet of waxed paper, then replace it loosely. Turn dough over and remove and discard top sheet of waxed paper. Cut out the cookies, using a 2¼- to 2½-inch scalloped or fluted round cutter or the rim of a similar-sized drinking glass. Transfer cookies to baking sheets, spacing about 1 inch apart.

Place in the center of the oven and bake for 8 to 10 minutes, or until cookies are almost firm to the touch. (They will puff up slightly during baking, then fall again.) Remove baking sheets from the oven and let stand for 1 minute. Transfer the cookies to wire racks to cool completely. When cooled, dip them in melted chocolate, or store plain and dip them the day you plan to serve them.

To prepare dipping chocolate, warm the chocolate and shortening in the top of a double boiler over barely simmering water, stirring frequently, until the chocolate melts and the mixture is smooth. Remove double boiler from the heat. With the pan tipped up so the chocolate pools in one side, dip each cookie so that the mixture covers only half the top. Gently scrape the underside of each cookie against the pan edge to remove any excess chocolate, then return the cookie to a wire rack set over waxed paper. (If the chocolate begins to cool and stiffen as you work, rewarm it slightly.) Let the cookies stand until the chocolate sets, about 45 minutes, or speed up the setting process by transferring them to the refrigerator or freezer for a few minutes. (Remove them from the freezer and refrigerate as soon as the chocolate sets.)

Store the plain crisps for up to 4 days. Freeze for longer storage. Chocolate-dipped cookies should be refrigerated in an airtight container with waxed paper between the layers. They will keep like this for 4 or 5 days, but the chocolate on top will gradually begin to discolor.

Makes about 45 2¾-inch cookies.

COOKIE HOUSE
(KNUSPERHAUS)

Germany

The custom of making colorful cookie houses at holiday time is as widely enjoyed in Germany as making gingerbread houses is in the United States. Cookie houses are so popular in Germany that stores sell make-your-own knusperhaus kits containing pattern pieces, instructions, and even the cookies for the project. (The word knusperhaus literally means "nibbling house.")

Though similar in appearance, cookie houses and gingerbread houses aren't made in exactly the same way. Gingerbread houses are prepared with ginger and molasses, and "knusper" houses are created with a honey-spice dough called lebkuchen.

In addition, gingerbread houses are made from rather fragile sheets of baked dough neatly joined with icing, while cookie houses are constructed from pieces of sturdy cardboard taped together and then covered with a layer of icing "mortar" and assorted cookies and candies. The advantage of this construction technique is that once the cardboard frame has been put together, even very young children can participate in the decorating. They can press the various cookie "roof tiles," "boards," and candies into place without any danger of breaking the structure. And due to the mortar lines in the design, the cookies don't have to be fitted precisely together to create an attractive effect.

MAKING THE FRAME PIECES

Referring to the pattern illustration on page 252, prepare pieces using cardboard at least ⅛-inch thick. The smooth cardboard used in *very sturdy* gift boxes works particularly well. Cut out and label the following pieces:

2 8½- by 10-inch rectangles for roof pieces. (Be sure to label so that the 10-inch dimension runs horizontally across the top.)

2 3½- by 8½-inch rectangles for house sides.

2 8½- by 10-inch rectangles for house front and back. To form the peaked shape, mark the center point of the top 8½-inch side. Then mark 3½ inches up from the bottom on each 10-inch side (see the pattern illustration). Using a ruler, draw lines from the center top to the 3½-inch-high points on each side to determine the roof angle. Cut along the lines to form the peaked front and back of the house. Measure and mark the placement of a front door, 2¾ inches high by 1¾ inches wide, in the center front as indicated on the illustration. Cut along the right side and top of the door, leaving the left side uncut so it will create a "hinge." Measure and mark the placement of the 1½-inch-high and 1¼-inch-wide upstairs windows in the back and front of the house by centering the top edge of each 2½ inches down from the roof peak. For front and back windows that open, cut away the right side and the top of each, leaving the left sides uncut as for the door. If desired, cutting can be omitted for windows that do not open.

2 5- by 1½-inch rectangles for chimney sides. Mark 2½ inches down on a 5-inch side of each rectangle. Using a ruler, draw

a line from the point marked *diagonally* across to an opposite corner of each rectangle. Cut away cardboard along the diagonal line (see the illustration on page 252).

1 5- by 2¼-inch rectangle for chimney front.

1 2½- by 2¼-inch rectangle for chimney back. (When labeling, *be sure a 2¼-inch side runs horizontally across the top*.)

Assembling the Cardboard Frame

To assemble the frame, lay cardboard front on a flat surface. Lay a side piece on each side of the front, matching up the 3½-inch-high edges and tape the pieces together using masking tape. Stand the unit up. Fit the back against the two sides, matching up the edges, and tape the pieces together using masking tape. If necessary, adjust the unit so the house frame is square and stands up straight. Tape with strapping tape (also called filament tape) or other sturdy tape to fix the pieces securely in place.

To attach the roof to the frame, match up two 10-inch-long sides of the roof pieces and tape together using masking tape. Fit the roof onto the house frame, adjusting the pitch and centering the roof seam so it overhangs an equal amount in front and back. Tape the roof to the frame in a few places using masking tape. Check to be sure the house looks square and the roof is straight, and make any necessary adjustments. Then tape with strapping tape to fix pieces securely in place.

To assemble the chimney, lay the cardboard chimney front on a flat surface. Lay the chimney side pieces with their long sides matching on either side of chimney front and their tapered parts both pointing up. Tape the front and sides together using masking tape. Stand the unit up. Fit the back of the chimney into place against the straight edges of the chimney sides to form a box. Tape the pieces into place using masking tape. Check to make sure the chimney unit is square and make adjustments, if necessary. Tape with strapping tape to fix pieces securely in place.

To secure the entire unit, turn the house upside down and tape all interior side and roof seams using strapping tape. Reinforce unit by taping outside seams with strapping tape.

To attach the chimney to the roof, center the chimney unit on one side of the roof, positioning it so that the chimney front is facing away from the roof and the angled sides line up with the pitch of the roof. Tape the chimney into place using masking tape. Check to be sure the chimney is straight; make adjustments if necessary. Secure the chimney by taping all roof-chimney seams using strapping tape.

To attach the house to a cardboard base, cut out an 11¾-inch or larger, if desired, square from sturdy (at least ¼-inch thick) cardboard. (If desired, cover the cardboard with decorative or white paper.) In the center of the square, cut a rectangle large enough for your hand to fit through. Center the house frame on the base. Working through the hole in the bottom of the base, securely tape the base to the house using strapping tape.

Making the Cookies

In this recipe, one basic mixture is flavored with different ingredients to make three different doughs—light lebkuchen, dark lebkuchen, and chocolate. Light lebkuchen dough is used to prepare cookie "boards" for covering the sides, front, and back of the house. Dark lebkuchen become roof shingles, front and back windows, optional decorative heart- or round-shaped pieces, and front door. And the chocolate dough is used to make chimney "bricks." Since the cookies need to be the specified sizes to fit the house neatly, it is best to use a ruler and mark before cutting them out. Don't worry about the natural variation that occurs during baking, however; the fact that there are spaces left between the pieces on the house means there is some margin for error.

The cookies can be made ahead, if desired. They will keep airtight for a week or two, or can be frozen for up to a month. To avoid confusion and to aid assembly, store the various sizes and shapes in separate, labeled plastic bags.

5	to 5¼ cups all-purpose or unbleached white flour
1	tablespoon plus 2 teaspoons ground cinnamon
1	tablespoon plus 1 teaspoon ground ginger
¼	teaspoon baking soda
½	teaspoon salt
¾	cup (1½ sticks) unsalted butter, slightly softened
⅔	cup granulated sugar
1	cup clover honey, or other light-colored honey
1	large egg
1	large egg yolk
1	tablespoon fresh lemon juice
4½	teaspoons unsweetened cocoa powder
¾	teaspoon ground cloves

DECORATION

½	cup slivered blanched almonds
	Candied cherry halves, cut into quarters

Thoroughly stir together 4 cups of the flour, the cinnamon, ginger, baking soda, and salt in a large bowl.

In a large mixing bowl, beat the butter with an electric mixer on medium speed until lightened. Beat in sugar and honey until well blended and smooth. Add the egg, egg yolk, and lemon juice and continue beating until incorporated. Beat in the reserved flour-spice mixture.

Divide dough into two equal parts. For the light lebkuchen dough, stir in ½ cup of the remaining flour until well blended and smooth. If dough seems too soft and sticky to handle, stir in a tablespoon or two more flour. For the dark lebkuchen dough, stir in 2½ teaspoons of the cocoa powder, the cloves, and remaining ½ cup flour until thoroughly incorporated. If dough seems too soft and sticky to handle, stir in a tablespoon or two more flour. For the chocolate dough, measure out ⅓ cup dough *each* from the light and dark lebkuchen doughs. Combine these two portions in a bowl, add the remaining 2 teaspoons cocoa powder, and stir or knead the mixture until thoroughly blended and smooth. Form dough portions into balls and wrap each separately in plastic wrap. Place in an airtight plastic bag. Refrigerate for at least 4 hours, or up to 48 hours.

Preheat the oven to 375 degrees F. Grease several baking sheets and set aside. Working with one dough ball at a time, roll, cut out, and bake cookies from the three types of dough as directed below. The directions allow for a few "extras" of each type in case of breakage. (There will also be plenty of extra dough so some cookies can be eaten as well.)

LIGHT LEBKUCHEN DOUGH
Roll dough out between sheets of waxed paper into a ¼-inch-thick rectangle, check-

ing the underside and smoothing out any creases in the paper. Turn dough over, peel off the bottom sheet of paper, and replace it loosely. Turn dough right side up, and peel off and discard top sheet of waxed paper. Measure, mark, and cut out the following cookies:

20 2¾- by 1½-inch rectangles for "boards" covering lower front, lower back, and sides of house

10 2- by 1½-inch rectangles for "boards" on upper front and back of house

Using a spatula, transfer cookies to baking sheets, spacing them about 1 inch apart. Press almond slivers into the four corners of all the *large* "boards" (see photograph). Press a candied cherry piece into the center of each large board. Press a cherry bit into the center of each of the *small* boards, and press 4 almond slivers around the cherry as shown in the photograph.

Place in the center of the oven and bake the cookies for 10 to 12 minutes, or until tinged with brown around the edges. Let stand on baking sheets for a minute or two. Transfer to wire racks until cooled completely.

DARK LEBKUCHEN DOUGH
Roll out dough between sheets of waxed paper to a scant ¼-inch thick, checking the underside and smoothing out any creases. Using cutters for the rounds and hearts and a sharp knife for rectangles, cut out the following:

30 1¾-inch rounds, using a 1¾-inch-diameter cutter or shot glass. (Immediately after baking, these will be cut in half to form half circles for roof shingles).

1 2¾- by 1¾-inch rectangle with rounded corners at one end for front door. Using a knife, score the door as shown in the photograph.

2 1½-inch-high by 1¼-inch-wide rectangles with rounded corners at one 1¼-inch end for front and back windows.

8 1-inch (*optional*) small hearts, stars, or rounds for decorating upper front and back of house, using a mini-cutter, aspic cutter, or bottle cap. (If optional pieces are omitted, Jordan almonds will be used in their place.)

Using a spatula, transfer the cookies to baking sheets, spacing them about 1 inch apart. Place in the center of the oven and bake for 8 to 9 minutes, or until tinged with brown around the edges.

Remove from the oven, immediately transfer "roof shingle" rounds to a cutting board, and cut each in half using a large, sharp knife. Let remaining cookies stand on baking sheets for a minute or two. Transfer to wire racks to cool completely.

CHOCOLATE DOUGH
Roll dough out between sheets of waxed paper into an 8-inch-long rectangle a scant ¼-inch thick, checking the underside and smoothing out any creases that form. Peel off bottom sheet of waxed paper, then replace it loosely. Peel off and discard the top sheet of waxed paper. Measure, mark, and cut out the following cookies:

6 2- by 1-inch rectangles for front and back chimney bricks

6 1½- by 1¼-inch rectangles for chimney side bricks. Cut one of these rectangles in half diagonally to form two triangles for chimney side half-bricks.

Using a spatula, carefully transfer the cookies to baking sheets, spacing them about 1 inch apart. Place in the center of the oven and bake for 6 to 8 minutes, or until tinged with brown around the edges. Remove from the oven and let stand on baking sheets for a minute or two. Transfer to wire racks to cool completely.

DECORATING THE COOKIE HOUSE

Have ready all the previously baked cookies and the prepared cardboard house frame.

DECORATION
75   to 80 ³/₈-inch round colored mints, M & M candies, or Skittles, for garnishing spaces between roof tiles and house front and back

80   mixed Jordan almonds, chocolate-covered almonds, and ³/₈-inch-diameter mints (or other candies) for decorating upper house front and back and trimming roof line

¹/₃   to ¹/₂ cup coarse crystal sugar or sanding sugar (optional), for sprinkling over house to add an icy, glistening look

1   egg white (if using crystal sugar)

Prepare a batch of royal icing as follows:

ROYAL ICING
³/₄   cup egg whites (6 to 7 large whites), completely free of any yolk and at room temperature

2   teaspoons fresh lemon juice

¹/₄   teaspoon salt

6   to 6³/₄ cups powdered sugar

In a large grease-free mixing bowl, combine egg whites, lemon juice, and salt and beat with an electric mixer on low speed until frothy. Increase speed to medium and gradually beat in the powdered sugar until mixture becomes fluffy and shiny and stands in firm but not dry peaks. The consistency should be smooth and spreadable but not too soft. If icing seems too soft, beat in a bit more powdered sugar; if too dry, beat in a few drops water. Remove one-third of icing, cover tightly, and set aside for final decorating. Cover remaining icing to prevent it from drying out as you work. If it does begin to stiffen, stir in a few drops of water.

Add the icing and decorations to the house as follows:

Using a flat-bladed spatula or large table knife, spread the house sides with an even layer of icing. Press 5 large cookie "boards" into icing along each side of the house, spacing them evenly (see photograph). Spread lower half of the house back with a ¹/₄-inch-thick layer of icing and press 5 large "boards" into place. Spread icing along the house lower front. Press 2 large "boards" into place on each side and press the front door into place in the middle. Place door in the desired position, open or closed, as it cannot be moved once the icing sets.

Spread the house upper back with a ¹/₄-inch thick layer of icing, being sure to spread it evenly under the eaves. Press a window-shaped cookie into place over the cardboard cut-away area, or center the top 2¹/₂ inches down from roof peak if window doesn't open. Place window in desired position, open or closed, since it likewise cannot be moved once the icing sets. Press the almonds, smaller "boards," small round candies, and heart-shaped (or round) cookies into place as shown. (If small heart-shaped or round cookies are omitted, fill in empty spaces with assorted almonds and candies of your choice.) Then repeat the process with the cookie house upper front, placing cookies and decorations in position as shown in the photograph.

Spread all sides of the chimney with a ¼-inch-thick layer of icing. Press 4 2- by 1-inch rectangles into place on the chimney front as shown and 1 2- by 1-inch rectangle into place on chimney back. Press 2 1½- by 1¼-inch rectangles and a triangular piece into each chimney side (see photograph).

Spread the roof side not containing the chimney with a ¼-inch-thick layer of icing. Working horizontally across the top and spacing evenly, press 5 "shingles" into place as shown in the photograph. Then, working vertically and spacing evenly, press a row of 6 "shingles" along one side. Continue adding rows, using the ones already in place as spacing guides. Decorate roof by pressing round, colored candies into the spaces between the shingles as shown.

Spread the roof side with the chimney with a ¼-inch-thick layer of icing. Add the "shingles" as for the preceding side, cutting off the ends of those on either side of the chimney as needed to fit neatly around it. Decorate roof by pressing round candies into the spaces between the shingles as shown.

Complete roof decoration by pressing a line of Jordan almonds, small candies, and chocolate covered almonds horizontally along the peak on both sides of the roof. Then, add a similar decorative line of mixed almonds and small candies horizontally along the bottom edge of both sides of the roof.

To complete the snow capping and icicle decorations, thin the reserved third of icing with water until it is soft enough to produce a graceful "dripped" look. Decorate the chimney top and crest of the roof by generously dropping the icing from a spoon along all the edges as shown. Add icicles along all the eaves by dropping the icing from a spoon or by piping it from a pastry bag fitted with a large writing tip. If desired, touch a spoon against the still soft icing along the eaves in a downward motion to create a more pronounced icicle effect. Let the cookie house stand until the icing is completely set, at least 6 hours.

If a crystal sugar garnish is desired, prepare an egg white wash by lightly beating 1 egg white with 2 teaspoons water. Working with small areas at a time, lightly brush icing-covered surfaces with the egg wash, then immediately sprinkle sugar crystals over the surface. Continue until all desired surfaces are garnished with the sugar.

Let the completed house stand, uncovered, for at least 2 hours to allow egg wash to dry out completely. Store the house loosely covered (*never airtight*) with cloth or plastic. The cookies, garnishes, and icing will be edible for several weeks and the house can be kept indefinitely.

Makes 1 11½-inch-high and 10- by 10½-inch-wide cookie house.

PEPPERNUTS
(PFEFFERNÜSSE)

Germany

The name comes from the fact that these cookies are small, brown crunchy-spicy tidbits about the size of nuts. Many peppernut recipes also contain a pinch or two of black or white pepper, which, along with ginger and cloves, gives the cookies a slight peppery bite. Pfeffernüsse were originally made without butter, but modern cooks frequently add it to produce cookies with better texture and flavor.

Some recipes call for rolling each peppernut into a ball, which can be time-consuming, but in this one, the dough is shaped into long thin logs and then simply cut crosswise into little slices.

3½ cups all-purpose or unbleached white flour
2½ teaspoons baking powder
1½ teaspoons ground cinnamon
1 teaspoon ground ginger
1 teaspoon ground cloves
    Pinch of ground white pepper
⅓ cup minced, mixed candied citrus peel
1 cup (2 sticks) unsalted butter, slightly softened
1 cup granulated sugar
¼ cup mild honey
1 large egg
    Finely grated zest of 1 large lemon

GLAZE (OPTIONAL)
2 cups sifted powdered sugar
2 tablespoons light or dark rum
2 teaspoons fresh lemon juice

Thoroughly stir together flour, baking powder, cinnamon, ginger, cloves, and white pepper. Stir in candied citrus peel and set aside.

Place the butter in a large mixing bowl and beat until light and fluffy. Add sugar and honey and beat until smooth. Beat in egg and lemon zest until thoroughly incorporated. Beat in about half the dry ingredients. Add remaining dry ingredients and stir until well blended and smooth.

Divide dough into four equal parts. Lay each quarter on a sheet of waxed paper and shape each into an evenly thick, 12-inch-long log. Smooth out and even the surface of logs by rolling them back and forth in the paper on a flat work surface until uniform. Slide logs onto a tray or baking sheet. Place in the freezer for at least 1½ hours or until firm. Slice and bake the cookies immediately, if desired, or pack the logs in a plastic bag and store in the freezer for up to 2 weeks.

Preheat the oven to 375 degrees F. Grease several baking sheets. Using a sharp knife, cut logs crosswise into generous ⅜-inch-thick slices and place on baking sheets, spacing them about ½ inch apart.

Place in the oven and bake until the tops of cookies are lightly browned, 8 to 9 minutes. Remove from the oven and let cool several minutes. Transfer cookies to wire racks and let stand until completely cooled.

To prepare glaze, combine powdered sugar, rum, lemon juice, and 1 teaspoon hot water in a large mixing bowl and stir until well mixed. Stir in enough additional hot water to make a rather fluid but still spreadable glaze. Using a blunt knife or pastry brush, very lightly coat the top of each cookie with glaze. Let peppernuts stand on wire racks set over waxed paper until glaze sets.

Store in an airtight container for up to 2 weeks. Freeze for longer storage.

Makes 110 to 120 1¼-inch cookies.

ALMOND MACAROONS
(MACARONS)

France

Aromatic and chewy-crisp, these classic French cookies are enjoyed the world over. They may actually have originated in Italy, but the French city of Nancy is said to have made them famous. They have been baked there for at least 700 years.

Legend has it that three nuns in Nancy produced extraordinarily good macaroons, and as a result, the cookies gradually grew in popularity throughout France and the rest of Europe. Sometimes the cookies are still called *macarons des sœurs*—macaroons of the sisters.

1⅔   cups (9 ounces) whole blanched almonds
1⅓   cups powdered sugar
1   3½-ounce package almond paste, cut into small pieces
⅓   cup (2 to 3 large) egg whites completely free of any yolk
½   teaspoon almond extract

DECORATION
30   candied cherry halves

Preheat the oven to 325 degrees F. Set out several baking sheets and cover each with aluminum foil cut to fit.

Spread the almonds in a large baking pan, place in the oven and toast, stirring occasionally, for 7 to 8 minutes, or until almonds are just beginning to color. Remove from the oven and set them aside. Reset oven temperature to 350 degrees F.

In a food processor fitted with a steel blade, combine cooled almonds and powdered sugar and process for 1½ to 2 minutes, stopping processor to scrape down the sides several times, until almonds are ground to a powder. With machine running, add almond paste pieces through the feed tube, processing until they are thoroughly incorporated and the mixture is smooth. Add egg whites and continue processing for 1 minute, or until mixture is well blended.

Transfer the mixture to a large heavy saucepan and place over medium-low heat. Cook, stirring constantly and scraping the bottom of saucepan for 4 to 5 minutes, or until mixture thickens slightly. Remove from the heat and stir in almond extract. Let mixture cool for about 15 minutes, or until slightly stiff but not firm.

Stand a large pastry bag fitted with a ½-inch-diameter star tip in a tall glass. Turn down edge into a deep cuff and spoon cooled macaroon mixture into bag until about half full. Unfold cuff and firmly twist bag closed. Pipe high, 1⅛-inch-diameter rosettes about 1½ inches apart onto foil-lined baking sheets. (If the mixture becomes too cool and stiffens too much to pipe, reheat it slightly.) Press a cherry half, cut side down, into the center of each macaroon.

Place in the upper third of the oven and bake the macaroons for 11 to 14 minutes until just tinged with brown but still soft inside. Remove from the oven and let macaroons stand on foil until cool. Then carefully transfer to wire racks to cool completely.

Store in an airtight container for 2 or 3 days. Freeze for longer storage.

Makes about 30 1½-inch macaroons.

Note: To make the macaroons without a pastry bag, simply drop small, rounded spoonfuls of the mixture onto the foil.

Almond Macaroons and Chocolate Macaroons (recipe on page 186).

CHOCOLATE MACAROONS
(MACARONS AU CHOCOLAT)

France

These are like the chocolate macaroons you see in French bake shops. They are often sold as double macaroons with the bottoms of two single macaroons fused together with water or egg white immediately after baking to make a smooth, double-domed shape. I think single macaroons are a little easier to eat.

1¼   cups slivered blanched almonds
2   cups powdered sugar
1   tablespoon unsweetened cocoa
       powder
       Pinch of salt
2   ounces unsweetened chocolate, finely
       chopped
3   large egg whites
½   teaspoon almond extract
½   teaspoon vanilla extract

Place almonds, powdered sugar, cocoa powder, and salt in a food processor fitted with a steel blade. Process for 1 to 1½ minutes, stopping processor to scrape down the sides several times, until almonds are ground to a powder. Add chocolate and process for 30 seconds longer. Add egg whites and continue processing for 1 minute, or until the mixture is smooth.

Transfer mixture to a large heavy saucepan and place over low heat. Heat, stirring constantly and scraping pan bottom to prevent sticking and burning, for 5 to 6 minutes, or until the chocolate melts and the mixture thickens just slightly. Remove from the heat, and stir in almond and vanilla extracts. Cover and refrigerate for 1 to 1½ hours, or until mixture is cold and fairly stiff. (Do not chill longer than 2 hours as the dough may become too stiff and dry.)

Preheat the oven to 350 degrees F. Line several baking sheets with waxed paper cut to fit.

To form macaroons, wet hands, then spoon a teaspoonful of dough into palms. Roll lightly between palms to form a smooth, 1-inch ball and immediately transfer to baking sheet. Repeat process until all dough is used, spacing balls about 2 inches apart on baking sheet.

Place in the center of the oven and bake for 13 to 15 minutes until puffed and crinkly, and almost firm to the touch. (It's normal for the waxed paper to smoke slightly.) Remove baking sheets from the oven and let stand for 30 seconds. Carefully lift waxed paper with the macaroons still attached, turn it over and lay on a work surface so the macaroons are facing down. Lay a wet cloth or towel over the back of waxed paper to soak thoroughly, and let stand for 20 seconds, while the steam that is produced loosens the macaroons. Wet paper again, then turn over so that macaroons face up. Immediately return waxed paper to the baking sheets and let stand 30 seconds longer. Carefully peel macaroons from the paper. Transfer them to wire racks to cool completely.

Store in an airtight container for 3 or 4 days. Freeze for longer storage.

Makes 25 to 28 2-inch macaroons.

CHOCOLATE-ALMOND MERINGUE COOKIES
(WESPENNESTER)

Germany

These chewy-crisp meringue drop cookies are a perennial favorite in Germany. They are included nearly every time a new cookie collection appears in a German food magazine or cookbook. The combination of caramelized almonds and chocolate makes this version particularly appealing.

3	tablespoons granulated sugar
1½	cups slivered blanched almonds
⅓	cup egg whites (2 to 3 large whites), at room temperature
½	teaspoon cream of tartar
⅛	teaspoon almond extract
1¼	cups powdered sugar
1	tablespoon unsweetened cocoa powder
2	tablespoons all-purpose or unbleached white flour
1	ounce very finely grated bittersweet or semisweet chocolate

Preheat the oven to 325 degrees F. Line several baking sheets with baking parchment or brown paper bags cut to fit and set aside.

Place granulated sugar in a large, heavy skillet and heat over medium heat, stirring occasionally, until the sugar begins to melt. Add almonds and heat them, stirring continuously, for 3 to 4 minutes longer, or until they are coated with sugar and nicely browned; lower the heat or lift the skillet from the burner if it begins to smoke or the almonds begin to turn too dark. Turn the almonds out into a large heatproof bowl and let stand until cooled completely. (If almonds have clumped together, break them apart with the fingers.)

In a completely grease-free mixing bowl, combine egg whites, cream of tartar, and almond extract, and beat with a mixer on low speed. Gradually increase mixer speed to high and continue beating until fluffy but not stiff. Gradually beat in powdered sugar until whites stand in very stiff, glossy peaks.

Sift cocoa powder and flour over cooled almonds. Add grated chocolate to the almonds, and toss ingredients until well mixed. Using a rubber spatula, fold almond-chocolate mixture into the beaten whites until blended but not overmixed. Drop the mixture by heaping teaspoonfuls onto the parchment-covered baking sheets, spacing about 2 inches apart.

Place in the center of the oven and bake for 20 to 23 minutes, or until firm to the touch. Remove baking sheets from the oven and let cookies stand on the parchment until cooled completely. Carefully peel cookies from the paper.

Store the cookies in an airtight container for up to 10 days. Freeze for longer storage.

Makes about 32 2-inch cookies.

MUSHROOM MERINGUE COOKIES
(CHAMPIGNONS EN MERINGUE)

France

French pastry chefs have long made these delightful trompe l'oeil creations. Traditionally, they are fairly plain and used as garnishes for the classic French Christmas dessert Bûche de Noël, or Yule Log cake roll.

In this version, however, the cookies are accented with almond flavoring and the undersides of the mushrooms are glazed with bittersweet chocolate, which makes them appealing and striking enough to stand on their own. I like to serve them arranged in a rustic basket surrounded by woodsy-looking plants. At first, people always think they are real, which makes them wonderful fun.

Meringue mushrooms do require a pastry bag fitted with a large decorator tip, but even cooks inexperienced with this equipment can turn out mushrooms that look real. Forming these sweets involves piping out and baking dome-like rounds for "caps" and stalagmite-like lengths for "stems." Then the two are "glued" together with melted chocolate.

⅓	cup egg whites (about 2 to 3 large egg whites), at room temperature
1	teaspoon cream of tartar
2⅓	cups powdered sugar
½	teaspoon almond extract

DECORATION

2	teaspoons unsweetened cocoa powder
3	ounces bittersweet or semisweet chocolate

Preheat the oven to 200 degrees F. Line several baking sheets with aluminum foil.

In a completely grease-free mixing bowl, combine egg whites and cream of tartar and beat with an electric mixer on medium speed until frothy. Increase mixer speed to high and beat until well-mixed and fluffy. Continue beating, gradually adding powdered sugar. Add almond extract and beat until mixture is very stiff, smooth, and glossy.

Fit a pastry bag with a large (⅜- to ½-inch diameter) plain decorator tip. Fill bag with the meringue mixture by standing it in a tall glass, turning down a deep cuff at the top, and spooning the mixture into the bag until no more than two-thirds full. Unfold the cuff and twist the bag closed. To form the mushroom "caps," pipe high, smooth 1- to 1½-inch domes onto foil-lined baking sheets, spacing them about 1½ inches apart. Using your finger or the tip of a blunt knife dipped in water, carefully smooth down any "tails" remaining from the piping. To form the mushroom "stems," pipe about ⅜-inch rounds onto the foil and then, still squeezing out meringue, draw the pastry tip upward off the baking sheet 1 to 2 inches to produce stalagmite-like lengths. Make a few extra stems, as some may fall over during baking. Very lightly sprinkle the caps and stems with the cocoa powder to suggest natural mottling of the mushrooms.

Place in the center of the oven and bake for 45 minutes, or until meringue pieces are firm and just beginning to color. Turn off the oven, open oven door, and let meringue pieces stand in the oven for 15 minutes.

Remove meringue pieces from the oven and let stand until cooled completely. Carefully peel the caps and stems from the foil. The pieces can be stored airtight for several weeks or frozen for longer storage. It's best not to assemble the mushrooms more than 48 hours before they will be

needed as the chocolate used to "glue" them together will gradually discolor, or "bloom." (Blooming won't affect the taste or edibility; the mushrooms just won't look quite as nice.)

To assemble the mushrooms, place the chocolate in the top of a double boiler and warm over barely simmering water until melted. Remove double boiler from the heat. Using a sharp paring knife, cut off pointed ends of the mushroom "stems" to make them perfectly flat. Then, with a blunt knife, spread a thin layer of choco-

late in a circle to within ⅛ inch of the edge on the underside of the caps and immediately press the cut end of a stem into the center of each cap. Carefully set aside the finished mushrooms, stem-side up, until the chocolate sets; prop them up if necessary, to prevent them from falling over.

Store the mushrooms in an airtight container at room temperature for up to 48 hours. (Do not refrigerate, as the caps and stems may separate.)

Makes 25 to 35 1¼- to 2-inch mushrooms.

BITTERSWEET AND WHITE CHOCOLATE BAR COOKIES
(SCHWARZ-WEIßSTÄNGERL)

Switzerland

The inspiration for this recipe was a little package of chocolate cookies I bought from a pastry shop in Geneva many years ago. The bar-shaped cookies had a rich almond and chocolate flavor and were cloaked in a bittersweet chocolate glaze. To complete the dramatic professional look, they were drizzled with white chocolate stripes.

My version of these cookies looks and tastes quite similar to the ones I remember.

2¼ cups all-purpose or unbleached white flour
¼ cup unsweetened cocoa powder
¾ teaspoon baking powder
⅛ teaspoon salt
1 large egg
3½ ounces almond paste, cut into small pieces
½ teaspoon almond extract
1 cup (2 sticks) unsalted butter, slightly softened
⅓ cup granulated sugar
2 ounces bittersweet or semisweet chocolate, finely grated

BITTERSWEET CHOCOLATE GLAZE
1 tablespoon solid vegetable shortening
6 ounces bittersweet or semisweet chocolate, coarsely chopped
1 ounce unsweetened chocolate, coarsely chopped

WHITE CHOCOLATE GLAZE
½ teaspoon solid vegetable shortening

190

1 ounce white chocolate, coarsely chopped

Preheat the oven to 350 degrees F. Grease several baking sheets and set aside. In a large bowl, stir together flour, cocoa powder, baking powder, and salt and set aside.

In a large mixing bowl, combine egg, almond paste, and almond extract and beat with an electric mixer on low speed for about 3 minutes, or until the almond paste is thoroughly incorporated and smooth. Add butter and continue beating until it is lightened. Beat in sugar until well blended and smooth. Gradually beat in the dry ingredients and grated chocolate until thoroughly incorporated.

Divide dough in half. Shape each portion into a smooth, evenly thick 13-inch log. Press down each log to form 2¼-inch-wide bars. Trim off and discard ends of bars. Mark and then cut each log crosswise into ½-inch-wide strips. Place strips upright on baking sheets, spacing them about 1¼ inches apart and flattening them slightly so they don't fall over as they bake.

Place on the center oven rack and bake for 11 to 13 minutes, or until tops are almost firm in the center. Remove baking sheets from the oven and let cookies stand for 3 to 4 minutes. Carefully transfer them to wire racks and let stand until cool.

To prepare dark chocolate glaze, combine shortening and bittersweet and unsweetened chocolates in the top of a double boiler over barely simmering water. Heat, stirring occasionally, until mixture is melted and smooth. Remove from heat. Dip the tops of the cookies, one at a time, into the glaze. It should cover their tops and sides. Place glazed bars, glazed side up, on wire racks set over sheets of waxed paper and let stand until glaze sets.

To prepare white chocolate glaze, combine shortening and white chocolate in a small, heavy saucepan over lowest heat. Warm, stirring frequently, until the chocolate is smooth and fluid.

When dark chocolate glaze on cookies is

completely set, drizzle diagonal lines of the white chocolate glaze across the tops of bars. (Piping the glaze through a pastry bag fitted with a fine writing tip will give the most professional finish, but drizzling the glaze from a spoon will look fine, too.) Let bars stand until the chocolate sets.

Store the bars in the refrigerator for up to 2 or 3 days. The cookies may be frozen unglazed, and then glazed after thawing. Once glazed, they should be kept refrigerated.

Makes about 40 2¾-inch bar cookies.

SPICED ALMOND CRISPS
(JANHAGEL)

The Netherlands

Janhagel, the Dutch cookie Americans are most familiar with, is a thin, crisp, cinnamon-spiced rectangle topped with sliced almonds. It is a simple cookie, but quite good.

2	*cups all-purpose or unbleached white flour*
¾	*cup granulated sugar*
1	*teaspoon ground cinnamon*
¼	*teaspoon ground allspice*
¼	*teaspoon salt*
¾	*cup plus 1 tablespoon (1 stick plus 5 tablespoons) cold unsalted butter*
1	*egg white*
1	*cup sliced unblanched almonds*

Preheat the oven to 350 degrees F. Generously grease and flour a 15- by 10-inch jelly roll pan.

Combine flour, sugar, cinnamon, allspice, and salt in a food processor fitted with a steel blade. Process in on/off pulses for 6 to 7 seconds to mix ingredients. Cut the butter into small pieces and sprinkle over dry ingredients. Processing in on/off pulses, cut butter into the flour until the mixture resembles fine crumbs. Continue processing in on/off pulses, gradually adding about 2 to 3 tablespoons cold water through the feed tube, until ingredients begin to hold together. Press into a ball.

Turn dough out onto a 15-inch-long sheet of waxed paper. Cover with another sheet of waxed paper, and using a rolling pin, roll dough out to form an evenly thick rectangle just slightly smaller than the jelly roll pan. (Patch or cut away any uneven places as needed to obtain the right dimensions.) Turn dough over and peel off bottom sheet of waxed paper. Turn dough over and center it directly on the jelly roll pan. Peel off top sheet of waxed paper and patch any tears by pressing dough together.

In a small bowl, beat egg white with 1 tablespoon water. Generously brush dough surface all over with the egg white mixture and immediately sprinkle with almonds, patting them down. Place a sheet of waxed paper over the almonds and press down firmly to imbed them slightly in dough. Using a sharp knife, cut dough into 6 2½-inch strips horizontally and 5 2-inch strips vertically.

Place in the oven and bake for 20 to 25 minutes, or until dough is golden and almonds are nicely browned. Remove baking pan from the oven and let stand on a wire rack for about 5 minutes. Using a sharp knife, retrace cuts previously made in dough. Separate the rectangles and, using a spatula, transfer them to wire racks to cool completely.

Store cookies in an airtight container for up to 1 week. Freeze for longer storage.

Makes 30 2- by 2½-inch rectangles.

CHAPTER 7

♡

SOUTHERN EUROPEAN
COOKIES

PERHAPS IT IS THE ABUNDANCE OF SUNLIGHT, OR the mellow climate, or the warm spirit of the people, but the cookies of Southern Europe seem especially festive and colorful. Often, the cookies of this area also seem to celebrate the bounty of the land: ingredients such as orange and lemon zest, candied citrus peel, almonds, walnuts, raisins, glacéed cherries, and figs frequently appear in recipes.

By far the greatest variety of cookies is produced by the Italians. Over centuries of assimilating and refining culinary ideas and utilizing foodstuffs from neighboring lands and invaders, regional Italian cooks have developed a large and sophisticated repertoire. For example, the Romans borrowed the custom of using almonds in sweets from the Greeks, and citrus fruits, dates, and figs were introduced by Crusaders returning from the Holy Land. A taste for elaborate cookies and pastries in Sicily evolved from sweets introduced by invading nomadic Arab tribes. The modern-day result is a wide variety of cookies, including thin, elegant almond Florentines, rusk-like lemon-scented Anise Biscotti, plump fruit- and honey-stuffed Holiday Fig Cookies, and Lemon-Iced Chocolate Spice Cookies.

The fondness of Italians for cookies is evident not only from their abundance in pastry shops, but also from their lighthearted, colorful names.

Small, square jam-filled butter cookie pockets are known as Sweet Ravioli, and irregularly-shaped, chunky hazelnut and cocoa meringue cookies are called Ugly but Good cookies.

Although the Spaniards and Portuguese don't prepare nearly as many cookies as the Italians do, they, too, enjoy giving their creations whimsical names. For example, thin, elongated butter wafers baked throughout Spain, as well as in France and Italy, are called Cats' Tongues, and the Portuguese have dubbed some simple meringue cookies Sighs.

Like the Italians, the Greeks' taste in sweets has been influenced by neighboring ethnic groups, and by the abundance of fruits and nuts. For example, Phoenician Honey Cookies, which are said to have originated in the ancient Mediterranean kingdom of Phoenicia, are filled with a delicious walnut-orange mixture and dipped in a spiced honey syrup. The Greeks also bake a number of mild-flavored shortbread cookies, (including the Chocolate-Powdered Sugar Fingers in this chapter) reminiscent of those prepared in the Middle East.

There is a strong sense of the color, vitality, and mingling of cultures of Southern Europe evident in the cookies included here. It comes through even when these sweets are recreated in a kitchen thousands of miles away.

Sweet Ravioli (recipe on page 194).

SWEET RAVIOLI
(RAVIOLI DOLCI)

Italy

Whimsical trompe l'oeil cookies that both amuse the eye and please the palate are found in Italy, as well as a number of other European countries. These "sweet ravioli" are, in fact, small square cookie dough pockets filled with cherry jam. The delicate, rich dough is set off nicely by the jam.

The directions for this recipe are particularly detailed and explicit, to make handling the rather soft, buttery dough as easy as possible. The cookies are actually simpler to assemble than it might at first seem.

2½ cups all-purpose or unbleached white flour
⅛ teaspoon salt
¼ teaspoon baking soda

1 cup (2 sticks) unsalted butter, slightly softened
⅔ cup granulated sugar
1 large egg
1½ teaspoons vanilla extract
¼ teaspoon almond extract
    Finely grated zest of 1 medium-sized lemon
¾ to 1 cup cherry preserves

Thoroughly stir together flour, salt, and baking soda. Place butter in a large mixing bowl and beat until light. Add sugar and egg, and beat until smooth and well blended. Add vanilla and almond extracts and lemon zest and beat a few seconds longer. Beat in about half the dry ingredients. As the mixture stiffens, stir in remaining dry ingredients with a wooden spoon until thoroughly incorporated.

Divide dough in half and lay each portion between 13-inch long sheets of waxed paper. Using a rolling pin, roll each half of dough as uniformly as possible into a 12-inch square, about ⅛ inch thick. Check the underside of the dough frequently and smooth out any wrinkles. Very gently peel off top layer of waxed paper and patch and trim dough as necessary to make it perfectly square. Replace waxed paper and slide dough squares onto a large tray or baking sheet. Refrigerate for at least 1 hour, or until very cold and firm. (To speed chilling process, place dough in the freezer for about 35 minutes.)

Preheat the oven to 350 degrees F. Grease several baking sheets and set aside.

Remove one dough square from the refrigerator. Peel off top sheet of waxed paper, and then replace it loosely. Carefully turn square over so underside is facing up and peel off and discard bottom sheet of waxed paper. Measure and mark dough vertically and horizontally at 1½-inch intervals. Using a pastry wheel or large knife, cut the dough as marked into 64 squares, trying not to cut through waxed paper underneath. While the squares are still cold and firm, transfer them to baking sheets, using a spatula, and space about 1¼ inches apart. (If dough becomes too soft to handle, simply slide the waxed paper onto a tray again and refrigerate a few minutes.) Place ½ teaspoon cherry preserves in the center of each square.

Remove the second dough square from the refrigerator. Turn dough over and peel off bottom layer of waxed paper. Replace paper loosely. Turn over dough and remove and discard top sheet of waxed paper. Measure, mark, and then cut the dough horizontally and vertically at 1½-inch intervals as for first half, to make 64 1½-inch squares. Using a fork, prick an "X" in the center of each square. While squares are still cold and firm, transfer them to baking sheets, carefully centering each one over a jelly-topped square; *do not* press down or try to crimp the edges of the two dough squares together at this point. Let the cookies stand for 4 or 5 minutes, or until squares on top begin to warm up and soften. Then, using the tines of a fork, press down around the edges of upper square to tightly seal the two layers. The dough should be soft enough to allow upper square to form a pocket around the preserves rather than causing the preserves to be squeezed out the edges. If necessary, dip fork into powdered sugar to prevent dough from sticking to the tines.

Place in the upper third of the oven and bake for 9 to 11 minutes, or until cookie edges are just tinged with brown. Reverse baking sheets from front to back halfway through baking to ensure even browning. Remove from the oven and let cookies stand on baking sheets for 3 or 4 minutes. Using a spatula, transfer ravioli to wire racks and let stand until cooled completely.

Store in an airtight container for 3 to 4 days. Freeze for longer storage.

Makes 64 1¾-inch cookies.

ANISE BISCOTTI
(PANE ANICE)

Italy

These are dry-crisp, double-baked cookies that look a bit like toasted slices of bread. They have a pleasing anise and lemon flavor.

Recipes for anise biscotti appear frequently in Italian cookbooks.

3	cups all-purpose or unbleached white flour
2	teaspoons ground anise (see Note)
2½	teaspoons baking powder
⅛	teaspoon salt
⅔	cup (1 stick plus 3 tablespoons) unsalted butter, slightly softened
1	cup granulated sugar
3	large eggs
	Finely grated zest of 2 large lemons
¼	teaspoon lemon extract

Preheat the oven to 375 degrees F. Grease a large baking sheet and set aside. Thoroughly stir together flour, anise, baking powder, and salt.

In a large mixing bowl, combine butter and granulated sugar and beat until well blended. Add eggs, lemon zest, and lemon extract and beat until light and fluffy. Gradually beat in about half the dry ingredients. As dough stiffens, stir in remaining dry ingredients with a large wooden spoon. Divide dough in half. Shape each half into a smooth, evenly shaped log about 11 inches long and 2 inches in diameter. (Shaping is easiest if dough is placed in waxed paper, then rolled back and forth until smooth.) Unroll logs from the paper directly onto baking sheet, spacing them as far from one another as possible. Press down logs to flatten them slightly.

Place in the center of the oven and bake for 25 to 28 minutes or until logs are lightly browned. Remove baking sheet from the oven and let logs stand until completely cooled, about 1½ hours. Cut logs diagonally into ½-inch thick slices using a large, sharp knife. Lay slices out flat on baking sheet, return to oven, and toast for 5 to 7 minutes. Turn over slices and bake 4 to 5 minutes on second side. (The longer the baking time, the crisper and drier the slices will be.) Remove from the oven and transfer biscotti to wire racks to cool completely.

Store in an airtight container for up to 2 weeks. Freeze for longer storage.

Makes about 30 3½- to 4-inch biscotti.

Note: A generous ¾ teaspoon anise extract may be substituted for ground anise. Add anise extract at the same time lemon extract is added.

SESAME SEED BISCOTTI
(BISCOTTI DI REGINE)

Italy

Called Queen's Biscotti in Italian, these are plain, crisp-dry, nutty-tasting cookies that Italians enjoy with dessert wine. In fact, these sesame-seed-covered cookies are often dunked in the wine as they are eaten. Thus, in some regions, dry, crisp cookies of this type are known as "wine dunkers."

3¼	cups all-purpose or unbleached white flour
1	tablespoon baking powder
¼	teaspoon salt
¾	cup (1½ sticks) unsalted butter, slightly softened
¾	cup granulated sugar
2	large eggs
2½	teaspoons vanilla extract
¼	teaspoon finely grated lemon zest
1	cup hulled (light colored) sesame seeds
3	tablespoons milk

Thoroughly stir together flour, baking powder, and salt. In a large mixing bowl, beat the butter until very light. Add the sugar and continue beating until fluffy and smooth. Add eggs, vanilla, and lemon zest and beat until blended. Gradually beat in about half the dry ingredients. Stir in remaining dry ingredients with a large wooden spoon.

Divide dough in half. Place each half on a sheet of waxed paper, and shape each into an evenly thick 12-inch long log. Roll logs back and forth in the waxed paper to smooth surface. Then slide them onto a tray or baking sheet. Press down with the hand to flatten logs until about 2½ inches across. Refrigerate for 30 to 40 minutes, or until chilled and firm enough to slice.

Preheat the oven to 350 degrees F. Grease several baking sheets. Spread sesame seeds in a large skillet and place over medium heat. Toast the seeds, stirring or shaking the pan constantly, for 5 to 7 minutes, or until they are just pale brown. Immediately remove from the heat, continuing to stir or shake for 30 seconds. Turn out the sesame seeds into a shallow bowl and let cool slightly. Stir in the milk and let seeds stand, stirring occasionally.

Using a sharp knife, trim off and discard uneven ends of the logs. Mark each log crosswise into about 22 even fingers. Then cut along markings. Roll each finger in moist sesame seeds until coated. Stand fingers upright on baking sheets, spacing about 1¼ inches apart. Carefully press down and flatten fingers slightly to help prevent them from falling over on their sides during baking.

Place in the center of the oven and bake for 17 to 18 minutes, or until golden on top and tinged with brown at the edges. Reverse baking sheets from front to back about halfway through baking to ensure even browning. Remove from the oven and transfer cookies to wire racks. Let stand until cooled completely.

Store in an airtight container for up to a week. Freeze for longer storage.

Makes about 44 2¾-inch-long biscotti.

CHOCOLATE POWDERED SUGAR FINGERS
(KOURAMBIETHES ME SOCOLATA)

Greece and Italy

Tender, buttery, and chocolatey, these little cookies are very appealing. They are rolled in a powdered sugar-cocoa coating, which makes them look attractive too. Brandy, a popular ingredient in Greek cookies, adds a complex flavor note.

Although this recipe is from Greece, I have found small ball-shaped cookies that tasted something like these in Italian bake shops—which proves once again that good food ideas cross international borders.

⅓	cup coarsely chopped walnuts
¾	cup (1½ sticks) unsalted butter, slightly softened
⅔	cup powdered sugar
1	large egg yolk
1	tablespoon brandy
1	tablespoon unsweetened cocoa powder
1½	ounces bittersweet or semisweet chocolate, grated
2	cups all-purpose or unbleached white flour

COATING

½	cup powdered sugar
1	tablespoon unsweetened cocoa powder

Preheat the oven to 325 degrees F. Grease several baking sheets and set aside. Spread the walnuts in a baking pan and toast in the oven, stirring occasionally, for 7 to 8 minutes. Remove from the oven and set nuts aside until cooled. Place cooled nuts in a nut grinder, food processor, or blender and grind to a powder.

Reset oven temperature to 350 degrees F. Place the butter in a large mixing bowl and beat with an electric mixer on medium speed until light and fluffy. Add ⅔ cup powdered sugar and continue beating until thoroughly incorporated and smooth. Beat in egg yolk, brandy, and 1 tablespoon cocoa powder. Beat in the ground walnuts and grated chocolate. Gradually beat in flour; if mixer motor begins to labor, stir in remaining flour by hand.

Pull off 1-inch pieces of dough and roll back and forth on a flat work surface to form plump 2-inch-long fingers. (The dough should be firm enough to handle, but if it is too soft and warm, refrigerate briefly.) Space dough fingers on baking sheets about ¾ inch apart.

Place in the center of the oven and bake for 15 to 16 minutes or until firm on top. Remove from the oven and let stand for 1 to 2 minutes. Using a spatula, transfer cookies to wire racks and let stand until completely cooled.

Sift remaining ½ cup powdered sugar and 1 tablespoon cocoa powder into a small bowl. Remove 2 tablespoons of the mixture and set aside. Dredge cookies in the sugar-cocoa mixture until coated. Just before serving, sift remaining 2 tablespoons of the mixture over the cookies.

Store cookies in an airtight container for up to a week. They may also be frozen before dredging in sugar-cocoa mixture. To serve, allow cookies to thaw, then dredge in coating mixture and sprinkle with reserved sugar and cocoa.

Makes about 45 2½-inch fingers.

PIZZELLE

Italy

Pizzelle are large, thin embossed wafers formed using a special iron a little like a waffle iron. However, most pizzelle irons are not electric and, thus, are held over a burner as they are used.

In the United States pizzelle irons can be purchased in some gourmet cookware stores and from mail order firms carrying European baking supplies (see page 13).

Traditionally, pizzelle are flavored with lemon and anise, but since anise is not as widely used or enjoyed in the United States, vanilla may be substituted in the following recipe.

10   *tablespoons (1 stick plus 2 tablespoons) unsalted butter*
2¼   *cups all-purpose or unbleached white flour*
¼   *teaspoon baking powder*
2   *large eggs*
⅔   *cup granulated sugar*
2   *teaspoons fresh lemon juice*
      Finely grated zest of 1 very large lemon
1   *teaspoon anise extract, or 1 teaspoon vanilla extract*
      Flavorless vegetable oil for brushing over the pizzelle iron

Place butter in a small saucepan and warm over low heat until melted. Remove from the heat and set aside until cooled. Thoroughly stir together the flour and baking powder in a bowl.

Beat the eggs in a mixing bowl with an electric mixer on medium speed until frothy. Add sugar and lemon juice and continue beating until the mixture is light. Beat in lemon zest and anise extract. Add dry ingredients, beating lightly until the mixture is smooth. Lightly beat in the cooled butter until incorporated.

Lightly brush the interior surfaces of a seasoned pizzelle iron (see Note) with vegetable oil, being sure to cover all the grooves and indentations. Heat the iron over medium-high heat on one side and then the other. Continue heating the iron until a drop of water sizzles when sprinkled on the interior surfaces.

Remove iron from the heat and, holding it over waxed paper, drop about 2 tablespoons batter onto the center of one side. Immediately close the iron and scrape off the batter that squeezes out the edges. Place the iron on the burner and bake, turning from one side to the other about every 20 seconds and opening the iron frequently to check the wafer for doneness. When it is light gold on both sides, quickly remove it from the iron, using tongs or a fork, and lay flat on a wire rack until cool. Repeat the process until all batter is used. (Wafers won't usually stick to the grooves of a properly seasoned iron, but if they are difficult to remove, very lightly brush the iron with a paper towel dipped in melted butter after each wafer.)

Store the wafers in an airtight container for 3 or 4 days. Freeze for longer storage.

Makes 14 to 15 5-inch wafers.

Note: Season a new pizzelle iron according to the manufacturer's directions. If no directions are provided, generously coat the interior surfaces of the iron with flavorless vegetable oil and heat the iron directly over medium-high heat. Heat on one side for 10 minutes, and then the other side for about 10 minutes. Let the iron cool to warm and then wipe off any excess oil.

FLORENTINES
(DOLCE ALLA FIORENTINO)

Italy

Brittle-crisp and wafer thin, these popular chocolate-glazed Italian cookies are flavored with orange peel and almonds. They remind me a bit of a thin chocolate brittle candy and are wonderful with after-dinner coffee.

1   cup sliced unblanched almonds
3   tablespoons unsalted butter
3   tablespoons milk
2   tablespoons clover or orange blossom
     honey
1   cup sifted powdered sugar
¼   cup all-purpose or unbleached white
     flour
⅓   cup very finely diced, candied orange
     peel
     Very finely grated zest of 2 medium
     oranges

CHOCOLATE GLAZE
½   teaspoon solid vegetable shortening
3½   ounces semisweet chocolate, coarsely
     chopped
2   ounces unsweetened chocolate,
     coarsely chopped

Preheat the oven to 350 degrees F. Line several baking sheets with aluminum foil cut to fit. Generously grease the foil. Coarsely chop ½ cup of the almonds. Set remaining almonds aside for decoration.

Combine butter, milk, honey, and powdered sugar in a medium saucepan. Bring to a boil, stirring, over medium heat and continue to boil the mixture, stirring, for 30 seconds. Remove saucepan from the heat. Sift flour over the boiled mixture, and stir until smooth. Stir in chopped almonds, candied orange peel, and orange zest.

Drop batter by very small, evenly shaped teaspoonfuls onto the foil, spacing about 3 inches apart. Don't crowd the cookies or make them too large, as they will spread a great deal. Generously sprinkle rounds with the reserved sliced almonds.

Place in the upper third of the oven and bake for 5 to 7 minutes, or until the wafers are rich golden brown, reversing baking sheets from front to back halfway through baking to ensure even browning. Check frequently, as the cookies bake very rapidly once they have begun to color, and make sure to remove them as soon as they are thoroughly baked but not overcooked. (They will be chewy and difficult to remove from the foil if undercooked and taste slightly burned if overcooked.) Remove baking sheets from the oven and let stand for 1 minute. Then carefully transfer foil along with the cookies to a flat surface, and let stand until *completely cooled*. Carefully peel cookies from the foil. (If the florentines stick, either they are under-cooked or the foil was not greased heavily enough.) The foil may be reused, if desired, but must be thoroughly regreased first, and baking sheets should be allowed to cool before reusing. Continue until all the cookies are baked, cooled, and removed from foil. Place them smooth side up on waxed paper.

To prepare the glaze, combine the short-ening and semisweet and unsweetened chocolates in the top of a double boiler over barely simmering water. Warm, stir-ring occasionally, until the mixture is completely melted and smooth.

Using a blunt knife, spread an even layer of warm chocolate glaze over the smooth underside of each cookie. (Don't worry if a bit of the glaze oozes through the lacy holes to the top of the wafers.) Let the wafers stand a few minutes, then draw a pastry comb or the tines of a fork across the chocolate in a wavy pattern for decorative effect, if desired. Let the florentines stand, glazed side up, until the chocolate sets, about 45 minutes. (Speed up setting by placing the wafers in the refrigerator for a few minutes.)

Store the cookies, refrigerated, in airtight containers with sheets of waxed paper between the layers for up to a week. Florentines may be frozen and then thawed in the refrigerator prior to serving, if desired.

Makes about 45 2½-inch wafers.

Cats' Tongues
(Lenguas de Gato)

Spain and France

Popular in both Spain and France, these are thin, crisp, mild-flavored wafers. Their whimsical name comes from the fact that the cookies are long and narrow and—if you stretch your imagination—resemble cats' tongues.

Although this recipe is quite easy to make, it is important to measure carefully. The exact proportion of the ingredients and temperature of the butter will determine how much the wafers spread.

6   tablespoons unsalted butter, very soft
      but not melted
½   cup granulated sugar
2   large egg whites
¼   teaspoon vanilla extract
⅛   teaspoon very finely grated lemon
      zest
½   cup plus 1 tablespoon all-purpose or
      unbleached white flour

Preheat the oven to 400 degrees F. Lightly grease several baking sheets and set aside.

In a small mixing bowl, beat the butter and sugar with an electric mixer on medium speed for 2½ to 3 minutes, or until very light and fluffy. Add the egg whites, vanilla, and lemon zest and beat for 30 seconds longer. Sift the flour over batter and, using a rubber spatula, gently fold it into the mixture until thoroughly incorporated.

Fill a pastry bag fitted with a ⅜-inch-diameter plain tip with the batter by standing the bag in a tall glass, tip down, and folding down the top edge in a cuff about 3½ inches wide. Spoon batter into it until two-thirds full. Then unfold the top and twist it tightly to close. Pipe out *thin*, 2½-inch lengths of batter onto baking sheet, spacing about 2 inches apart. (Do not crowd the cookies or make them too wide, as they spread a lot.) Pat down any "tails" on the lengths of batter using a blunt knife dipped in water.

Place in the upper third of the oven and bake for 4 to 5 minutes, or until cookies are deep golden brown at the edges. Remove baking sheets from the oven and let cookies firm up for 30 seconds. Then, using a spatula, carefully but quickly transfer cookies to wire racks before they become brittle. If they firm too rapidly, return baking sheets to the oven to warm and soften slightly. Let stand until cooled completely. (Let the baking sheets cool completely between batches, or the dough will overheat and spread too much. Re-grease baking sheets before reusing.)

Store the wafers in airtight containers for up to a week. Freeze for longer storage.

Makes about 50 3-inch-long wafers.

HAZELNUT SUGAR DUSTIES
(POLVORONES DE AVELLANAS)

Spain

These cookies remind me of pecan butter balls, the powdered-sugar-coated little pecan shortbreads popular in the American South. However, since sugar dusties are made with hazelnuts, they have an entirely different taste. People who like the distinctive flavor of hazelnuts always love these rich, tender cookies.

A writer friend of mine who set one of her recent novels in Spain brought this recipe back from a research trip to Madrid.

⅔	cup whole hazelnuts
¾	cup (1½ sticks) unsalted butter, slightly softened
⅓	cup granulated sugar
1	egg yolk
⅛	teaspoon salt
1¾	cups all-purpose or unbleached white flour

COATING
½	cup sifted powdered sugar

Preheat the oven to 325 degrees F. Grease several baking sheets and set aside. Spread hazelnuts in a large baking pan and toast in the oven, stirring occasionally, for 16 to 17 minutes, or until the hulls begin to loosen and the nuts are tinged with brown. Set the nuts aside to cool. Reset oven temperature to 375 degrees F.

When hazelnuts are cool enough to handle, remove hulls by vigorously rubbing a handful of nuts at a time between palms or in a clean kitchen towel. Discard the bits of skin as you work. (It's difficult to remove all bits sticking to nuts, but they should be relatively free of hull.) Grind hazelnuts to a powder using a nut grinder, food processor, or blender.

Place butter in a large mixing bowl and beat with an electric mixer on medium speed until light and fluffy. Add granulated sugar and continue beating until thoroughly incorporated and smooth. Beat in egg yolk and salt. Stir in the hazelnuts. Gradually beat in the flour. If the mixer motor begins to labor, stir in last of the flour with a wooden spoon. Pull off small pieces of dough and shape into 1-inch balls. Place on baking sheets about 1 inch apart.

Place in the upper third of the oven and bake for 15 to 17 minutes or until just barely brown at the edges. Remove baking sheets from the oven and let stand for 1 to 2 minutes. Using a spatula, transfer cookies to wire racks and let stand until completely cooled.

Place powdered sugar in a shallow bowl and dredge cooled cookies in sugar until coated all over.

Store in an airtight container for up to a week. If freezing cookies for longer storage, freeze before dredging in sugar. Allow to thaw and dredge just before serving.

Makes about 45 1¼-inch cookies.

Ugly but Good Chocolate Cookies
(Brutti ma Buoni al Cacao)

Italy

Despite the whimsical name, these cookies are not really ugly, just homey rather than chic looking. The flavor combination, on the other hand, is rather sophisticated.

The cookies taste like chocolate hazelnut macaroons, but have a chunky texture and irregular shape. They smell wonderful as they bake, and most chocolate and hazelnut fans love them.

½   cup whole, unblanched hazelnuts
½   cup slivered blanched almonds
1   ounce unsweetened chocolate
3   large egg whites, completely free of any yolk
     Pinch of salt
½   teaspoon instant coffee powder or granules
2¾   cups powdered sugar
6   tablespoons unsweetened cocoa powder
½   teaspoon almond extract
½   teaspoon vanilla extract

Preheat the oven to 325 degrees F. Spread hazelnuts in a baking pan and place in the oven. Toast, stirring occasionally, for 16 to 17 minutes or until the hulls begin to loosen and the nuts are fragrant. Spread almonds in a separate pan and toast, stirring occasionally, for 6 minutes. Set nuts aside to cool. Place chocolate in the top of a double boiler set over barely simmering water and warm until melted. Set aside to cool to barely warm.

Reset oven temperature to 350 degrees F. Line several baking sheets with baking parchment.

When the hazelnuts are cool enough to handle, remove hulls by vigorously rubbing a handful of nuts at a time between the palms or in a clean kitchen towel, discarding bits of skin as you work. (It's usually difficult to remove all bits sticking to nuts, but they should be relatively free of hull.) Coarsely chop hazelnuts and almonds and set aside.

In a completely grease-free mixing bowl, combine egg whites, salt, and coffee powder. Let stand for 5 minutes to allow coffee powder to soften. Then beat with electric mixer on medium speed until frothy. Increase mixer speed to high and beat until well mixed and fluffy. Continue beating, gradually adding powdered sugar, then cocoa powder and vanilla and almond extracts. Beat until mixture is stiff, smooth, and glossy. Stir in melted chocolate and chopped nuts until thoroughly incorporated, but do not overmix.

Drop dough by heaping teaspoonfuls onto parchment-lined baking sheets, spacing cookies about 1½ inches apart. Place in the center of the oven and bake for 11 to 13 minutes, or until almost firm to the touch. (For chewy cookies underbake slightly; for crispy, dry ones overbake slightly.) Cookies will puff and enlarge during baking. Remove baking sheets from the oven and let cookies stand for 1 to 2 minutes. Then slide the parchment from baking sheets to a flat surface and let the cookies stand until cooled completely. Carefully peel cooled cookies from parchment.

Store in an airtight container for 3 or 4 days. Freeze for longer storage.

Makes 40 to 45 2¼- to 2½-inch cookies.

LEMON-ICED CHOCOLATE SPICE COOKIES

(BISCOTTI DI CIOCCOLATA)

Italy

The flavors of chocolate, raisins, citrus, and spice blend beautifully in this traditional Southern European cookie. The cookies bake into small evenly shaped mounds which are then lightly iced with a lemon glaze. During the holidays, these cookies are often decorated with bits of candied citrus peel. They are particularly popular in Sicily, but are baked in other parts of Italy also.

1¼   cups dark seedless raisins
3   tablespoons orange juice
3   cups all-purpose or unbleached white flour
½   cup unsweetened cocoa powder
¾   teaspoon baking powder
½   teaspoon baking soda
1   teaspoon ground cinnamon
1   teaspoon ground allspice
¾   teaspoon ground ginger
½   teaspoon ground nutmeg
1   cup plus 2 tablespoons (2¼ sticks) unsalted butter, slightly softened
1   cup granulated sugar
1   large egg
2   teaspoons vanilla extract
  Finely grated zest of 1 small orange
  Finely grated zest of 1 small lemon
4   ounces bittersweet or semisweet chocolate, coarsely grated

LEMON GLAZE
1½   cups powdered sugar
2   tablespoons fresh lemon juice
1   tablespoon orange juice

DECORATION
¼   cup diced candied citrus peel (optional)

Preheat the oven to 350 degrees F. Grease several baking sheets.

Combine raisins and orange juice in a small bowl, and set aside to allow raisins to plump for at least 10 minutes. Meanwhile, sift together flour, cocoa powder, baking powder, baking soda, cinnamon, allspice, ginger, and nutmeg.

Place butter in a large mixing bowl and beat until light. Add sugar and continue beating until well blended and smooth. Beat in egg, vanilla, and orange and lemon zests. Beat in about half the dry ingredients. Stir in raisin-orange mixture and grated chocolate. Stir in remaining dry ingredients using a large wooden spoon.

Pull off pieces of dough and roll between palms into 1-inch balls. (If dough seems too soft to roll, cover and refrigerate briefly before continuing.) Space the balls about 1¼ inches apart on baking sheets.

Place in the center of the oven and bake for 7 to 9 minutes, or until cookies are almost firm when gently pressed on top. Remove baking sheets from the oven and let cookies firm for 2 to 3 minutes. Using a spatula, transfer them to wire racks. Glaze cookies while they are still slightly warm.

To prepare glaze, sift powdered sugar into a small, deep bowl. Add lemon juice and orange juice and stir until smooth. The mixture should be thin and rather runny; add a few more drops of orange juice, if needed.

One at a time, dip tops of warm cookies into the glaze, then immediately turn each cookie right side up and place on wire racks set over waxed paper. If desired, press a piece of candied citrus peel into the center of each cookie. Let cookies stand until the glaze sets, about 40 minutes.

Store glazed cookies in an airtight container for up to a week. Freeze for longer storage.

Makes 60 to 65 1¾-inch cookies.

Chocolate-Orange Sandwich Wafers
(Biscotti Milano)

Italy

In this recipe, buttery, orange-flavored oblong wafers are sandwiched together with chocolate, and their ends are dipped in a satiny chocolate glaze. The finished cookies look wonderful, and are an irresistible accompaniment to a cup of cappuccino.

1⅓   cups all-purpose or unbleached white flour
⅛   teaspoon salt
¾   cup (1½ sticks) unsalted butter, slightly softened
⅔   cup granulated sugar
1   large egg
1¼   teaspoons vanilla extract
    Finely grated zest of 1 small orange
    Finely grated zest of half of a small lemon

Chocolate Glaze
1½   ounces unsweetened chocolate
1¼   cups powdered sugar
1   tablespoon unsweetened cocoa powder
¾   teaspoon light corn syrup
4   to 5 tablespoons hot coffee or water

Preheat the oven to 375 degrees F. Lightly grease several baking sheets. Thoroughly combine flour and salt; set aside.

Place the butter in a small mixing bowl and beat with an electric mixer on medium speed for about 2½ minutes, or until very light and fluffy. Add sugar and beat until smooth. Add egg and continue beating until thoroughly blended and smooth. Add vanilla and beat a few seconds longer. Gradually beat in dry ingredients until thoroughly incorporated. Stir in orange and lemon zests until well mixed.

Spoon dough into a pastry bag fitted with a ⅜-inch-diameter plain or star tip. Pipe dough out onto baking sheets to form thin 2-inch-long strips about 3 inches apart. (Do not crowd the cookies, as they spread quite a bit.) Using a table knife, gently smooth down any points left at the ends of the strips.

Bake wafers, one baking sheet at a time, in the upper third of the oven for 7 to 9 minutes, or until cookies are golden brown around the edges. Reverse baking sheet from front to back about halfway through baking to ensure even browning. Remove baking sheet from the oven and let cookies firm up for 30 seconds. Using a spatula, carefully but quickly loosen cookies from baking sheet before they become brittle and transfer them to wire racks. (If the cookies cool too rapidly and are difficult to remove, return baking sheet to the oven for 1 to 2 minutes to reheat.) Let stand until cool. Baking sheets must be scraped with a spatula to remove crumbs, cooled thoroughly, and then regreased before being used again. Repeat with remaining dough.

To prepare glaze, warm chocolate in the top of a double boiler set over very gently simmering water, stirring occasionally, until melted and smooth. Remove from the heat. Sift powdered sugar and cocoa powder into a small bowl. Stir in corn syrup and 3 tablespoons of the hot coffee until smooth and well blended. Add mixture to the melted chocolate and stir until glossy and smooth. If necessary, add a bit more coffee until glaze is fairly thin but not runny.

Using a blunt knife, place a dab or two of glaze in the center of the underside of one wafer. (It isn't necessary to spread out the glaze as it will be squeezed outward when the two wafers are sandwiched together.) Gently press the bottom of another wafer against the glaze to form a sandwich. Repeat until all the wafers are used.

Return double boiler to the heat and gently rewarm the glaze, stirring occasionally, until warm but not hot. Add enough of the remaining hot coffee to give the glaze a liquefied, slightly runny consistency. One at a time, dip about ½ inch of one end of each cookie into the glaze until coated, tipping saucepan slightly if necessary. Remove cookie, and hold vertically over saucepan for a moment to allow the excess glaze to drip off. Then lightly scrape the tip of the end against the saucepan to remove more excess glaze. Place cookies on wire racks and let stand a minute or two until glaze is partially set. Then, one at a time, holding cookies in the middle, dip the other end of each into the chocolate. Drain, scrape off, and return to wire rack, allowing ends to overhang rack. Let stand until the glaze is completely set, about 45 minutes.

Store cookies in an airtight container for 4 or 5 days. The plain wafers may also be frozen for up to 10 days, and then assembled and glazed shortly before serving time, if desired.

Makes about 30 2¾-inch-long sandwich cookies.

RICOTTA-ORANGE-CHOCOLATE TARTLETS (CASSATINE)

Italy

A specialty of Sicily, cassatine are dainty cookie shells filled with ricotta cheese, citrus, chocolate, and almonds. Sicilian cooks have a reputation for producing wonderful desserts and pastries, and these delicious tartlets are doubtless one of the reasons why. Cassatine are similar to the well-known fried pastries, cannolis.

The cookie shells and ricotta filling can be prepared ahead, but the tartlets should not be assembled until an hour or two before serving time or they will lose their crispness.

DOUGH
⅔ cup slivered blanched almonds
7 tablespoons unsalted butter, slightly softened
⅓ cup granulated sugar
¼ teaspoon finely grated lemon zest
⅛ teaspoon finely grated orange zest
⅛ teaspoon salt
1 tablespoon plus 1 teaspoon orange juice
1 cup plus 2 tablespoons all-purpose or unbleached white flour

FILLING
1⅓ cups well-drained ricotta cheese
⅓ cup powdered sugar
½ teaspoon vanilla extract
⅛ teaspoon finely grated lemon zest

⅛   teaspoon finely grated orange zest
⅛   teaspoon ground nutmeg
4   ounces bittersweet or semisweet
     chocolate, finely chopped

Preheat the oven to 325 degrees F. Spread the almonds in a baking pan. Place in the oven and toast, stirring occasionally, for 6 to 8 minutes, or until nicely colored. Remove from the oven and let stand until cool. Divide almonds in half and set one half aside for decorating tartlets. Place remaining almonds in a food processor or blender and process until finely ground.

Reset the oven temperature to 375 degrees F. Very generously grease two 12-muffin, mini-muffin tins. (The cups of the tins should be about 1¼ inches in diameter at the bottom and 1¾ inches in diameter at the top.)

To prepare the dough, combine butter, granulated sugar, lemon zest, and orange zest in a small mixing bowl and beat with an electric mixer on medium speed until smooth and fluffy. Beat in the salt, orange juice, and ground almonds. Beat in the flour until incorporated but not overmixed.

Divide the dough in half. Place each half between sheets of waxed paper and roll out to ⅛-inch thick, smoothing out any creases that form on the underside. Slide the dough sheets onto a baking sheet and refrigerate for 15 to 20 minutes, or until cool and firm but not hard.

Working with one dough sheet at a time and leaving the other refrigerated, peel off the bottom sheet of waxed paper and then replace it. Turn dough right side up and peel off and discard the top sheet of waxed paper. Using a plain 2¼-inch cutter or the rim of a liqueur or sherry glass, cut out rounds. Gather dough scraps and re-roll between sheets of waxed paper. Repeat with

the second dough sheet and continue cutting out the dough until there are 24 rounds; discard any excess dough. Center each round of dough in a muffin cup and firmly press and smooth into the bottom and sides of each cup. Prick the dough all over with the tines of a fork. Continue until all the tartlet shells are formed.

Place in the center of the oven and bake shells 8 to 10 minutes, or until they are lightly browned at the edges. Remove muffin tins from the oven and immediately run the point of a small knife around the edges of the shells to loosen them. Let stand a few minutes until the shells are cool. Carefully lift shells from the cups, using the point of a knife if further loosening is necessary, and place on wire racks until cooled completely.

To prepare the filling, gently stir together ricotta cheese, powdered sugar, vanilla, lemon zest, orange zest, and nutmeg in a medium bowl until blended. Stir in about 3 ounces of the chopped chocolate, reserving the remainder for decoration.

Spoon about 1 tablespoon filling into each cookie shell (or enough to completely fill it). Sprinkle the top of each tartlet generously with some of the reserved almonds. Then sprinkle lightly with the reserved chocolate. Continue until all the tartlets are assembled.

The tartlets should be served within an hour or two of being assembled. The cookie shells may be stored, airtight, for 2 or 3 days or frozen for longer storage. The filling may be prepared and stored in the refrigerator for 24 hours, if desired.

Makes 24 1½-inch tartlets.

PHOENICIAN HONEY COOKIES
(PHOENÉKIA)

Greece

These are popular in Greece, particularly on the islands, where they are baked for New Year's celebrations. Soaked with honey and flavored with orange, spice, and walnuts, the oblong cookies are aromatic and pleasantly crisp. They are said to have been brought to the region by the Phoenicians; hence their name. Early versions called for olive oil, but modern cooks generally use butter or a combination of butter and vegetable oil.

Phoenician honey cookies aren't difficult to make, but they are a bit time-consuming. Traditionally, they are stamped with a design, using either a special cookie stamp or the raised lines of a cut-glass bowl pressed into the surface. The tines of a fork may be pressed into cookie tops if neither a stamp nor a cut-glass bowl is available.

FILLING
¾   cup clover honey, or other mild honey
½   cup granulated sugar
½   cup orange juice
1   4-inch cinnamon stick
5   whole cloves
    Pinch of finely grated orange zest
½   tablespoon brandy
1   cup finely chopped walnuts
    Finely grated zest of 1 medium orange

DOUGH
3   cups all-purpose or unbleached white flour
½   teaspoon baking soda
½   teaspoon baking powder
¼   teaspoon salt
¾   teaspoon ground cinnamon
½   teaspoon ground cloves
¼   teaspoon ground nutmeg
½   cup (1 stick) unsalted butter, slightly softened
½   cup granulated sugar
½   cup flavorless vegetable oil
¼   cup orange juice
2   tablespoons brandy

DECORATION
¼   cup finely chopped walnuts (optional)

To prepare filling, combine honey, sugar, orange juice, cinnamon stick, cloves, and pinch of orange zest in a medium saucepan. Bring to a boil over medium-high heat and boil, stirring occasionally, for 5 minutes. Strain syrup through a fine sieve, discarding spices. Stir brandy into syrup. Pour ¼ cup of warm syrup into a small bowl and stir in 1 cup chopped walnuts, and zest of medium orange; set aside. Pour remaining syrup back into saucepan and set aside.

Preheat the oven to 350 degrees F. Grease several baking sheets.

To prepare dough, thoroughly stir together flour, baking soda, baking powder, salt, cinnamon, cloves, and nutmeg. Place butter and sugar in a large mixing bowl and beat with an electric mixer on medium speed until light. Add oil, orange juice, and brandy and beat on low speed until well blended and smooth. Gradually beat in about half the dry ingredients. Using a large wooden spoon, stir in remaining dry ingredients to form a smooth, soft dough.

Pinch off pieces of dough and roll each between palms to form small logs about 1¾ inches long and ½ inch in diameter. Using a finger, press down along the length of each log to form a trough. Spoon a generous ¾ teaspoon walnut filling along indentation of each log. Then, pinch the

dough back together around filling to seal well. Place logs, seam-sides down, on a baking sheet, spacing them about 1½ inches apart. Smooth and reform each into an evenly shaped, 2¼-inch long log. Continue in this manner until all cookies are formed. If desired, decorate tops of logs by imprinting with a deeply grooved cookie stamp, the rim of a cut-glass bowl, or the tines of a fork. Smooth cookies back into a log shape if necessary.

Place in the center of the oven and bake for 18 to 22 minutes, or until light brown all over. Remove from the oven and let stand for several minutes.

Meanwhile, warm syrup remaining in saucepan gently over low heat. Remove cookies from baking sheets and dip the top of each into the warm syrup. Arrange dipped cookies on large plates or serving platters. If desired, sprinkle cookies with a few chopped walnuts.

Cover platters tightly with plastic wrap and let cookies stand overnight, or for at least 4 hours, until the honey is absorbed and the flavors mellow. Store cookies in an airtight container for up to a week. Freeze for longer storage.

Makes 34 to 36 2½-inch long cookies.

ORANGE COOKIES
(KOULOURAKIA)

Greece

Traditionally, koulourakia are formed into rings, half circles, figure 8's, S-curves, Greek letters, and other simple shapes before baking. The cookies have an unusual orange and walnut flavor. A food processor is needed for this recipe.

¼	cup chopped walnuts
2	cups all-purpose or unbleached white flour
¾	teaspoon baking powder
½	teaspoon baking soda
	Pinch ground cloves
	Zest of 1 small orange
	Zest of 1 small lemon
¾	cup granulated sugar
2	tablespoons flavorless vegetable oil
6	tablespoons (¾ stick) unsalted butter, slightly softened
1	large egg
1	large egg yolk
1	tablespoon brandy, or orange juice
2	to 3 tablespoons powdered sugar for garnish (optional)

Preheat the oven to 325 degrees F. Spread the walnuts in a baking pan and place in the oven. Toast, stirring occasionally, for 7 to 8 minutes. Set aside to cool.

Thoroughly stir together flour, baking powder, baking soda, and cloves. Combine orange and lemon zests and sugar in a food processor fitted with a steel blade.

Process for several minutes until zests are finely minced. Stop the processor and scrape down sides several times. Add cooled walnuts and vegetable oil and continue processing until walnuts are puréed. Transfer the zest-walnut mixture to a small bowl and set aside.

Place butter in processor and process for about 1 minute or until light and creamy. Add zest-walnut mixture, egg, egg yolk, and brandy and continue processing until well mixed. Sprinkle in dry ingredients and process in on/off pulses until ingredients are just mixed; do not overprocess. Divide dough in half and wrap each half in waxed paper. Refrigerate until cold and fairly stiff, at least 1½ hours.

Reset oven temperature to 350 degrees F. Lightly grease several baking sheets. Working with one dough half at a time and keeping the other half refrigerated, pull off 1-inch pieces of dough. Quickly roll each piece back and forth on a sheet of waxed paper to form a 4½- to 6-inch long rope. Try not to overhandle dough or it will become too warm and be difficult to manage. Space the ropes about 2 inches apart on baking sheets and form each into a ring, half-circle, S-curve, cane, loop, horse shoe, or other simple shape.

Place in the center of the oven and bake for 10 to 12 minutes, or until light golden brown on top and slightly darker at edges. Turn baking sheets from front to back about halfway through baking to ensure even browning. Remove from the oven and let stand for about 3 minutes. Then transfer cookies to wire racks and let stand until cooled completely. If desired, very lightly sift powdered sugar over the cookies just before serving.

Store in an airtight container for up to a week. Freeze for longer storage.

Makes about 30 2½-inch cookies.

HOLIDAY FIG COOKIES
(CUCIDATA)

Italy

These attractive holiday cookies are stuffed with a colorful mix of figs, candied cherries, golden raisins, and nuts. They are made by tucking filling into the center of logs of dough and then cutting the logs crosswise into slices.

FILLING
1½	cups (about 10 ounces) finely chopped dried Calimyrna figs
1	cup (about 6 ounces) chopped candied cherries
1	cup coarsely chopped golden raisins
½	cup clover honey, or other mild honey
2	tablespoons orange juice
1	teaspoon ground cinnamon
½	teaspoon ground allspice
	Finely grated zest of 1 medium orange

DOUGH
3⅔	cups all-purpose or unbleached white flour
1½	teaspoons baking powder
⅛	teaspoon salt
¾	cup (1½ sticks) unsalted butter, slightly softened
¾	cup granulated sugar
2	large eggs
	Finely grated zest of 1 medium orange

In a large bowl, stir together figs, cherries, raisins, honey, orange juice, cinnamon, allspice, and orange zest until well mixed. Cover and refrigerate for at least 30 minutes or up to 24 hours, if desired.

Thoroughly stir together flour, baking powder, and salt in a large bowl. In a large mixing bowl, beat together butter and sugar until well blended. Add eggs and orange zest and beat until light and fluffy. Gradually beat in dry ingredients. If the mixer motor labors, stir in the last of the dry ingredients using a large wooden spoon. Divide dough in half. Shape each half into a smooth, evenly thick log 1¾ inches in diameter and 13 inches long. Press and mold the dough with the side of the hand to make a 2-inch-wide trough down the center of each log. Spoon half the filling down the length of each trough. Pinch the dough back together to cover the filling and smooth logs by placing each in waxed paper and rolling back and forth. Wrap each log tightly in waxed paper. Slide logs onto a baking sheet and freeze for 2½ to 3 hours, or until firm. (The logs may be held in the freezer for up to 2 weeks if wrapped airtight.)

Preheat the oven to 350 degrees F. Generously grease several baking sheets and set aside. Using a large, sharp knife, cut the frozen logs crosswise into ¼-inch-thick slices. Lay them with a cut side down about 1¼ inches apart on the baking sheets.

Place in the center of the oven and bake the cookies for 13 to 15 minutes, or until lightly browned at the edges. Remove from the oven and, using a spatula and working carefully, *immediately* transfer the cookies to wire racks and let stand until completely cooled. (The filling will stick to the sheets as it cools.)

Store in an airtight container for up to 10 days. Freeze for longer storage.

Makes 70 to 80 2¾- to 3-inch slices.

CHAPTER 8

EASTERN EUROPEAN
COOKIES

IN EASTERN EUROPE COOKIES HAVE AS MUCH TO DO with heritage and tradition as sustenance. Many popular recipes are centuries old and provide glimpses into the culinary tastes as well as the political and social history of the region.

Among the most often prepared sweets here are simple honey cookies, descendents of the very earliest little dessert cakes eaten in Europe. Once international trade made cane sugar abundant on the Continent, the use of honey as a sweetener gradually declined in many areas, and more sophisticated sugar-based recipes were devised. However, throughout the Balkan and Baltic states and in neighboring areas people steadfastly preserved the old customs. The Poles, who are famous for producing superior honey and have had a beekeeping industry since pagan times, bake numerous "honey cakes," including the chewy-crisp Almond-Honey Cookies in this chapter. The Yugoslavians also make honey cookies, most notably thick, cinnamon-flavored cakes called Medenjaci. In Hungary, gaily iced heart-shaped cookies sold as love tokens have long been a favorite at country fairs.

Particularly distinctive among Eastern European sweets are those that pair honey and poppy seeds, another hallmark regional ingredient. In some recipes, such as the appealing Bulgarian Honey-Poppy Seed Rolled Cookies presented here, the tiny bluish-black seeds are simply sprinkled over the cookies to add a pleasant crunch and nutty flavor. In others, like the tender Poppy Seed-Filled Cookies, ground poppy seeds and honey combine to form an unusual, exotic-tasting filling.

In addition to honey cakes, there are some fine old-fashioned butter cookies in the Eastern European repertoire. In Hungary, where the dazzling baking tradition of the Hapsburg Empire lingers, elegant jam-topped Hussar's Kisses, Rum-Butter Cookies, and Almond Tea Cakes are typical offerings. During Easter and other holidays, cooks in Poland and the Baltic states also make a variety of butter- and egg-rich cookies. Indeed, the incredible abundance of these ingredients in some heirloom recipes indicates that most local societies were (and still are) agrarian; even in hard times farming could satisfy family dairy needs.

Over the centuries, change and turmoil have been a part of the social landscape in Eastern Europe. Nevertheless, the custom of traditional cookie baking endures. This simple pleasure provides a comforting link with the past and a sense of continuity for succeeding generations.

Apricot Tea Cookies (recipe on page 218).

APRICOT TEA COOKIES
(CIASTKA Z KONSERWA)

Poland

Studded with almonds and garnished with dabs of apricot preserves, these tender, citrus-scented cookies are delicious, with tea or without. Tea time in Poland lasts from about three to six p.m., and tea is usually served, garnished with lemon slices, in tall, thin glasses. The Poles take their afternoon tea at home or in tea shops.

1	cup (2 sticks) unsalted butter, slightly softened
1/8	teaspoon salt
1/3	cup granulated sugar
3/4	cup apricot preserves
1	large egg yolk
1/2	teaspoon baking powder
1/8	teaspoon almond extract
	Finely grated zest of 1 large lemon
1/4	teaspoon finely grated orange zest
2½	cups all-purpose or unbleached white flour
1	cup finely chopped blanched almonds

Preheat the oven to 375 degrees F. Grease several baking sheets. Place butter in a mixing bowl and beat with the mixer on medium speed until light and smooth. Add the salt, sugar, and ¼ cup of the apricot preserves and beat until well blended and smooth. Beat in egg yolk, baking powder, almond extract, lemon zest, and orange zest until well blended. Gradually beat in flour until incorporated. Spread almonds in a shallow bowl.

Pinch off 1-inch diameter pieces of dough and roll into balls between the palms. (The dough should be firm enough to handle at this point, but if it seems too soft refrigerate it for 5 to 10 minutes until it firms slightly.) Roll each ball in the chopped almonds until coated and space on baking sheets about 1½ inches apart. Press a deep indentation in the center of each cookie using your knuckle or thumb.

Place in the center of the oven and bake for 5 minutes. Remove from the oven and fill the indentations with about ½ teaspoon apricot preserves. Return cookies to the oven to bake 6 to 8 minutes longer, or until they are just tinged with brown and the preserves are melting. Remove from the oven and let stand on the baking sheets for 2 to 3 minutes. Then transfer cookies to wire racks to cool, handling carefully as they are fragile and slightly crumbly.

Store the cookies in an airtight container with waxed paper between the layers for up to a week. Freeze for longer storage.

Makes about 45 1½-inch cookies.

ALMOND-HONEY COOKIES
(PIERNICZKI Z MIGDAŁAMI)

Poland

Honey and almonds are both used frequently in Polish baked goods, and their flavors blend nicely in this recipe. Decorated with an almond half and egg white glaze, these cookies are handsome and crunchy-crisp.

2½   cups all-purpose or unbleached white
     flour
½   teaspoon baking soda
⅛   teaspoon salt
¾   cup (1½ sticks) unsalted butter,
     slightly softened
⅓   cup clover honey, or other mild
     honey
⅔   cup granulated sugar
1   teaspoon vanilla extract
½   teaspoon almond extract
1   large egg, separated
20   to 25 whole blanched almonds,
     halved lengthwise

Thoroughly stir together flour, baking soda, and salt. Place butter, honey, and sugar in a large mixing bowl and beat until lightened and smooth. Beat in vanilla and almond extracts and egg yolk. (Reserve egg white for brushing over cookies.) Beat in about half the dry ingredients. Stir in remaining dry ingredients using a large wooden spoon. Divide dough in half and wrap each half in plastic wrap. Refrigerate dough for at least 1½ hours or until chilled and slightly firm, but not stiff.

Preheat the oven to 350 degrees F. Grease several baking sheets. Working with one portion at a time and leaving the other refrigerated, roll dough out on a floured surface to a generous ⅛-inch thick. Lift dough several times and dust rolling pin frequently to prevent dough from sticking.

Cut out cookies using a 2¼-inch or slightly larger scalloped, fluted, or plain round cutter or the rim of a drinking glass. Using a spatula, transfer cookies to baking sheets, spacing about 1½ inches apart. Gather dough scraps, re-roll, and continue cutting out cookies until all dough is used. Repeat the rolling and cutting out process with the second half of dough.

In a small bowl, beat together reserved egg white and 1½ tablespoons water with a fork until well blended. Press an almond half into the center of each cookie, then, using a pastry brush or paper towel, very lightly but thoroughly brush entire top of each with egg wash.

Place in the center of the oven and bake for 8 to 10 minutes, or until cookies are golden all over and just slightly darker around edges. (The longer the baking time, the crunchier cookies will be.) Remove baking sheets from the oven and let stand for about 2 minutes. Using a spatula, transfer cookies to wire racks and let stand until completely cooled.

Store cookies in an airtight container for up to 10 days. Freeze for longer storage.

Makes 40 to 50 2½- to 2¾-inch cookies.

Almond Tea Cakes
(Kis Sütemény)

Hungary

These resemble American sugar cookies, except that the dough contains finely ground almonds and has a light almond flavor. The cookies are also garnished with chopped almonds instead of cinnamon-sugar or nonpareils as sugar cookies often are.

Hungarians serve these with afternoon tea or coffee, but you don't have to wait for tea time to enjoy them. They are just fine with milk, apple cider, cocoa—or with nothing at all.

2¼	cups all-purpose or unbleached white flour
¾	teaspoon baking powder
⅔	cup finely chopped slivered blanched almonds
¾	cup (1½ sticks) unsalted butter, slightly softened
¾	cup plus 1 tablespoon granulated sugar
2	large egg yolks
1¼	teaspoons vanilla extract
¼	teaspoon almond extract
1	large egg white

Thoroughly stir together the flour and baking powder in a bowl. Grind ⅓ cup almonds to a powder in a food processor, blender, or nut grater. Set the remaining almonds aside for decoration.

Place the butter in a mixing bowl and beat with an electric mixer on medium speed until light. Add sugar and beat until fluffy. Add egg yolks and vanilla and almond extracts and continue beating until thoroughly blended and smooth. Gradually beat in dry ingredients. If the mixer motor labors, stir in the last of the dry ingredients using a large wooden spoon. Divide dough in half, and wrap each half in plastic wrap. Refrigerate for about 45 minutes, or until cool and firm but not hard.

Preheat the oven to 375 degrees F. Grease several baking sheets and set aside.

Working with half of dough at a time and keeping the other half refrigerated, roll out between sheets of waxed paper to ⅛-inch thick. Check the underside of the dough frequently and smooth out any creases that form. Turn dough over and peel off the bottom sheet of waxed paper, then replace it loosely. Turn dough right side up again and peel off and discard top sheet of paper. Cut out cookies using a 2½-inch or similar scalloped round cutter or assorted 2- to 3-inch cutters. Then using a spatula, transfer cookies to baking sheets, spacing about 1½ inches apart. Gather dough scraps and re-roll between sheets of waxed paper. Repeat the cutting out process. Repeat the procedure with the second dough half.

In a small bowl, lightly beat egg white with 1 tablespoon water. Lightly brush cookie tops with egg white mixture. Immediately sprinkle tops with the reserved chopped almonds.

Place in the center of the oven and bake for 6 to 9 minutes, or until cookies are just beginning to brown at the edges. Remove baking sheets from the oven and allow cookies to firm up for 2 minutes. Using a spatula, immediately transfer them to wire racks and let stand until cooled completely.

Store the cookies in an airtight container for up to 1 week. Freeze for longer storage.

Makes about 40 2¾-inch scalloped cookies.

DOUBLE-BAKED HAZELNUT SLICES
(SUKHARIKI)

Russia

Like Italian biscotti, these dry, crisp cookies are formed by shaping the dough into a loaf and cutting it into slices after baking. The slices are then returned to the oven and baked again until they develop a wonderful crunchy, rusk-like texture. They are loaded with hazelnuts and have a great flavor. Hazelnut slices are often served with tea.

1½   cups whole hazelnuts
2   cups all-purpose or unbleached white
     flour
½   teaspoon baking powder
⅛   teaspoon salt
¼   cup (½ stick) unsalted butter, slightly
     softened
1   cup granulated sugar
2   large eggs
¼   teaspoon vanilla extract

Preheat the oven to 325 degrees F. Grease a large baking sheet and set aside.

Spread hazelnuts in a baking pan. Place in the oven, and toast, stirring occasionally, for 17 to 18 minutes, or until the hulls begin to loosen and the nuts are slightly colored. Remove nuts from the oven and set aside to cool. Reset the oven temperature to 350 degrees F.

When the hazelnuts are cool enough to handle, remove the dark hulls by vigorously rubbing a handful of nuts at a time between the fingers or in a clean kitchen towel, discarding the bits of hull as you work. (It's all right if some bits of hull don't come off completely.) Coarsely but evenly chop hazelnuts, preferably by hand. (The nuts should be in distinct pieces, and most food processors produce too many small crumbly bits.) Set the nuts aside.

Thoroughly stir together flour, baking powder, and salt in a bowl.

In a large mixing bowl, beat the butter and granulated sugar together until well blended. Add the eggs and vanilla and beat until light and fluffy. Gradually beat in about half the dry ingredients. Using a large wooden spoon, stir in hazelnuts until distributed throughout. Stir in remaining dry ingredients.

Divide dough in half. Shape each half into a smooth, uniformly thick log, 7-inches long by 2-inches wide. (Shaping is easiest if each log is placed in waxed paper and then rolled back and forth until smooth.) Unroll logs from the paper directly onto the baking sheet, spacing them as far apart from one another as possible.

Place in the center of the oven and bake for 35 to 40 minutes, or until lightly browned and cracked on top. Remove baking sheet from the oven and let the logs stand until completely cooled, at least 2 hours.

Reset the oven temperature once again to 350 degrees F.

Transfer logs to a cutting board and cut them crosswise into ⅜-inch-thick slices using a large, sharp knife. Lay slices flat on the baking sheet.

Place in the center of the oven and bake for about 10 minutes, or until cookies are just barely tinged with brown. Transfer to wire racks and let stand until cooled completely.

Store in an airtight container for up to 2 weeks. Freeze for longer storage.

Makes about 30 3-inch slices.

Raisin-Orange Cookies
(Ciastka z Bakaliami)

Poland

222

Polish cooks love to use a lot of eggs when they bake. In this recipe, egg yolks are creamed with butter and sugar for richness, and whites are beaten separately and folded in to lend lightness. Finally, raisins, nuts, and candied orange peel are gently incorporated into this rich yet airy suspension. The result is an unusual *and* delicious cookie with a delicate, feather-light texture and lovely orange flavor. The texture is best when the cookies are very fresh.

3	large eggs
1	cup (2 sticks) unsalted butter, very soft, but not melted
1⅓	cups powdered sugar
½	teaspoon baking powder
	Finely grated zest of 1 large orange
	Finely grated zest of 1 large lemon
	Pinch of ground cloves
⅛	teaspoon salt
½	teaspoon fresh lemon juice
1	cup all-purpose or unbleached white flour
1	cup coarsely chopped dark, seedless raisins
½	cup finely chopped blanched almonds
½	cup finely chopped candied orange peel

Preheat the oven to 325 degrees F. Very generously grease several baking sheets and set aside.

Separate the eggs, making sure the whites are completely free of yolk. Beat the butter in a mixing bowl until light and fluffy. Beat in 1 cup of the powdered sugar until well blended. Beat in the egg yolks, one at a time, followed by the baking powder, orange zest, lemon zest, and cloves.

In a completely grease-free mixing bowl, beat the egg whites, salt, and lemon juice with an electric mixer on medium speed until frothy. Gradually increase mixer speed to high and beat for about 1 minute. Gradually beat in remaining ⅓ cup powdered sugar and continue beating until the whites stand in firm but not dry peaks. Pour egg yolk mixture into the whites. Gradually sift the flour into the whites, gently folding with a rubber spatula until the yolk mixture and flour are incorporated into the whites. Then fold in the raisins, almonds, and candied orange peel until just incorporated but not overmixed.

Drop the mixture by rounded teaspoonfuls about 3½ inches apart on the baking sheets. Don't crowd the cookies or make them too big, as they spread a great deal.

Place in the center of the oven and bake for 11 to 13 minutes, or until cookies are rimmed with a ¼-inch deep ring of tan, reversing baking sheets from front to back about halfway through baking to ensure even browning. Remove baking sheets from the oven and let the cookies stand for about 30 seconds. Before they firm up, immediately transfer to wire racks, using a thin-bladed spatula; the edges are fragile and may crumble a bit. (If the cookies become too cool and crisp to remove from baking sheets easily, return them to the oven to warm up for a minute or two.) Let the cookies stand until cooled completely. Clean off and re-grease the baking sheets before reusing them.

Store the cookies flat with waxed paper between the layers for 2 or 3 days. Freeze for longer storage.

Makes 50 to 55 2¾- to 3-inch cookies.

CHOCOLATE DROP COOKIES
(CIASTKA CZEKOLADOWE)

Poland

These chocolate drop cookies are at once light and tender and rich and chocolatey. The delicate, almost cake-like texture is due to the somewhat unusual mixing method, so be sure to follow the directions carefully. I have seen this same technique employed in several other Polish recipes, including the raisin-orange cookies on the opposite page.

These cookies are best when very fresh, so plan to make them when you need them.

2	*large eggs*
1	*large egg white*
¼	*teaspoon instant coffee powder or granules*
¼	*teaspoon fresh lemon juice*
⅛	*teaspoon salt*
1¼	*cups all-purpose or unbleached white flour*
¼	*cup unsweetened cocoa powder*
¾	*teaspoon baking powder*
¾	*cup (1½ sticks) unsalted butter, very soft, but not melted*
1	*cup granulated sugar*
2½	*ounces bittersweet or semisweet chocolate, chopped moderately fine*

Preheat the oven to 350 degrees F. Generously grease several baking sheets and set aside.

Separate the eggs, making sure the whites are completely free of any yolk. Set yolks aside in a small bowl. Combine the 3 egg whites, coffee powder, lemon juice, and salt and set aside, stirring occasionally, until coffee dissolves. Thoroughly stir together flour, cocoa powder, and baking powder in a bowl.

Place butter in a mixing bowl and beat with the mixer on medium speed until light. Add ¾ cup of the sugar and continue beating for about 2 minutes, or until the mixture is very light and fluffy. Beat in reserved egg yolks until well blended and smooth.

In a completely grease-free large mixing bowl, beat the egg white-coffee mixture on low speed until frothy. Gradually increase mixer speed to high and beat for about 1 minute. Gradually beat in remaining ¼ cup sugar and continue beating until the mixture stands in firm but not dry peaks. Pour the egg yolk mixture into the whites. Sift the flour mixture over the whites. Then sprinkle the chocolate over the whites. Using a rubber spatula, gently fold the ingredients into the whites until thoroughly incorporated but not overmixed.

Drop dough by small rounded teaspoonfuls about 2½ inches apart on baking sheets. Don't crowd the cookies as they spread quite a bit.

Place in the center of the oven and bake for 8 to 10 minutes, or until the edges are just slightly darker, reversing baking sheets from front to back about halfway through baking to ensure even baking. Remove baking sheets from the oven and let cookies stand for about 30 seconds. Immediately transfer to wire racks and let stand until cooled completely.

Store the cookies flat with waxed paper between the layers for 2 or 3 days; if stored longer they tend to dry out rapidly. Freeze for longer storage.

Makes 35 to 40 2½- to 2¾-inch cookies.

Overleaf: *Chocolate Drop Cookies and Raisin-Orange Cookies.*

Walnut Finger Cookies
(Paliushky)

Ukraine

This recipe was inspired by a cookie baked by the mother of a former schoolmate. Her family immigrated to the United States from the Soviet Union when she was a small child, and her mother brought along some favorite recipes, including one similar to this.

These are mild, tender cookies dusted with vanilla- and lemon-scented powdered sugar.

⅓	cup chopped walnuts
½	cup (1 stick) unsalted butter
2½	tablespoons solid shortening, or top-quality lard
½	cup powdered sugar
	Pinch of salt
1	large egg yolk
2	tablespoons dairy sour cream
	Finely grated zest of 1 large lemon
2	cups all-purpose or unbleached white flour

DECORATION

3	tablespoons granulated sugar
1	1-inch long piece of vanilla bean, chopped (see Note)
1	¾- by ½-inch strip of lemon zest, chopped
½	cup powdered sugar

Place walnuts in a nut grinder, food processor, or blender and grind until very fine, keeping the ground nuts aerated and fluffy rather than clumped and oily while grinding. Set aside.

Place the butter and solid shortening in a large mixing bowl and beat with an electric mixer on medium speed until light and fluffy. Add the powdered sugar and salt and continue beating until thoroughly incorporated. Beat in egg yolk, sour cream, and lemon zest until well blended. Beat in ground walnuts. Add the flour and stir with a wooden spoon until thoroughly incorporated.

Cover and refrigerate dough for about 1½ hours, or until firm. (If dough chills for more than 4 hours, you may need to let it warm up just slightly before shaping cookies.)

Preheat the oven to 350 degrees F. Lightly grease several baking sheets and set aside. Remove about a third of the chilled dough from the refrigerator. Pull off ½-inch-round pieces and roll each piece back and forth between the palms to form a 2¼-inch-long finger about ¼ inch in diameter. Space cookies about 1 inch apart on the baking sheets. Repeat the shaping process with the second and third dough portions.

Place in the upper third of the oven and bake cookies for 9 to 11 minutes, or until just browned at the edges. Remove baking sheets from the oven and let stand for 2 or 3 minutes. Using a spatula, gently transfer cookies to wire racks and let stand until cool.

Combine granulated sugar, chopped vanilla bean, and lemon zest in a blender or food processor. Blend or process until vanilla bean and lemon zest are completely ground. (A blender is preferable for this task as it grinds the vanilla bean and lemon zest more finely than a processor.) Turn the mixture into a bowl and toss with the powdered sugar. Press the mixture through a fine sieve into a large shallow bowl, discarding any bits of vanilla bean or lemon zest that remain. In 3 or 4 batches, dredge the cookies in the sugar mixture until they are lightly but thoroughly coated.

Store in an airtight container for up to a week. The cookies may be frozen before dredging for longer storage. Allow them to thaw and dredge in sugar shortly before serving.

Makes 55 to 65 2½-inch fingers.

Note: If a vanilla bean is unavailable, 2 packets of vanilla sugar (a European vanilla-flavored baking product found in some gourmet shops), may be substituted. Add the vanilla sugar along with the lemon zest.

RUM BUTTER COOKIES
(VAJAS PISKÓTA)

Hungary

These small, tender butter cookies have a pleasant rum and lemon flavor. Their tops are attractively decorated with a cross-hatch pattern created using the tines of a fork.

2	*cups all-purpose or unbleached white flour*
¼	*teaspoon baking powder*
⅛	*teaspoon salt*
1	*cup (2 sticks) unsalted butter, slightly softened*
½	*cup granulated sugar*
1	*large egg yolk*
	Finely grated zest of 1 large lemon

½	*teaspoon vanilla extract*
2	*teaspoons light or dark rum*

DECORATION
1	*to 2 tablespoons powdered sugar (optional)*

Thoroughly stir together the flour, baking powder, and salt in a large bowl.

Place the butter in a mixing bowl and beat until light and fluffy. Beat in the sugar until well blended and smooth. Add the egg yolk, lemon zest, vanilla, and rum and beat until blended. Beat in about half the flour mixture. Stir in the remaining flour using a large wooden spoon. Cover and refrigerate dough for about 30 minutes, or until cool and firm, but not stiff.

Preheat the oven to 350 degrees F. Grease several baking sheets and set aside. Pull off generous ¾-inch pieces of dough and roll into smooth balls. Space about 1 inch apart on baking sheets. Press the tines of a fork into the cookies horizontally and then vertically to flatten them slightly and to create a decorative design. (If the tines stick to the dough, dip them into powdered sugar before each use.)

Place in the center of the oven and bake cookies for 11 to 13 minutes, or until just tinged with brown at the edges. Remove baking sheets from the oven and let stand for about 2 minutes. Transfer cookies to wire racks and let stand until cooled completely. Very lightly sift powdered sugar over tops of cookies, if desired.

Store in an airtight container for 3 or 4 days. Freeze for longer storage.

Makes about 50 1½-inch cookies.

Overleaf: Honey-Poppy Seed Rolled Cookies (recipe on page 232) and Poppy Seed-Filled Cookies (recipe on page 230).

POPPY SEED-FILLED COOKIES
(MÁKOS KIFLI)

Hungary

Using poppy seeds as the base for a sweet filling for baked goods is a common practice in Eastern and Central European countries. In this recipe the dough is rich, tender, and only lightly sweetened. The filling is dark, aromatic, sweet, and slightly crunchy. Almost anyone who enjoys the subtle yet distinctive taste of poppy seed filling will find this combination—and cookie—pleasing.

2¼ cups all-purpose or unbleached white flour
½ teaspoon baking soda
⅛ teaspoon ground cinnamon
¼ teaspoon salt
½ cup plus 6 tablespoons (1¾ sticks) unsalted butter, slightly softened
⅓ cup granulated sugar
1 large egg
½ teaspoon very finely grated lemon zest

FILLING AND DECORATION
½ cup poppy seeds
2½ tablespoons granulated sugar
¼ cup dark seedless raisins
¼ cup mild honey
1 tablespoon fresh lemon juice
½ teaspoon finely grated lemon zest

Thoroughly stir together flour, baking soda, cinnamon, and salt and set aside. Place butter in a mixing bowl and beat with an electric mixer on medium speed until light. Add sugar and continue beating until mixture is very light and fluffy. Beat in egg and lemon zest. Gradually beat in dry ingredients until thoroughly incorporated and dough is smooth.

Divide dough in half and place each half between large sheets of waxed paper. Using a rolling pin, roll each half out into a circle about 10 inches in diameter and ⅛ inch thick. The circle doesn't have to be perfectly round, but for best appearance the edges should be fairly even. Slide rolled dough sheets onto a tray or baking sheet and refrigerate for 15 to 20 minutes, or until cold and slightly firm but *not stiff*. Preheat the oven to 375 degrees F. Grease several baking sheets and set aside.

To prepare filling, combine poppy seeds and sugar in a blender and blend until seeds are completely ground; stop motor several times and stir to redistribute mixture. Transfer mixture to a bowl. Combine raisins, honey, lemon juice, and lemon zest in the blender and blend until mixture is smooth and puréed. Add raisin mixture to poppy seeds and stir until well combined.

Working with one chilled dough sheet at a time and leaving the other refrigerated, carefully peel off top layer of waxed paper, and replace loosely. Turn dough over and gently peel away and discard bottom layer of waxed paper. Using a pastry wheel or large sharp knife, cut circle into 8, then 16 equal wedges. Spoon a generous ½ teaspoon filling down the center of each wedge. Using a table knife, spread filling to within ¼ inch of the edges of each wedge. Working from outer edge of circle toward center, tightly roll up wedges and place on a baking sheet, spacing about 1 inch apart. Repeat the process with the remaining dough sheet until all cookies are formed.

Place in the center of the oven and bake cookies for 11 to 13 minutes or until just slightly colored on top and lightly browned at edges. Reverse baking sheets from front to back about halfway through baking to ensure even browning. Remove baking sheets from the oven and let stand for about 2 minutes. Transfer cookies to wire racks to cool completely.

Store in an airtight container for 3 or 4 days. Freeze for longer storage.

Makes 32 2¾-inch cookies.

JAM-FILLED BUTTER COOKIES
(HUSZÁRCSÓK)

Hungary

Known as Hussar's Kisses in Hungary, these cookies are not only delectable and pretty, but are also easy to make. The dough is wonderfully buttery and flavorful, and each cookie is enhanced with a colorful dab of jam and almond slivers. When finished, these look a bit like American thumbprint cookies, but are more elegant and delicate.

1½	cups (3 sticks) unsalted butter, slightly softened
¼	teaspoon salt
1	cup granulated sugar
3	egg yolks
2¼	teaspoons vanilla extract
⅛	teaspoon almond extract
3½	cups all-purpose or unbleached white flour
½	to ⅔ cup red currant or seedless raspberry jam
½	to ⅔ cup slivered blanched almonds

Preheat the oven to 375 degrees F. Grease several baking sheets.

Place butter in a mixing bowl and beat until lightened and smooth. Add salt and sugar and beat until light and fluffy. Beat in egg yolks and vanilla and almond extracts. Gradually add flour and mix until thoroughly incorporated. Pinch off pieces of dough and roll between palms into 1-inch balls. Space about 1½ inches apart on baking sheets. Press a deep indentation in the center of each cookie using your knuckle or thumb.

Place in the center of the oven and bake for 7 minutes. Remove baking sheets from the oven and fill each cookie indentation with about ½ teaspoon jam. Sprinkle a few almond slivers over the center top of each cookie. Return baking sheets to the oven and bake about 5 minutes longer, or until cookies are just tinged with brown and jam is melting. Transfer cookies to wire racks to cool.

Store in a single layer in airtight containers for up to a week. Freeze for longer storage.

Makes 55 to 60 1¼-inch cookies.

Honey-Poppy Seed Rolled Cookies
(Medenki S Makovo Seme)

Bulgaria

These unusual honey-spice cookies are garnished with poppy seeds, which add a subtle nutty flavor, a pleasant crunch, and eye appeal. The finished cookies are lightly spiced, fragrant, and a beautiful tan color.

4⅓   cups all-purpose or unbleached white flour
1   teaspoon baking soda
¾   teaspoon baking powder
2½   teaspoons ground cinnamon
1¾   teaspoons ground cloves
1½   cups (3 sticks) unsalted butter, slightly softened
1¼   cups granulated sugar
⅓   cup clover honey, or other mild honey
2   large eggs
       Finely grated zest of 2 large lemons

DECORATION
1   egg
2   to 3 tablespoons poppy seeds

Thoroughly stir together flour, baking soda, baking powder, cinnamon, and cloves.

Place butter in a mixing bowl and beat until light and smooth. Beat in sugar and honey until well blended. Add eggs and lemon zest and beat until blended. Beat in about half the dry ingredients. Stir in remaining dry ingredients using a large wooden spoon.

Divide dough into thirds and place each portion between large sheets of waxed paper. Using a rolling pin, roll each third out to ¼-inch thick, checking underside and smoothing out any wrinkles in paper as you roll. Stack the rolled dough sheets on a tray or baking sheet and place in the refrigerator for 20 to 25 minutes, or until chilled and slightly firm. (To speed up chilling process, place the dough in freezer for 10 to 15 minutes, being careful not to let it get too cold and hard.)

Preheat the oven to 375 degrees F. Grease several baking sheets and set aside.

Working with one chilled dough sheet at a time and leaving the others refrigerated, carefully peel away bottom layer of waxed paper, then replace paper loosely. Turn the dough over and peel off and discard top layer of waxed paper. Using assorted 2- to 3-inch cutters, cut out cookies. Carefully lift cookies from waxed paper with a spatula and space about 2 inches apart on baking sheets. Gather and re-roll dough scraps between waxed paper sheets. Chill and then continue cutting out cookies until all dough is used. Repeat process with second and third dough sheets.

In a small bowl, beat egg with 1 tablespoon water. Brush the tops of a few cookies with egg-water mixture using a pastry brush or paper towel, then sprinkle each generously with poppy seeds. Repeat until all the cookies are decorated.

Place in the center of the oven and bake for 9 to 11 minutes or until cookies are a rich tan color all over and just slightly darker around edges. Remove from the oven and let stand for about 2 minutes. Transfer cookies to wire racks and let stand until completely cooled.

Store in an airtight container for up to a week. Freeze for longer storage.

Makes 50 to 65 cookies, depending on size of cutters used.

Cinnamon-Honey Cookies
(Medenjaci)

Yugoslavia

There are many recipes for honey-spice cookies in Eastern Europe. In this simple, yet very good, version the flavors of cinnamon and orange predominate. As is typical, the cookies are thick, cake-like, and homey.

1 cup (2 sticks) unsalted butter, slightly softened
½ cup clover honey, or other mild honey
  Finely grated zest of 2 large oranges
3⅓ cups all-purpose or unbleached white flour
1¼ cups granulated sugar
2 teaspoons baking powder
1 tablespoon plus 1 teaspoon ground cinnamon
1½ teaspoons ground cloves
½ teaspoon ground nutmeg
3 large eggs

Combine the butter and honey in a large saucepan. Warm over medium heat, stirring, until the butter melts. Remove saucepan from the heat. Stir in orange zest and let stand until mixture cools to room temperature.

Meanwhile, thoroughly stir together the flour, sugar, baking powder, cinnamon, cloves, and nutmeg in a large bowl and set aside.

Separate one of the eggs and set the white aside in a small bowl. Add egg yolk and remaining 2 eggs to the cooled honey mixture and beat with a wooden spoon. Stir in the dry ingredients until thoroughly incorporated and smooth. Turn dough out onto a sheet of plastic wrap. Wrap the dough in plastic wrap and refrigerate for at least 1½ hours or up to 4 hours.

Preheat the oven to 375 degrees F. Grease several baking sheets and set aside.

Turn dough out onto a floured surface. If it seems too stiff to roll out, knead briefly to soften slightly. Roll dough out to ¼-inch thick, dusting rolling pin frequently with flour and lifting the dough to make sure it isn't sticking. Using a 2¼-inch plain round cutter or the rim of a small drinking glass, cut out the cookies. Transfer them to baking sheets with a spatula, spacing about 2 inches apart. Gather and re-roll dough scraps and continue cutting out cookies until all the dough is used. (If the dough is too soft and sticky to roll out, refrigerate it briefly.)

In a small bowl, beat together the reserved egg white and 2 teaspoons water with a fork. Using a pastry brush or a paper towel, evenly brush cookie tops with the wash.

Place in the center of the oven and bake the cookies for 15 to 17 minutes, or until nicely browned all over and just slightly darker at the edges. Remove baking sheets from the oven and let cookies stand 1 minute. Immediately transfer to wire racks and let stand until cooled completely.

Store in an airtight container for up to 2 weeks. Freeze for longer storage.

Makes 35 to 40 2¾-inch cookies.

CHOCOLATE MERINGUE-TOPPED BAR COOKIES
(PLIATZOK)

Ukraine

T his traditional Eastern European bar cookie is from the collection of Joanna Chmilewsky, who came to the U.S. from the Soviet Union.

BOTTOM LAYER
1½	cups all-purpose or unbleached white flour
1¼	teaspoons baking powder
1	cup (2 sticks) cold unsalted butter, cut into small pieces
3	large egg yolks
1	tablespoon dairy sour cream
¼	cup granulated sugar

TOP LAYER
1½	ounces bittersweet or semisweet chocolate, coarsely chopped
1	cup finely grated or ground walnuts
1	tablespoon powdered sugar
1	cup red currant jelly (if unavailable, substitute red raspberry jelly)
3	large egg whites, free of any yolk
1	teaspoon cream of tartar
⅓	cup granulated sugar

DECORATION
1	to 2 tablespoons powdered sugar (optional)

Preheat the oven to 350 degrees F. Grease a 7½- by 11¾-inch glass baking pan.

To prepare bottom layer by hand, thoroughly stir together flour and baking powder in a medium bowl. Sprinkle butter pieces over the flour. Using a pastry blender or forks, cut butter into the flour until mixture resembles fine crumbs. In a separate bowl, combine egg yolks, sour cream, and sugar and beat until well blended and frothy. Add egg yolk mixture to flour mixture. Stir until well blended and smooth, being careful not to overmix. Dough should be very moist and soft.

To prepare bottom layer using a food processor, combine flour and baking powder in a processor fitted with a steel blade and process in on/off pulses for about 5 seconds to mix dry ingredients. Sprinkle butter pieces over dry mixture. Process in on/off pulses for 1 to 1½ minutes or until butter is cut into dry ingredients and mixture resembles coarse crumbs. In a small bowl, combine egg yolks, sour cream, and sugar and beat with a fork until well blended. Pour egg yolk mixture into processor through feed tube, processing in on/off pulses. Continue to pulse until ingredients are well blended and dough just begins to mass, but is still very moist and soft.

Spoon dough into baking pan and spread evenly over bottom and out to the edges. Place in the upper third of the oven and bake for 20 minutes. Remove pan from the oven and let cool to lukewarm.

To prepare top layer, place chocolate in a small heavy saucepan and warm over lowest heat, stirring frequently, until melted. Remove from the heat and set aside to cool. In a small bowl, toss together ground walnuts and 1 tablespoon powdered sugar. Stir currant jelly until slightly liquefied.

When bottom layer has cooled, brush currant jelly evenly over the surface.

In a large, grease-free mixing bowl, combine egg whites and cream of tartar and beat with an electric mixer on medium speed until frothy. Raising speed to high, gradually beat in granulated sugar and continue beating until egg whites form firm but not dry peaks. Gently fold cooled chocolate and walnuts into the meringue mixture, working lightly and quickly to avoid deflating meringue.

Using a table knife or long-bladed spatula, spread meringue evenly over bottom layer. Immediately return baking pan to the oven and bake for 20 to 23 minutes, or until meringue is puffy and just tinged with brown. Remove from the oven and let stand until completely cooled.

If desired, dust top lightly with powdered sugar shortly before serving. Cut into small rectangles. Bars are best when very fresh, but they will keep in an airtight container for 2 or 3 days. Or they may be frozen for up to a week.

Makes 15 to 18 2- to 3-inch bars.

GOLDEN EGG COOKIES
(DOTTERPLÄTZCHEN)

Rumania

This recipe is unusual to Americans in that the dough contains sieved hard-cooked egg yolks as well as uncooked yolks. The cooked yolks lend a pale gold color, and a special tenderness and richness, to the cookies.

3   *large hard-cooked eggs, cooled and peeled*
10 *tablespoons (1¼ sticks) unsalted butter, slightly softened*
¾   *cup granulated sugar*
2   *large egg yolks*
½   *teaspoon baking powder*
⅛   *teaspoon salt*

Very finely grated zest of 2 medium lemons
2   *to 3 drops almond extract*
½   *cup finely ground blanched almonds*
1½ *cups all-purpose or unbleached white flour*
1   *large egg white*

Separate the cooked egg whites from the yolks. Press yolks through a fine sieve. Reserve whites for another purpose or discard.

Place the butter in a mixing bowl and beat until light. Add sugar and sieved egg yolks and continue beating until well blended and smooth. Beat in the uncooked egg yolks, baking powder, salt, lemon zest, almond extract, and almonds. Beat in flour.

Divide the dough in half and wrap each portion in plastic wrap. Refrigerate for at least 1 hour, or until cold and slightly firm.

Preheat the oven to 350 degrees F. Grease several baking sheets. Working with one half of dough at a time and leaving the other half refrigerated, roll dough on a floured surface to ⅛-inch thick. Lift the dough several times and dust the rolling pin frequently to prevent dough from sticking to it. Cut out the cookies using a 2¼-inch or slightly larger scalloped or fluted round cutter or the rim of a drinking glass. Using a spatula, transfer cookies to baking sheets, spacing about 1¼ inches apart. Gather and re-roll scraps and continue cutting out cookies until all the dough is used. Repeat with the second dough half. In a small bowl, beat egg white with 1 tablespoon water. Lightly brush tops of cookies with the egg white mixture.

Place in the center of the oven and bake for 7 to 9 minutes, or until cookies just begin to brown around the edges. Remove baking sheets from the oven and let stand for 2 minutes. Transfer the cookies to wire racks and let stand until completely cooled.

Store the cookies in an airtight container for up to a week. Freeze for longer storage.

Makes 40 to 45 2½-inch cookies.

APPENDIX

NAPOLEON'S HATS
SEE PAGE 121

SCANDINAVIAN SUGAR PRETZELS
SEE PAGE 120

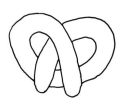

GLAZED SWEET PRETZELS
SEE PAGE 158
&
CHOCOLATE PRETZELS
SEE PAGE 144

1

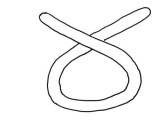

2

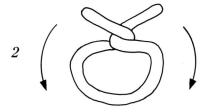

3

COOKIE HOUSE PATTERN PIECES
DOTTED LINES INDICATE
PLACEMENT OF PIECES
SEE PAGE 177

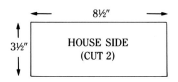

8½″

HOUSE SIDE
(CUT 2)

3½″

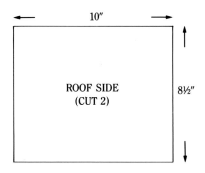

10″

ROOF SIDE
(CUT 2)

8½″

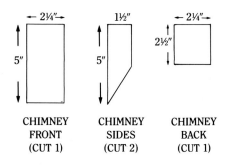

2¼″   1½″   2¼″

5″   5″   2½″

CHIMNEY
FRONT
(CUT 1)

CHIMNEY
SIDES
(CUT 2)

CHIMNEY
BACK
(CUT 1)

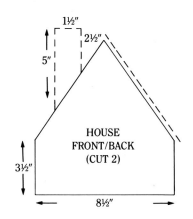

1½″   2½″

5″

HOUSE
FRONT/BACK
(CUT 2)

3½″

8½″

CREDITS

All locations are in New York City unless
otherwise noted.

page 14:   plates courtesy of
Rogers-Tropea

page 21:   shawl courtesy of Vito
Giallo Antiques

page 27:   glass courtesy of Mood
Indigo; toys and books
courtesy of Darrows Fun
Antiques

page 31:   flag, plate, and figures
courtesy of Somethin'
Else, Englewood, New
Jersey

page 39:   plates courtesy of
Rogers-Tropea

page 42:   plate courtesy of
Bernardaud Limoges

page 55:   teddy bears courtesy of
The Enchanted Forest;
plates courtesy of Paper
Art

page 67:   plate courtesy of Jenny
B. Goode; quilt courtesy
of Laura Perry Epstein

page 82:   pottery courtesy of Pan
American Phoenix

page 97:   plate, cup and saucer
courtesy of Jenny B.
Goode

pages 100–101:   tablecloth, tea caddy, jar,
and cup and saucer
courtesy of Somethin'
Else

page 108:   plate, cup and saucer,
and birds courtesy of
Rande Lynne, Inc., En-
glewood, New Jersey

page 112:   plate courtesy of Royal
Copenhagen

pages 118–119:   painted wooden board
by Michael Del Sapiro of
La Carezza

page 138:   plates courtesy of
Rogers-Tropea

page 143:   plates courtesy of
Rogers-Tropea

pages 168–169:   stein courtesy of Man-
tiques

page 185:   tablecloth and plate
courtesy of Pierre Deux

page 196:   Bacas cordial glasses
courtesy of Somethin'
Else

page 201:   plate, cup and saucer,
and candlesticks cour-
tesy of Rande Lynne,
Inc., Englewood, New
Jersey

page 204:   plate and bells courtesy
of Cobweb

page 216:   lace runner and plate
courtesy of Rande
Lynne, Inc., Englewood,
New Jersey

INDEX

Pages in *italic* have illustrations

Almond Cookies
  -Chocolate Meringue, 187
  -Honey, 219
  Jam Filled Shorties, 94, *95*
  Macaroons, 184, *185*
  "Petticoat Tails" Shortbread, 91
  Ring Cake, 130
  Spiced Crisps, 191
  Tea Cakes, 220
  "Tile" Wafers, *156,* 157
  Viennese Crescents, 163
Anise Biscotti, 196, *197*
Anise Cookies, Holiday, 74, *75*
Anthea's Ginger Biscuits, 104
Apple-Raisin Rum Cookies, 58, *59*
Apricot Sandwich Cookies, Chocolate-
    Glazed, Viennese, 160, 161
Apricot Tea Cookies, *216,* 218
Austrian Cookies
  Chocolate Pretzels, 144, *145*
  Little Rascals, *138,* 140
  Nut Wreaths, 164
  Raspberry-Chocolate Bars, 146, 173
  Viennese Almond Crescents, 163
  Viennese Chocolate-Glazed Apricot

    Sandwiches, *160,* 161
  Viennese Stamped Butter, 167

Basel "Brown" Cookies, 172, *173*
Basler Brunsli, 172
Belgian Speculaas, *148,* 153
Biscochitos, 74
Biscotti
  Anise, 196, *197*
  di Cioccolata, 207
  Milano, 209
  Sesame Seed, 198
Black Walnut Icebox Cookies, *Frontispiece,* 65
Brandy Snaps, 98
Brazilian Coconut Chews, 81
British Cookies, 87-107. *See also* English,
    Irish, Scottish, Welsh
Brown Sugar Cookies, 73. *See also* Sugar
    Cookies
  -Chocolate Chunk Supreme, 37
  Molded, 62, *63*
  -Peanut Bars, *70,* 72
Brownies
  Butterscotch, *39,* 41
  Extra Chocolatey, with Shiny Chocolate

Glaze, *39,* 40
Fudge, 38, *39*
Brutti ma Buoni al Cacao, 206
Bulgarian Honey-Poppy Seed Rolled
    Cookies, *228,* 232
Butter, about using, 8
Butter Cookies
  Cherry Half Moons, *108,* 110
  Chocolate, 125
  Jam-Filled, 231
  Rum, 227
  "S," *118,* 129
  Sablés, 166
  Spritz, 124
  Viennese Stamped, 167
Buttercream Sandwich Cookies, 136
Butterscotch Brownies, *39,* 41

Canadian Cookies
  Apple-Raisin Rum, 58, *59*
  Caramel Walnut Slices, 34
  Nanaimo Bars, 44
  Raisin Spice, Soft and Chewy, 57
  Sooke Harbour House Salal Berry, 68
Caramel Walnut Slices, 34

Cardamom Wafers, Embossed, *112,* 113
Cassatine, 210
Cats' Tongues, 203
Cherry Half Moons, *108,* 110
Chocolate. *See also* Brownies, White
   Chocolate
  -Almond Meringue Cookies, 187
  Basel "Brown" Cookies, 172, *173*
  Bittersweet, and White Bars, 190
  Chews, Double, 17
  Chip Cookies, *27,* 33
  Chip, Ice Cream Sandwiches, 36
  Chocolate Chip Cookies, 32
  Chunk-Brown Sugar Supreme Cookies, 37
  "Dark Bread" Cookies, *168,* 170
  Drop Cookies, 223, *224*
  -Glazed Apricot Sandwich Cookies, Vien-
    nese, *160,* 161
  -Glazed Hazelnut Spritz Wafers, 142, *143*
  Hazelnut Crisps, *173,* 174
  Icebox Slices, 29
  Kiss-Peanut Butter Cookies, 54, *55*
  Macaroons, *185,* 186
  Meringue-Topped Bar Cookies, 234
  Nanaimo Bars, 44
  -Orange Sandwich Wafers, *208,* 209
  Powdered Sugar Fingers, 199
  Pretzels, 144, *145*
  -Raspberry Bars, 146, *173*
  -Ricotta-Orange Tartlets, 210
  Spice Cookies, Lemon-Iced, 207
  Spritz Cookies, 125
  -Tipped Pecan Bars, 30
  Ugly but Good, 206
Chunky Macadamia Nut-White Chocolate
    Cookies, 28
Cinnamon Cookies
  -Honey, 233
  Stars, *148,* 155
Cochinitos, 78, *79*
Coconut Cookies
  Chews, Brazilian, 81
  Crunchies, 99
  Dream Bars, Toasted, *42,* 43
  -Peanut, 85
Columbian Cookies, Brown Sugar-Peanut
    Bars, *70,* 72
Cookie House, *176,* 177-82
Cornish Fairings, 107
Cornmeal Cookies, *82,* 83
Costa Rican Cookies, Coconut-Peanut, 85
Country Fair Cookies, 106
Cuban Brown Sugar Cookies, 73

Danish Cookies
  Almond Ring Cake, 130
  Butter Spritz, 124; Chocolate, 125
  Iced Honey, 134

Sand Tarts, 114
Sugar Pretzels, Scandinavian, *118,* 120
"Dark Bread" Cookies, *168,* 170
Date-Orange Pinwheel Cookies, 56
Date Rocks, 69
Double-Baked Hazelnut Slices, 221
Double Chocolate Chews, 17
Dreams, 137
Dutch Cookies. *See* Netherlands

Eastern European Cookies, 217-35. *See
    also* name of country
Egg, Golden, Cookies, 235
Embossed Cardamom Wafers, *112,* 113
English Cookies. *See also* Irish, Scottish,
    Welsh
  Anthea's Ginger Biscuits, 104
  Brandy Snaps, 98
  Coconut Crunchies, 99
  Cornish Fairings, 107
  Jam-Filled Almond Shorties, 94, *95*
  Lemon Tea Biscuits with Lemon Curd,
    100, 102
  Melting Moments, 92
  Orange-Ginger Creams, 105
  Orange Meltaways, 96, *97*
  Shrewsbury Biscuits, 89
Extra Chocolatey Brownies with Shiny
    Chocolate Glaze, *39,* 40

Fig Holiday Cookies, 215
Finnish Cookies
  Butter "S," *118,* 129
  Ginger Thins, *118,* 123
  Holiday Prune-Filled Pinwheels, 126, 127
Florentines, 202
French Cookies
  Almond Macaroons, 184, *185*
  Almond "Tiles," *156,* 157
  Chocolate Macaroons, *185,* 186
  Madeleines, 141
  Mushroom Meringues, 188, *189*
  Pretzels, Glazed Sweet, 158
  Sablés, 166
Fudge Brownies, 38, *39*

German Cookies
  Chocolate Hazelnut Crisps, *173,* 174
  Chocolate Pretzels, 144, *145*
  Chocolate-Almond Meringues, 187
  Cinnamon Stars, *148,* 155
  Cookie House, *176,* 177–82
  "Dark Bread," *168,* 170
  Honey Lebkuchen, *148,* 150
  Little Rascals, *138,* 140
  Nut Wreaths, 164
  Peppernuts, 183
  Raspberry-Chocolate Bars, 146, 173

"Sausage" Cookies, *168,* 171
Springerle, *148,* 152
Viennese Almond Crescents, 163
Viennese Chocolate-Glazed Apricot
    Sandwich Cookies, *160,* 161
Ginger Cookies
  Anthea's Biscuits, 104
  Parliament, *86,* 90
  Snaps, 61; Brandy, 98
  Thins, *118,* 123
Gingerbread People, 60
Gingersnaps, Swedish, 135
Glazed Sweet Pretzels, 158
Golden Egg Cookies, 235
Golden Oat Cookies, *86,* 93
Grandmother Ellison's Oatmeal Cookies,
    18, 21
Greek Cookies
  Chocolate Powdered Sugar Fingers, 199
  Orange, 214
  Phoenician Honey, 212, *213*

Hazelnut Cookies
  Chocolate Crisps, *173,* 174
  Slices, Double-Baked, 221
  Spritz Wafers, Chocolate-Glazed, 142, *143*
  Sugar Dusties, *204,* 205
Honey Cookies
  -Almond, 219
  -Cinnamon, 233
  Iced, 134
  Lebkuchen, *148,* 150
  Phoenician, 212, *213*
  -Poppy Seed Rolled, *228,* 232
Hungarian Cookies
  Almond Tea Cakes, 220
  Jam-Filled Butter, 231
  Poppy Seed-Filled Cookies, *228,* 230
  Rum Butter Cookies, 227

Ice Cream Chocolate Chip Sandwiches, 36
Icebox Cookies
  Black Walnut, *Frontispiece,* 65
  Pecan Butter with Orange Zest, 45
  Chocolate Slices, 29
Icelandic Little Sugar Cakes, 117
Irish Cookies. *See also* English, Scottish,
    Welsh
  Almond "Petticoat Tails" Shortbread, 91
  Shortbread, *86,* 88
Ischler-Plätzchen, 161
Italian Cookies
  Anise Biscotti, 196, *197*
  Cats' Tongues, 203
  Chocolate-Orange Sandwich Wafers,
    208, 209
  Chocolate Powdered Sugar Fingers, 199
  Florentines, 202